The
Changing Face
of the
Royal Masonic
Benevolent Institution

The Changing Face of the Royal Masonic Benevolent Institution

RMBI

John Reuther

Lewis Masonic

First published 2016

ISBN 978 0 85318 535 2

Published by Lewis Masonic in conjunction with the RMBI

an imprint of Ian Allan Publishing Ltd, Addlestone, Surrey KT15 2SF.

Printed in Bulgaria.

CONTENTS

ACKNOWLEDGEMENTS

It is without doubt that this book would never been written had not Brigadier Willie Shackell, the then President of the Royal Masonic Benevolent Institution, suggested, after a board meeting, that it would be a good idea to write an updated history of the RMBI. Then, turning around to those assembled, he stated that this was a job for Reuther. Thus began a two-year search through the archives of the Freemasonry to produce this book. I was ably assisted throughout this project by the kind help of the staff of the Library and Museum of Freemasonry, in particular, Diane Clements, Martin Cherry, Susan Snell, Harriet Sandvall and Peter Aitkenhead. I would also like to thank Lt Col Chris Head for his guidance throughout this project and the continued support of Chris Caine, the Grand Vice President of the RMBI, who maintained my enthusiasm when times became difficult. I cannot thank enough the time given by the Nadine Plumley, who painstakingly proof read and corrected the document. I would also like to thank past Chief Executives of the RMBI, namely Noel Grout and Peter Gray, as well as the current Chief Executive, Brigadier David Innes, for their advice and guidance and as witnesses of many of the events in the narrative. I am grateful to the Past President, Willie Shackell, for the original idea and the current President, James Newman, for his continued support. I must also thank Edna Petzen and the staff of the RMBI for their guidance and assistance. I would also like to thank Peter Waller for his guidance and patience throughout the production of this work without which it would never have left the draft stage. Finally, I would like to thank my wife, Maggie, for all her patience and understanding whilst I locked myself away for hours researching and writing this story.

FOREWORD
by the Deputy Grand Master

I am pleased to introduce this illustrated history of the RMBI by Dr. John Reuther.

As a senior Freemason, long serving Trustee of the RMBI and recognised academic, he is extremely well qualified to write this impressive and very readable account of one of the foremost Masonic charities.

The RMBI has come a long way from its formation by Robert Crucefix but the founding principle remains intact; to help our Brethren live with dignity and care in the final years of their lives. Provision of residential care has changed dramatically over the last 173 years, as has society itself, and this is vividly reflected within these pages.

I hope the reader will find the journey the RMBI has taken throughout the years interesting and informative; they will find that history has a habit of repeating itself and nothing worth doing comes easily.

I commend this book in the hope it will reassure you, should the need arise, that you would find a warm and caring welcome in an RMBI care home.

Jonathan Spence
October 2015

CHAPTER I

THE PROBLEM

What to do with the poor, especially the poor and elderly, was a problem that had vexed the conscience of the country since the Middle Ages. Prior to the reign of Henry VIII this had been largely the responsibility of the Church, but the Reformation created a vacuum in the medieval social structure. Charity had now moved from a voluntary framework, previously controlled by the monasteries, to a compulsory tax administered and raised by the local parish. The failure to manage the problem became part of our heritage, with songs that have now become popular nursery rhymes:

Hark, hark, the dogs do bark,
The beggars are coming to Town.

Throughout the Tudor period the presence of large numbers of beggars preyed on the fears of the people, especially those in isolated communities such as farms and lonely villages. A large proportion of these itinerant vagrants had no trade and would wander the countryside looking for casual or seasonal work. Those who had a trade would be paid by the day, hence the expression 'journeyman', from the French *jour*, and having completed their task would move on. There was also a large group of individuals who through reasons of sickness and age remained where they were and became the parish's problem. Vagabonds were divided into two simple groups: those who could not work and those who would not work. The former were licensed to beg within their own community, but if they strayed into a neighbouring parish they could expect the stocks and a whipping, as received by those who were not in possession of a licence. Those who could work were forced to labour under the threat of extreme punishments. The decline of the Roman Church in England destroyed the ability to administer parochial poor relief on a consistent national basis. Local officials, mayors and churchwardens were permitted to collect charitable alms to support the helpless, and preachers pricked the conscience of their parishioners to assist the needy.

The able-bodied people who refused to work could be imprisoned; punishments were extreme and often disabling. Most of these barbaric laws were repealed by 1576 and more humane laws introduced, such as the Poor Relief Act of 1597, later updated in 1601. The definition of a vagrant was clarified into two groups: individuals who were sick or disabled, and those 'mighty of body but refused to work'. A law passed in 1576 required every city and town to provide wool, hemp, flax, iron or other materials so that the 'honest poor' could be suitable employed. The others — the so-called rogues — were to be incarcerated into houses of correction and disciplined until they did work. Each parish was responsible for assisting its own aged and helpless. It became their responsibility to train orphans to fill the workforce, and to provide labour for those who were unemployed. Unpaid churchwardens or parish overseers were elected to take on the responsibility for collecting poor relief from local inhabitants, and failure to pay could result in criminal convictions. Each town or city now had the prototype for a workhouse or, as more familiarly known at the time, a poorhouse. This Act would ultimately lead to the great and dismal Union Workhouses of the late Georgian and Victorian eras. The Settlement Act of 1662 allowed new incoming vagrants to be moved on, out of the parish, if they were considered by the local justices to be potential dependants on local charity. A man wishing to move to another parish had to have a Settlement Certificate that guaranteed his home parish would pay if ever he became a claimant. These were unpopular and were rarely issued, resulting in inhabitants staying where they were.

The Poor Laws would change over the next two hundred years, with minor modifications to adapt to the changing environment. In the late 17th century, recipients of the poor relief were obliged to wear a pauper's badge, which consisted of the letter 'P' preceded by the initial of their local parish. The designation of pauper was a great stigma, causing both suffering and embarrassment.

Some religious groups, such as the Quakers, set up

LEFT **Beer Street.** *Hogarth*

TOP **Gin Lane.** *Hogarth*

BELOW **March of Bricks.** *Cruikshank*

workhouses in London and Bristol as an act of charity to help and assist the poor. In some parishes poorhouses were converted into spinning schools. The workhouses in the larger towns took the form of factories where paupers were forced into unskilled manufacturing work.

Sir Edward Knatchbull in 1722 sponsored an act to permit local parishes to build housing especially for the poor and penniless. The management of such establishments could contract out to a third party who, though obliged to provide work for the inmates, could take all the profits. This became known as farming the poor and, although some were well run, it was inevitable that many ended up as grim establishments.

The Old Poor Law can generally be described as parish centred, haphazard and with no continuity from one part of the country to another. However, it was the administration of Poor Law Relief that ultimately brought about the introduction of change and the formation of the New Poor Laws. Relief could take two forms: indoor relief, for those working within the workhouse; or outdoor relief, for those in need but living away from the institution. This could be help for those too ill to work, who became known as the impotent poor. Relief often came in the form of food, hence the so-named parish loaf. The overseer of the poor under Elizabethan law would know the deserving from the undeserving poor; he would also be aware of the size of the population, making the administration relatively simple and

TOP **Holborn Hill across the Fleet ditch.** *Thornbury*

ABOVE **Edwin Chadwick 26 Jan 1846.** *Illustrated London News*

RIGHT **Jeremy Bentham.** *J. Watts*

comparatively cheap. However, the arrival of the industrial revolution saw an increase in population and a rise in administration costs to £7 million. Something had to be done, otherwise the country was doomed to bankruptcy.

The beginning of the 19th century was unequalled in the history of Great Britain; the industrial revolution had created an enormous population migration travelling from the country into the growing urban centres. The 'march of bricks' — as illustrated by George Cruikshank — created an exceptional and virtually uncontrolled increase in the size of the great cities. Many assumed that the streets would be paved with gold, but sadly for the greater number life would be full of hardship and, in many cases, the only reward was an early grave.

The newly created buildings in the leafy suburbs would soon be filled by the middle classes, whilst their vacated properties in the centre of the cities were filled by the labouring classes and tradesmen, the majority of whom lived in appalling accommodation. The centres of towns were crowded, as illustrated in evidence given by William Dryer in court at the Old Bailey in 1787:

> *The place that I did lodge in, there is neither a bolt, nor a latch to the door; the last that goes out, takes a bit of a padlock and locks the door ... several people lodge in the same room; there are three beds all occupied and there was one woman drunk in bed when they came there, that was a ballad-singing woman; my wife and I went out to sell some cabbage nets and white rags ...*

These areas became known as rookeries and existed in every large town. In London a particularly large area became known as the rookeries of St Giles and extended from Holborn to Leicester Square and from Bloomsbury to the Strand. The cost for a night's accommodation in one of the cheaper houses in this area was around 3d per night, whilst one in an ale house with food included could be as much as 6d. It is not surprising, therefore, that many slept rough in the street or crammed into a single room to reduce expenditure. Overcrowding on this scale led to disease, and throughout the early part of the century the towns were visited by such plagues as typhoid and cholera, leading to tremendous loss of life. William Budd, a physician working in Bristol in 1847, discovered a small epidemic of typhoid in the neighbourhood and was surprised to find that the distinguishing characteristic of the healthy from the afflicted was the latter's use of a common well. In a similar case John Snow, working in the slums of Soho in London in 1854, connected the use of a particular water pump and an outbreak of cholera that was rampaging through the area. In 1798, Thomas Robert Malthus, a Fellow of Jesus College Cambridge, published *An Essay on the Principle of Population* in which he argued that increases in population would eventually outpace the ability of the population of the world to feed itself. His argument was:

> *We will suppose the means of subsistence in any country just equal to the easy support of its inhabitants. The constant effort towards population ... increases the number of people before the means of subsistence are increased. The food therefore which before supported seven millions must now be divided among seven millions and a half or eight millions. The poor consequently must live much worse, and many of them be reduced to severe distress. The number of labourers also being above the proportion of the work in the market, the price of labour must tend toward a decrease, while the price of provisions would at the same time*

> *tend to rise. The labourer therefore must work harder to earn the same as he did before. During this season of distress, the discouragements to marriage, and the difficulty of rearing a family are so great that population is at a stand. In the meantime the cheapness of labour, the plenty of labourers, and the necessity of an increased industry amongst them, encourage cultivators to employ more labour upon their land, to turn up fresh soil, and to manure and improve more completely what is already in tillage, till ultimately the means of subsistence become in the same proportion to the population as at the period from which we set out. The situation of the labourer being then again tolerably comfortable, the restraints to population are in some degree loosened, and the same retrograde and progressive movements with respect to happiness are repeated.*

Malthus' solution was one of catastrophe where diseases and epidemics destroyed the population and reduced the balance:

> *The power of population is so superior to the power of the earth to produce subsistence for man that premature death must in some shape or other visit the human race.*

ABOVE **John Ricardo.** *Illustrated London News*

RIGHT **Thomas Carlyle.** *Illustrated London News*

FAR RIGHT **John Stuart Mill.** *Illustrated London News*

The vices of mankind are active and able ministers of depopulation. They are the precursors in the great army of destruction, and often finish the dreadful work themselves. But should they fail in this war of extermination, sickly seasons, epidemics, pestilence, and plague advance in terrific array, and sweep off their thousands and tens of thousands. Should success be still incomplete, gigantic inevitable famine stalks in the rear, and with one mighty blow levels the population with the food of the world.

Malthus had a far-reaching impact on the academic population and even influenced Darwin and his theory of natural selection. It was self-evident to the city dwellers that the increase in population would ultimately create famine and disease that were an ever-present threat. This was not helped by the large consumption of cheap spirits such as gin. Hogarth demonstrated the advantages of drinking beer over gin in his engravings 'Gin Lane' and 'Beer Street'. The towns

were overcrowded and the graveyards in the cities were packed to capacity. By the middle of the 19th century, London churchyards were so overcrowded that they were a severe health risk to those living nearby. Bodies were buried in shallow graves, and the stench of rotting bodies became overpowering. Charles Dickens illustrates this in *Bleak House*:

... comes with his pauper company to Mr. Krook's and bears off the body of our dear brother here departed to a hemmed-in churchyard, pestiferous and obscene, whence malignant diseases are communicated to the bodies of our dear brothers and sisters who have not departed, while our dear brothers and sisters who hang about official back- stairs — would to heaven they HAD departed! — are very complacent and agreeable. Into a beastly scrap of ground which a Turk would reject as a savage abomination and a Caffre would shudder at, they bring our dear brother here departed to receive

Christian burial. With houses looking on, on every side, save where a reeking little tunnel of a court gives access to the iron gate — with every villainy of life in action close on death, and every poisonous element of death in action close on life — here they lower our dear brother down a foot or two, here sow him in corruption, to be raised in corruption: an avenging ghost at many a sick-bedside, a shameful testimony to future ages how civilization and barbarism walked this boastful island together. Come night, come darkness, for you cannot come too soon or stay too long by such a place as this! Come, straggling lights into the windows of the ugly houses; and you who do iniquity therein, do it at least with this dread scene shut out! Come, flame of gas, burning so sullenly above the iron gate, on which the poisoned air deposits its witch-ointment slimy to the touch! It is well that you should call to every passerby.

The movement from the rural to the urban environment during the industrial revolution created a population explosion that was difficult to control. The competition for work amongst the labouring classes led to a decline in wages as more and more competed for fewer jobs. To many in the affluent middle and upper classes the solution again was self-evident — that these individuals should work. Thomas Carlyle was later to look upon work as a religion, stating that there was 'nobleness, even sacredness in Work'. However, the working man knew that in order to live and support his family he would have to work until the day he died unless he was frugal enough to save for his old age.

At the same time, the English economist and banker David Ricardo published his view that wages could not fall below subsistence level because labourers would ultimately be unable to work. However, competition for employment would drive wages down to the lowest level that would maintain work. This complemented Malthus' theory that population increases only when wages are above the lowest level and falls when wages are below this level. This delighted the industrialists and factory owners; as a result of competition, they were now able to pay their workers at the lowest sustainable level. The third great contemporary movement was utilitarianism, based upon the concept developed by Jeremy Bentham. Bentham had been born in Spitalfields, London, in 1748 and was educated in Oxford. He proposed many social as well as legal reforms and was instrumental at suggesting that there should be a non-sectarian secular university; most in this country were still attached to religious institutions. This ultimately led to the foundation of the University of London. His principles on utilitarianism argued that policies and deeds should cause 'the greatest good for the greatest number of people', also known as 'the greater happiness principle'. His eminent pupil, John Stuart Mill (1806-1873), defined 'the greater happiness principle' to mean that one must always act in a manner so as to produce the greatest happiness for the greatest number of people, within reason.

The movement influenced much in late Georgian and early Victorian England, including the construction of new houses of correction such as Pentonville Prison (which was a distinct improvement on the then still functional Newgate Prison). Houses were constructed in areas such as Bloomsbury around a central communal garden, enabling the residents to appreciate a country garden in an urban environment. Bentham believed in the equality of the sexes, but also suggested that people did what was pleasant and would tend to claim relief rather than work and that the interest of the majority of the community was the outcome to be achieved.

Based upon the three doctrines of Bentham's utilitarianism, Malthus' population explosion and Ricardo's iron law on wages, the Whig government, under Lord Melbourne, considered the time was right for a review of the

LEFT **Rioting at the Union Workhouse 1842.**

BELOW **Christmas Distribution of Coal.**
Foster

Poor Law Act of 1601, and a Royal Commission was set up in 1832 to examine the problem and find a solution. There were 26 Commissioners appointed to the Committee headed by Dr Blomfield, the Bishop of London, and the Secretary was the noted Benthamite Edwin Chadwick. They suggested some fundamental changes to the Poor Law, which included the abolition of outdoor relief with the exception of the sick and the elderly. Those, however, who could not be supported from home — and this included orphans — should be admitted to the workhouse. They also recommended the grouping of small parish workhouses into larger Unions, often consisting of several thousand inmates divided strictly into men, women, children and the elderly. These were to be governed centrally by a Board of Commissioners. The aim for the able-bodied pauper was to make his or her position worse than the worst paid labourer outside the institution, thereby encouraging individuals to work hard to get out and return to the general workforce in the community. This was to be the last resort. The general principles were accepted by both senior members from the Tory and Whig parties, and it passed into law in 1834.

Although the Act was considered by many to be the most far-reaching piece of legislation — it certainly reduced the cost to each individual property-owning taxpayer — it did have a great many critics. Most of the newspapers at the time were against it in some form or other. The abuses of the system were shown in a dramatic form by Charles Dickens in his novel *Oliver Twist* (published monthly from February 1837), which highlighted the effects on a middle class boy born by chance in a workhouse and his eventual rehabilitation into his own family. This was aimed at the literate middle class families to illustrate the harshness of the institutions; but, for the Grace of God, this could happen to them.

Opposition following the passing of the Poor Law Amendment Act of 1834 varied throughout the country. In southern England the introduction was relatively peaceful with only minor disturbances, but in the northern parts and in Wales acts of violence and riots were more intense and troops were often seen on the streets to quell the disturbances. Many considered the building of large Union Workhouses as not cost-effective and the distribution of dole more beneficial. In 1841, the Tory radical G. R. W. Baxter published *The Book of the Bastiles*, which consisted of extracts from virtually every publication that was set against the new Act. The word 'Bastiles' was an obvious corruption of the French *Bastille* and a popular contemporary expression for the new Union Workhouses. The book was directed towards the upper and middle classes and emphasised what he called a crisis mainly attributable to the operation of such harsh biting statutes as the New Poor Law, and in his opening chapter he related to it through the character of John Bull:

And when any of the poor wretches complain of their wrongs and wretchedness, what is the constant reply they receive? 'Go and Work.' Yes, they bid the aged cripple, the bed-ridden man of eighty, and the widow woman of seventy, to Go and Work!!

The unforeseen problem with the introduction of the new Union Workhouses was that they soon became refuges for the elderly. A typical example can be illustrated by the life of John Lander, a bootmaker who worked and sold his produce in the Brill Market of Somers Town in St Pancras. As a young man he built a modest business with his wife; he would cut the leather whilst his wife, Elizabeth, would sew the pieces together. As their family grew, their children were trained as bootmakers, but the problem came as John and Elizabeth grew old and were no longer capable of working. Their children had flown the nest and become potential rivals as they strove to feed their own children. The elderly couple had no other recourse than to retire to the St Pancras Workhouse. In 1809, the workhouse housed 500, but by 1856 the number of inmates had increased to between 1,500 and 1,900, of whom 1,000 were elderly or infirm. Children often slept six to eight per bed, and the ventilation was so poor that patients and staff frequently complained of headaches and nausea. When John Lander died he was buried as a pauper in 1874, aged 78. It could be said that before the 1834 Poor Law Amendment Act parish workhouses were almost paternalistic; now, with the introduction of this new law, the lives of many poor, infirm and elderly people would change for ever. It was with great fear and trepidation that they looked towards their futures. The workhouse under the new Act was to be a deterrent to all who were considered able-bodied paupers but the only refuge for the elderly poor.

CHAPTER 2

ROBERT THOMAS CRUCEFIX: THE PRIVATE LIFE

One particular individual for whom the New Poor Law was to have a profound effect was Robert Thomas Crucefix, a charismatic, middle-aged London doctor whose influence on Freemasonry is still evident today. His workload was unrelenting and truly 'filled the unforgiving minute with 60 seconds' worth of distance run'. There is limited information on his personality, but the Rev Slade in a letter to Dr Oliver in 1842 compared him to Charles Dickens' Mr Pickwick:

> The little doctor truly enjoyed himself and fascinated all with his speeches, whilst others compared him to Mr Pickwick, the hero of The Pickwick Papers.

The *Freemasons' Quarterly Magazine* published on 30th September 1849 described him as follows:

> Despite 60 years of age, middle stature and of easy deportment, he possesses a highly intelligent countenance, quick dark eyes, and expressive features. His eloquence is subdued and chaste, his style nervous, and his manner persuasive. Sadly he is 'sicklied o'er with the pale cast of Thought'.

His ancestors were Huguenots who came from Dieppe around 1685 when Louis XIV repealed the Edict of Nantes. They had initially settled in Spitalfields, London, and were clockmakers. The first Robert Crucefix became a Brother of the Worshipful Company of Clockmakers in 1689, but he was not a liveryman, having learned his trade in France. His lantern clocks are now very collectable. Robert Thomas Crucefix, the eldest son of middle class, well-educated parents, was the fifth generation since his family's exodus, and all traces of his French ancestry had long since gone. His father, also called Robert, was a commercial traveller at the time he married Maria Charlotte Mason on 15th September 1787. They lived on Holborn Hill in the Parish of St Andrew's. Holborn is situated on the western boundary of

the City of London and named after the Holeborne, a small tributary of the River Fleet, both now piped beneath the streets. To the north of Holborn Hill stands Saffron Hill, noted for its rookeries, thieves and paupers, and reputed to be the scene of Fagin's house in Dickens' *Oliver Twist*; a filthy and muddy area with no proper paved roads. Dickens described it as follows:

> ... filthy shops are exposed for sale huge bunches of second-hand silk handkerchiefs, of all sizes and patterns; for here reside the traders who purchase them from pickpockets. Hundreds of these handkerchiefs hang dangling from pegs outside the windows or flaunting from the door-posts; and the shelves, within, are piled with them. Confined as the limits of Field Lane are, it has its barber, its coffee-shop, its beer-shop, and its fried-fish warehouse. It is a commercial colony of itself: the emporium of petty larceny: visited at early morning, and setting-in of dusk, by silent merchants, who traffic in dark back-parlours, and who go as strangely as they come. Here, the clothesman, the shoe-vamper, and the rag-merchant, display their goods, as sign-boards to the petty thief; here, stores of old iron and bones, and heaps of mildewy fragments of woollen-stuff and linen, rust and rot in the grimy cellars.

Just to the west of Holborn Hill lies Ely Place, the one-time home of the Bishop of Ely, but by the late 18th century the area had become squalid and dilapidated. Holborn was also the centre of the great Inns of Court such as Staple Inn, Lincoln's Inn and Gray's Inn, all within a few hundred yards of Holborn.

At the top of the hill the Parish Church of St Andrew's still stands, where the young Crucefix was baptised on 15th July 1788. There has been a church on this site since the Middle Ages; the first was destroyed during the Great Fire of London in 1666 and rebuilt by Christopher Wren. Seriously damaged during the Blitz of the Second World War, it was rebuilt after the war.

LEFT
John Crucefix Clock.
Brian Loomes

BELOW
St Andrews Church Holborn Hill.

school had been founded in 1561 by members of the Merchant Taylors' Company and was situated in an old manor house known as the Manor of the Rose in the parish of St Laurence Pountney in the City of London. The reputation of the various City schools at the time was somewhat notorious. In 1796, two pupils were expelled for flying the French tricolour in support of the French Revolution, and City records tell of many school riots such as a pitched battle fought between the boys of St Paul's School at the bottom of Cheapside in 1811.

Crucefix left school in July 1804 to become apprenticed to Mr William Chamberlaine of the Royal College of Surgeons, a celebrated general practitioner who worked in and around the district of Clerkenwell. Traditionally practitioners of medicine could be divided into physicians, surgeons and apothecaries. Physicians were usually university educated and were considered to know most about the science of medicine. They were, however, not allowed to dispense medicine nor permitted to perform surgery; examination and diagnosis were their parameters. They were invariably licensed by the Royal Colleges of Physicians in the cities of Edinburgh and London. Surgeons, however, were usually apprenticed, learning their craft in the same manner as other trades. They were affiliated to the Barber Surgeons' Company and were permitted to perform operations and set bones. The old surgeon-barbers and their apprentices had unfortunately little opportunity to become skilled in anatomy as only four bodies a year, taken from those recently executed, were selected for dissection. The beadle of the Company usually attended public executions specifically to select suitable subjects. Apothecaries made and distributed medicines and, like their surgeon colleagues, learned their skills by apprenticeship. They were members of the Company of Apothecaries and later the Royal College of Surgeons after its formation in 1800. They, unlike physicians, could dispense medicines and were often known as surgeon-apothecaries.

In the early 19th century there was a general desire for a

Robert Thomas Crucefix was born on 15th June 1787, and his parents were sufficiently affluent to send him to one of the livery company schools within the area. Young Robert first attended the Merchant Taylors' School in 1801. The

greater understanding of the science of medicine. Universities and academic institutions were beginning to introduce practical training into their curriculum, combining academia with the science of medicine. This was the beginning of the medical schools. The famous Hunter brothers had first established such a school in Great William Street in London in the late 18th century, declaring that the study of anatomy was the only way to perform and understand surgery. In 1781, William Blizzard asked permission from the Governors of the London Hospital in Whitechapel to deliver two courses of lectures on anatomy and surgery, and within four years this had developed into the first recognisable medical school.

These new medical schools, however, were still few in number and heavily subscribed. The usual form of medical education had until then been by apprenticeship, preferably with a reputable general practitioner or surgeon. This was the basis of Robert Crucefix's training. It took the form of a formal legal document binding the young man to serve his master for a set period of time; in return he would receive the education to become a physician or surgeon, but the qualities of an apprenticeship were by their very nature varied. Some physicians and surgeons were excellent and caring doctors, whilst others cared little beyond the fee they were paid. The core of his education was the development of manual skills. Initially the apprentice would be employed as his master's servant, waiting on table and fulfilling other domestic duties. Eventually he would be taught the art of using a razor, bleeding and cupping, preparing bandages and dressing wounds. Finally he would be permitted to attend and assist during surgical operations. This was the basis of his medical training, but to become a qualified surgeon it was essential to study anatomy and witness a number of dissections under one of the recognised experts in the field. To this end, Crucefix attended St Bartholomew's Hospital during 1809 and 1810 and initially trained under Sir Ludford Harvey, a surgeon who practised at the hospital between 1807 and 1824. Inevitably Crucefix would also have attended the dissections conducted by one of the greatest surgeons of the day, the highly talented and eccentric John Abernethy, who had opened his house to demonstrate dissections. Abernethy had himself been a pupil of the great William Blizzard, whom he frequently quoted:

Let your search be after truth, be eager and constant. Be wary of admitting propositions as fact before you have submitted them to the strictest examination. Should you perceive truths to be important make them motives for

ABOVE **Merchant Taylors' School Suffolk Lane.** *Thornbury*

action. But truth is only important in so far as it influences conduct.

This statement may have had a profound effect on the young Crucefix later in his life. John Abernethy began giving lectures and private anatomy demonstrations at his home in Bartholomew Close in 1801, and these soon became so popular and profitable that the hospital governors erected an anatomy theatre especially for him. Although St Bartholomew's had existed since the Middle Ages, it could be argued that Abernethy was one of the founders of its medical school. His *Surgical Observations on the Constitutional Origin and Treatment of Local Diseases* was one of the earliest popular works in medical science. Robert Crucefix eventually qualified on 6th July 1810 with a Diploma from the Royal College of Surgeons.

There was clearly a need for reform in the training of medical students, especially in standardising the quality of the eventual qualifications, and the Apothecaries' Act was passed for this reason in August 1815. It entitled the Worshipful Company of Apothecaries to license medical students and qualified surgeons intending to dispense medicines.

Sometime during Robert Crucefix's training, news came from India that his father's only brother, John Henry Crucefix, had died on 31st December 1805, aged 43 years, at Fort George in Madras. He was buried in the garrison church of St Mary's situated next to the Residency. John Crucefix had been an Ensign in the 108th Regiment of Foot before becoming an officer in the army of the Nawab of Arcot, a

ABOVE **The Holborn Valley from Holborn Hill.** *Thornbury*

BELOW **St Bartholomew's Hospital 1750.** *Thornbury*

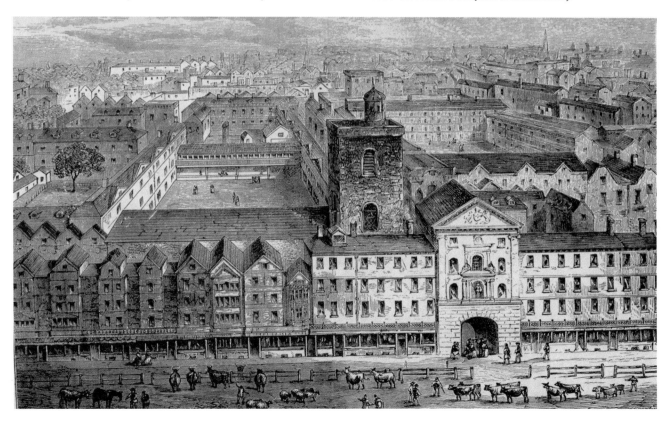

principality on the Carnatic Coast thought to be pro-British. There is, however, some evidence that these Nawabs played a somewhat Machiavellian game with the British, playing them off against neighbouring hostile princes. Promotion in the British Army cost a great deal, and as such, profit would be greater serving in a foreign army. John Crucefix was also a Freemason and had served as Master of the Unity, Peace and Concord Lodge No IX in 1801, meeting on the Coromandel Coast.

There was a great deal of similarity in the conduct of both Robert Thomas Crucefix and his uncle John; both fell foul of Masonic authority and were chastised for it. John Henry had upset the Grand Lodge in Madras because he thought they were interfering in the affairs of his Lodge in a heavy-handed manner, the outcome being that other Freemasons were then forbidden to attend his Lodge. When John died he left substantial properties, which may have been the reason for Robert's decision to travel to India. Robert knew that fortunes could be made in the East India Company, but sickness was rife and life could be cut short, especially around the big cities of Madras, Calcutta and Bombay where disease was endemic. The route was long, travelling around the Cape of Good Hope and then across the Indian Ocean, and the passage would have been hot and extremely tedious. Conditions for passengers were exceedingly cramped, as the average boat could take anything up to a hundred passengers, but Crucefix must have thought this was worth enduring especially if his uncle had left a substantial sum. But his time in India was short, for soon after completing his business he was making the return journey home. There is, however, currently no evidence that he went to India in the time between completing his training on 6th July 1810 and terminating his partnership on 24th June 1811 — barely a year and, although practically possible, the window of opportunity is short.

The terminated partnership was entitled 'James, Burnett & Crucefix, Surgeons, Apothecaries, Men-Midwives, Chemists, and Druggists'. His partners were William James and James Burnett, and there is every likelihood that the more affluent Burnett bought him and James out, for the company continued under his name.

In or around 1813, Crucefix met either Thomas Goss, or more probably his widow, Jane Goss. Goss had been born in Rosemary Lane near to the Royal Mint in 1781, the son of Dorothy and John Goss, and was baptised in St Botolph's Church, Aldgate. By the age of 16 years he had been apprenticed to the apothecary J. W. Pearce. He eventually became a purveyor of medicines, which he combined with

his duties as a medical practitioner, dispensing these products under the title Goss & Co. On 14th October 1802, Dr Thomas Goss married a young widow named Jane Bannister at St Leonard's Church, Shoreditch. Jane had been born into a large family in Hackington on the outskirts of Canterbury on 7th April 1782, and her parents, William Taylor and Susannah Dove, were poor and lived in tithed accommodation. She was one of the younger members of her family, and on the death of her parents (William died in 1785, and Susannah in 1800) she went to live with her eldest sister, Elizabeth, and her husband William Coatsworth, a wine cooper, of St Martin's in Canterbury. He died within the year and Elizabeth quickly married James Smith, a prominent member of Mrs Sarah Baker's theatrical company. They looked after Jane until, aged 18 years, she married Thomas Bannister of Northgate, Canterbury. The marriage was short, and on Thomas's death she moved to London where she married Thomas Goss.

Life was not easy, for on two occasions, in 1802 and then in 1808, whilst living in Hackney, Thomas was declared bankrupt. Jane appears to have been illiterate at the time of her marriage to Goss, signing the marriage certificate with an 'X', but within a few years she had learned to read and write, for on marrying Crucefix she was able to write her own name. Dr Goss died at 13 Bouverie Street, near St Bride's Church in Fleet Street, on 24th September 1813, aged 32 years. He left virtually all his estates to his wife, with strict instructions on how the business should be conducted should she ever remarry. Dr Robert Thomas Crucefix married Goss's widow Jane at St Mary's Church, Lambeth, on 2nd July 1814. His brother, John Clarke Crucefix, was one of the witnesses. Robert and Jane's relationship was private, for in the reams of letters and writings of Dr Crucefix, Jane is rarely mentioned. However, in one of the early editions of the *Freemasons' Quarterly Review*, he wrote a poem to a Freemason's wife that must reflect his own relationship:

> *To Her*
> *Whose value as a Friend*
> *Can only be estimated by him*
> *Whose adversity has been cheered by her patience and*
> *her smiles*
> *And whose prosperity*
> *Owes its only charm to her sharing its advantages:*
> *Whose least beauty is her personal Grace,*
> *And whose charms upon her husband's gratitude*
> *For the cheerful acquiescence in her utility of his*
> *Masonic Avocations*

RIGHT **Barber Surgeons Hall about 1800.** *Thornbury*

Has enabled him, if may be successfully, to perform of his
Duty to the Craft;
To a woman whose heart is charitable
To a Freemason's Wife
This volume is most affectionately dedicated.

Later, when he received his testimonial from his fellow Freemasons, he spoke lovingly of his wife:

It is true I have no Lewis to share with me the heat and burden of the day, who can hereafter look on this testimonial as a record of a sire's zeal, but there is one at home now waiting my return, as she often has with far different feeling, in whose bosom this splendid proof of your attachment will enkindle the gentle consolation that her husband has equally gained the approbation of his friends, as he has proved deserving of her health.

The Napoleonic War ended in 1815 and soon thousands of doctors from the Army and Navy were added to what was becoming an overcrowded profession. The many doctors who had qualified by the old system found themselves in open competition with their more academic colleagues now leaving the newer medical schools. Doctors, like Crucefix, had to expand their business into other areas to survive. Many did this by manufacturing remedies and potions, often of questionable value, as well as extending their practices into the less socially attractive and less popular forms of medicine. This would include the sexually transmitted diseases, the gynaecological diseases, and those where cures were, at that time, unknown. In many cases they had no alternative other than to join the ranks of the quacks to make a living. (So much harm came from quack remedies claiming success, that in 1917 the treatment of syphilis by an unqualified person was made a criminal offence.)

In the upper classes of society syphilis was accepted within reason. The symptoms could in the early stages of the disease be disguised, but inevitably as it progressed it led to disfiguring ulcers and ultimately invaded other organs such as the brain, resulting in dementia. Death was inevitable. There was no satisfactory cure yet people were desperate, and embarrassment led to panic. Victims would go to any length to alleviate the disease. An advertisement placed in *The Times* of 23rd August 1815 by Dr Crucefix shows how, by using a combination of pseudoscience and personal qualifications, the innocent could be enticed into any form of cure:

Messrs Goss & Co Members of the Royal College of Surgeons in London continue to direct their attention to those diseases by which the power of constitution becomes enfeebled: and their experience in such cases, during a long and successful practice, enables them to offer to persons so affected, a safe and speedy restoration to sound and vigorous health. A certain disorder frequently contracted in a moment's intoxication, as also its concomitants, are by their plan of treatment (without

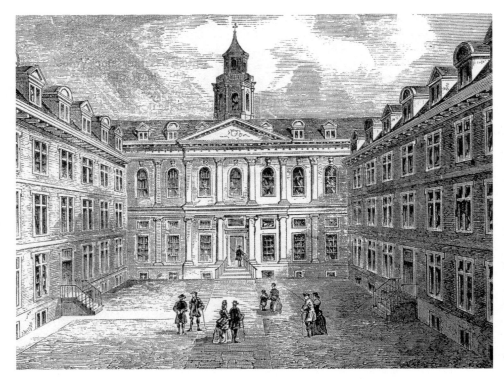

LEFT **College of Physicians Warwick Lane.** *Thornbury*

was particularly scathing, and maintained a continued campaign against Goss & Co. Publishing in the *Medical Adviser and Guide to Health and Long Life*, he wrote:

Goss and Company! Good God! Was there ever such a heap of filth and infamy as this swindling firm of straw! Was there ever such a cancer upon society — such an adroit and plausible system of rapacious plundering?

No matter how much Robert protested and advertised that

restraint in diet and exercise) speedily and effectually cured: and whereas early application is made, on discovery of the infection, the complaint is frequently removed within two days. By professing exclusively the cure of such complaint, and in order that they may not be marked by a mistaken few with the obloquy so justly attached to the ignorant empiric, Messrs Goss & Co think it but justice to themselves to state that they have been regularly educated in every branch of the profession (certificates of which from different hospitals and testimonials from most eminent physicians they have to convince any enquiry) that the success resulting from their endeavours first induced them to quit the practice of the general practitioner: and they presume that their pretensions constitute a fair ground for the unprecedented confidence for which they have, by the public, been so liberally honoured. To be consulted at their house daily, by either sex, personally or by letter, with secrecy, delicacy, and attention. Letters for advice and medicine to contain a banknote, — Goss and Co, surgeons, 13 Bouverie Street, Fleet Street.

Crucefix found this new pursuit contributed towards the income derived from his medical practice; however, his drug company had an appalling reputation. Alexander Burnett

his qualifications as a surgeon were legitimate, the magazine continued to persecute him with such statements that the letters MRC after his name did not stand for Member of the Royal College, but for MURDERING, ROBBING CHARLATAN.

On 30th June 1824, Crucefix was presented by the Chamberlain to the Board of the Court of Admissions for the Freedom of the City of London to receive the benefits of Freedom by redemption to the Company of Scriveners. This cost him 40s 8d but gained him another potential source of income, as since 1821 the Scriveners' Company had secured the Public Notaries Act compelling all who wished to become notaries to fall under its jurisdiction. The Company was now responsible for ensuring that all its members were properly qualified and licensed to draw up deeds and perform other legal formalities. Whatever the strengths and weaknesses of Crucefix's scientific skills, he was not prevented from obtaining a doctorate of medicine (MD). This was gained from the University of St Andrews on 2nd July 1825, and was validated by the signatures of Henry Harrington MD and John B. James MD, two Fellows of the University of Edinburgh. Sometime in the 1840s, Crucefix ceased to use his MD qualification and began to put LLD after his name, implying he had now become a Doctor of Law.

RIGHT **John Abernethy.** *J. Cochran*

In 1827, he published under his company's name the first of a series of journals entitled *The Aegis of Life*, stating that these were:

> a non-medical commentary on the indiscretions arising from human frailty, in which the causes, symptoms, and baneful effects of venereal disease, gonorrhoea, stricture, seminal weakness, &c. are explained in a familiar manner : to which are added very extensive practical observations on sexual debility, and its attendant sympathies : the whole illustrated by striking cases : addressed to youth and maturity.

Crucefix's practice now expanded into the realm of female medicine, thereby embracing both sexes, and today he would be described as a urogenital specialist. Pioneering work had been done by William Hunter (1718-1783), the renowned anatomist and obstetrician, who had performed innumerable dissections of the female reproductive system, publishing his results in *Anatomia uteri humani gravidi* (The anatomy of the human gravid uterus) (1774) with plates engraved by Jan van Rymsdyk (1730-1790). However, in the first half of the 19th century there was little understanding of these diseases and limited reliable experimental research. Crucefix in 1829 saw this as a niche market and began publishing a series of articles stating clearly that they were for 'the use of females only'. He describes his work in his book *Hygeiana* as:

> a non-medical analysis of the complaints incidental to females, in which are offered some important admonitions on the peculiar debilities attending their circumstances, sympathies and formation, illustrated by cases, intended for the use of females only, and addressed to the youth and maturity of that sex.

There is little science in these writings; most are in a poetic language that, in the 21st century, appears patronising. It does not take a great deal of imagination to see through the writings and realise that, although written for the female market, they are ultimately designed to titillate the male:

> Equally, if not more malignant, are the disease instances to the softer sex, than those maladies which are peculiar to men. As the beautiful colouring of the delicate flowers wither beneath the incipient breathings of the destructive mildew, so the frail texture of female beauty gives way when the worm of disease has made its earliest lodgement. Alike the fair and the flower — both forms of beauty, designed by nature to attract and fix our admirations — are susceptible of the lightest touch of corruption, which too soon insinuates itself into sanctuary, converting it into gloomy ruin. Imagination can scarcely conceive a more heart-desolating scene than the destruction of fascinating beauty — when morbid ugliness usurps the prerogative of time, and anticipates his despotic ravages.

This paragraph appeared in the 1834 edition of *Hygeiana*. It is a thinly disguised description of venereal disease and promises, by the use of various potions, that a cure could be achieved. Although Goss & Co appeared frequently in both the general and medical press, there is little to associate Dr Robert Thomas Crucefix MD with such a company. There is only one contemporary reference, and that appeared in the 1825 edition of the *Monthly Gazette of Health*, where it stated:

> ... the proprietor of Goss & Co was a former shop assistant going by the unlikely name of Mr. Crucifix [sic].

Events did not always run smoothly, for Dr Crucefix was declared to be a bankrupt in September 1828. Subsequently printed in the *Law Advertiser* on 25th May 1830 was a notice

ABOVE **The London Hospital Whitechapel**

that a certain printer of Bouverie Street had appeared before the Court of Common Bankruptcy, stating:

> *Crucefix, Robert Thomas, Bouverie Street, Fleet Street, London, printer; June 16 and 12 precisely, C.C.B, as to disposing of two debts. To the estate of a printer of Bouverie Street, had appeared before the Court of Common Bankruptcy at 12pm on 6th June to account for two debts to the estate, or otherwise compounding the same, and on other special affairs.*

These, however, may not have been too serious and may just relate to having failed to pay outstanding money owed.

His third book, entitled *The Syphilist: A Familiar Treatise on the Nature, Symptoms, and Effects of Lues Venerea, Gonorrhoea, Gleet, Stricture, and a Variety of Incidental Diseases; with Many Interesting Observations and Remarks Occurring in a Most Extensive Practice to which is Appended a Series of Cases Explanatory of Each Subject*, was published in 1830.

In 1830, for whatever reason, he moved from Bouverie Street to 7 Lancaster Place, Waterloo Bridge, London, a middle class street connecting the Strand with the Thames riverbank. This was before the construction of the Thames Embankment by Joseph Bazalgette, designed to hold part of the London sewage system. Until the 1860s, the area stank from the polluted river and must, at times, have been unbearable. Thomas Cubitt in 1840 described it as follows:

> *Fifty years ago nearly all London had every house cleansed into a large cesspool ... Now sewers having been very much improved, scarcely any person thinks of making a cesspool, but it is carried off at once to the river. The Thames is now made a great cesspool instead of each person having one of his own.*

Crucefix and his wife lived here until he eventually retired to the country and, as the decade continued, his Masonic career began to expand. His business took him all over Great Britain, and his repertoire developed from the *Diseases of Venus* into the realms of an agony aunt. This was in a society that found talk of sex distasteful — the word was never to be mentioned.

In the *Belfast Newsletter* he invited ladies to attend his surgery as follows:

> *Surgeon Goss, from London, is now in Dublin, and can be consulted everyday (except Sunday) at 11 Upper North Gloucester St from 9 until 2, and on Mon, Wed, Fri from 6 til 9. He will leave on the 15th Oct.*

He took advantage of his business travels to advance his versions of Freemasonry and its other orders. However, his reputation, created from specialising in the treatment of unfashionable diseases with improbable cures, was to haunt him throughout his Masonic career. A broadsheet published by I. O. Truman in 1840 made just such an accusation. In 1841, Crucefix and his wife took in his 18-year-old nephew, Robert Richard Crucefix (the son of Robert Clarke Crucefix), who was studying medicine at Charing Cross Hospital in the Strand. That year, Crucefix's health began noticeably to deteriorate. He must have been fully aware from his symptoms that he had contracted tuberculosis, announcing at his testimonial celebrations in November of that year:

> *Brethren, failing strength and impaired health admonish me to limited duty; but there is honour in retirement. I feel that when I shall reflect on the transactions of this auspicious day, as if my spirits would reanimate and my health improve: in such a case, I doubt my resolution to keep from among you.*

Nevertheless a deteriorating health did not appear to limit his heavy workload. In 1844, he published under his own name *Time versus Life: an enigma*. This covers a variety of physiological and psychological conditions associated with sexual diseases.

By 1845, Robert Crucefix, now 57 years old, was continually tired and frequently coughing up blood. The general consensus at the time, and the only hope for a cure, or at least remission, was to seek a cleaner environment away from London — the miasmic theory that diseases were transmitted by foul air was extremely topical at the time. There could be nowhere worse than living near the River Thames, then one of the most polluted rivers in the world, and the sensible thing to do was to go to the country. Crucefix realised he still had much to do in a limited time; he particularly wished to finish his work on popular events in English Freemasonry. He moved from Lancaster Place on the north bank of the river to the countryside of Kent at Grove, Gravesend. Here he had a peaceful, clean environment with ready access to London, the Gravesend & Rochester Railway having opened a line between London and Gravesend earlier that year.

RIGHT **St Brides' Church, Fleet Street.** *Thornbury*

CHAPTER 3

THE GRAND MASTER

At the time of Robert Crucefix's initiation into Freemasonry, the Duke of Sussex had been the Grand Master for 13 years. The nation as a whole was benefiting from a time of peace since Waterloo, and prosperity as a consequence of the industrial revolution. It was, however, split into three social economic groups or classes. The differences between these classes were profound and they rarely if ever inter-mixed. The largest was the great working masses, largely illiterate, who worked or starved. Crucefix came within the smaller, middle or professional class — well-educated and financially sound, but not of independent means. The Duke was at the pinnacle of the ruling class, and as such, Crucefix and the Duke could not have been more different. The concept of *trade* was etched in the minds of the aristocracy as something if not distasteful, not quite acceptable within their social circle.

The Duke was baptised Augustus Frederick by the Archbishop of Canterbury in Buckingham House (later Palace) on 25th February 1773, just one month after his birth. He and his brothers, Prince Ernest and Prince Adolphus, attended the University of Göttingen in Germany as befitted a member of the House of Hanover. Ideally he would have followed his brother William (later King William IV) into the Royal Navy, but as a severe asthmatic he was spared military service. Therefore, to alleviate his medical condition and, perhaps more importantly, to keep him away from English women, he was sent to Prussia.

In 1793, whilst staying in Rome, he had a romantic affair with Lady Augusta Murray, the daughter of the 4th Earl of Dunmore, and they secretly married. When the news of this reached the King he had the young prince escorted back to London in disgrace and the marriage annulled. Augustus Frederick was not, however, perturbed and went through a second secret marriage to Lady Augusta in St George's Church, Hanover Square, London, which again was annulled. Although unable to marry his love, he remained with her until 1801. They had two children, but as they were both born in contravention of the Royal Marriages Act, the children — Augustus Frederick d'Este (1794-1848) and Augusta Emma d'Este (1801-1866) — were declared illegitimate. In 1801, ever short of money, he was offered a dukedom with a hefty endowment if he left her. Bowing to royal pressure, they went their separate ways. She was also given £4,000 per annum and retired to live at Mount Albion House, Ramsgate, with their children. She continued to live in Thanet until her death in 1831, and lies in St Laurence's Church in Ramsgate, Kent. Given the titles of Duke of Sussex, Earl of Inverness and Baron Arklow, along with a grant from parliament of £12,000 a year, Augustus Frederick became a member of the Privy Council and represented the King at Weymouth in September 1804. He was the fifth of his brothers to join Freemasonry when he was initiated in the Lodge Victorious Truth during his stay in Berlin in 1798. This Lodge belonged to the Royal York of Friendship, the Grand Lodge of Prussia, and he eventually became its Master. Prussian Lodges were at this time devoutly Christian, which suited the Duke who was a fervent believer, reportedly spending anything up to two hours a day contemplating religious script. His love of books, especially religious writings, was his great delight in life. His library was said to contain over 50,000 books, including 1,000 editions of the Bible and innumerable Hebrew and other ancient manuscripts. The *Christian Observer* (1843) recorded that he was convinced of the divine origin of the Scriptures, 'which contain matters beyond human understanding', and that he did not 'concern himself with dogmas, which are of human origin'. It continued that he was 'not to be thought a Freethinker, which imputation I would indignantly repel; nor to pass for a person indifferent about religion'.

When he returned to England in 1800, he joined the Prince of Wales' Lodge. He participated in the work of several other Lodges, and had a special liking for Pilgrim Lodge No 238, which to this day is German-speaking and uses the Berlin workings of its founder, Bro Johann Daniel Siegfried Leonardie. His promotion within Freemasonry was rapid, as befitted his social standing. Augustus Frederick was said to be unlike most of his family; he was a most liberal and social individual, interested in current affairs and scientific discoveries, and was said to be competent in several languages. He became the President of the Royal Society — a position he held for nine years. His support of liberal views and his association with the Whig Party distanced him from his father and brothers from an early age and excluded him from lucrative employment enjoyed by others in his family. When only seven years old, the King had locked him in his nursery for wearing Admiral Keppel's election colours. Keppel (1725-1786) was a member of a prestigious Whig family and had served as a senior officer in the Royal Navy during the Seven Years War and the American War of Independence. The Duke supported many reforming acts throughout his life, including the abolition of the slave trade, the repeal of the Corn Laws, and Catholic emancipation, all

BELOW **King George IV painted by Thomas Lawrence.** *Library and Museum of Freemasonry*

RIGHT **Augustus Frederick (1773–1843), Duke of Sussex, by an unknown artist.** *Library and Museum of Freemasonry*

BELOW RIGHT **Field Marshal HRH Edward (1767–1820), Duke of Kent and Strathearn, by George Henry.** *Library and Museum of Freemasonry*

contrary to the beliefs of his father and brothers. He was appointed Grand Principal of the Grand and Royal Chapter in 1810, and two years later became Deputy Grand Master. However, in 1813, he succeeded his brother George, the Prince Regent, as the Grand Master of the Premier Grand Lodge of England. He took his Freemasonry very seriously and was reported as saying:

> *When I first determined to link myself with this noble Institution, it was a matter of very serious consideration with me; and I can assure the Brethren that it was at a period when, at least, I had the power of well considering the matter, for it was not in the boyish days of my youth, but at the more mature age of 25 or 26 years. I did not take it up as a light and trivial matter, but as a grave and serious concern of my life.*

Throughout the 18th century there had been two groups of Freemasons, both often vehemently opposed to each other. They were known as the Antients and the Moderns. The Antients, or as it is now known the Antient Grand Lodge of

England, traced its origins from Prince Edwin of York and was formed in AD926. It flourished in England between 1751 and 1813, and was known informally as the Atholl Grand Lodge. It became clear during the Napoleonic War that in order to prevent their Lodges becoming proscribed organisations they needed to act together. The Moderns, who had been formed in 1721, invited the Prince Regent to become their Grand Master, which he accepted, relinquishing that post to his younger brother, the Duke of Sussex, in 1813. The Antients, not to be outdone, chose his brother the Duke of Kent to be their Grand Master. The actual process of unification did not start until 1811, and it was largely due to the efforts of these two brothers that the two parties eventually merged.

The events relating to the merger are complex and have been recorded by many worthy writers. The result was that on 27th December 1813 the Premier Grand Lodge of England united with the Antient Grand Lodge of England to form the United Grand Lodge of England (UGLE). The Duke of Sussex became its first Grand Master, a position he would hold until his death in 1843. His brother, the Duke of Kent, had no wish to compete for the title and chose to stand down. It was accepted by both sides that their separate rituals would have to be combined into something mutually agreeable. A Lodge of Reconciliation was consecrated to enforce the ritual and regulations which centred on

RIGHT **Tomb of Lady Augusta Murray, St Laurence, Ramsgate.** *Author*

the basic degrees of Craft masonry and the Holy Royal Arch rather than concentrating on the additional degrees that, as a consequence of union, began to emerge from all over the Masonic world.⬚

The Coronation of Sussex's brother William in 1830 once again restored the Duke's popularity within court circles, but this was to be short-lived as he again supported the Whig Party by endorsing the passing of the Reform Bill in the House of Lords. The Reform Act or the Representation of the People Act of 1832, presented by the Whig Party under Lord Grey, was designed to rebalance the seats in the House of Commons to favour the rapidly changing population. People were leaving the country and moving to large industrial towns, and rotten boroughs were seen as undemocratic when populations often in the tens had equal voting powers to areas measured in thousands. The Act was vehemently opposed by the Tory Party under the Duke of Wellington. In the early days, Lord Grey's election victory had given him enough seats to get the act passed in the Commons, but it was defeated in the strongly Tory dominated House of Lords, resulting in street rioting. An approach was made to William IV to create more Whig peers, which he refused, becoming increasingly suspicious of these parliamentary reforms, forcing Lord Grey to resign. Wellington was invited to form a Tory government, but without the support of many Tories, including Sir Robert Peel, he failed. The King had no option other than to concede and create more reformist peers. He did, however, gain some concessions; only one in seven males were given the vote, and a number of constituencies still had fewer than 300 electors. Both sides of the House of Commons were surprised at how far-reaching the new Bill was to become.

Meanwhile, Sussex's attitude towards marriage and his regard for the Royal Marriages Act did not change. He married a second time, on 2nd May 1831, after the death of his first wife (there was to be no question of bigamy). This time it was to Lady Cecelia Letitia Buggin, the widow of Sir George Buggin. The marriage took place at Great Cumberland Place and the couple resided at Kensington Palace. However, the marriage was again considered void and she was never permitted to use the title of Duchess of Sussex, but Queen Victoria — as the Duke was her favourite uncle and had given her away at her marriage to Prince Albert — graciously ennobled her in 1840 by investing her as Duchess of Inverness. She continued to live at Kensington Palace until her death in 1873 and was buried next to her husband.

In 1832, the Duke began to go blind from cataracts, which although operable were thought too dangerous to perform.

ABOVE **Duke of Sussex as Grand Master.** *Library and Museum of Freemasonry*

P. R. James, in his 1962 Prestonian Lecture, described the Duke's deterioration in health towards the end of his life. He was now blind and unable to read his beloved books, and many of his friends and advisers had died. He became dispirited, bad tempered, perhaps unjust and despotic, and looked with malice on what he considered the organised conspiracies of Crucefix and Oliver, whom he considered were bringing his life's work crashing down. His death came as a relief to the fraternity and probably to himself.

He died in 1843, having noted that he did not want a state funeral but wished to be interred in a simple grave. He had been so appalled by the protocol of his brother William IV's funeral at Windsor that he declared, 'I would not be buried there after this fashion for all the world.' He therefore made it known in his will that he wished to be buried in Kensal Green Cemetery, Harrow Road.

The 1962 Prestonian Lecture ends with this statement: 'He was not a great Grand Master, but he was a good one.'

CHAPTER 4

THE GATHERING STORM

Six sons of George III were Freemasons, and this inevitably increased the Craft's popularity with the general public. The recent union of the two Masonic Grand Lodges in 1813 brought to an end the bickering that had occurred throughout the 18th century. The Duke of Sussex was considered a radical, and now as Grand Master he found himself in charge of an organisation that, at grass roots level, also wished to benefit from the new reforms that were beginning to change the country.

These reforms were not universally popular and many at the centre of Freemasonry did not support them. William Howley, the Archbishop of Canterbury and a Freemason, opposed the repeal of the Test and Corporation Acts (1828), the Emancipation of Catholics (1829) and the passing of the great Reform Act (1832), his outspoken views having led to his coach being attacked in the streets of Canterbury. The Duke, as Grand Master, had to balance these conflicting views within the Craft, although he himself had strong political sympathies with these new laws. It was, however, inevitable that many of these new equalities did not extend into his Freemasonry. The Craft had always been non-political; in fact the discussion of politics was, and still is, discouraged. This approach had given Freemasonry exemption from the Unlawful Societies Act of 1799, which had not been granted to other groups such as early trade unions and friendly societies. Some of these alliances had even incorporated and copied aspects of Masonic ritual, and the fear of comparison was a constant threat. The arrest and subsequent transportation in 1834 of the Tolpuddle Martyrs, under the Unlawful Societies Act, demonstrated the value of Grand Lodge's approach. Grand Lodge continually urged its Brethren not to be complacent but to check that there was no subversion within their Lodges, thereby preventing any infringement of the Act. All Lodges were required to make a list of their members, along with their professions, and copies were to be sent to the Grand Secretary and to the local magistrate; failure to do so would result in exclusion of that Lodge.

The Duke controlled the Craft within an inner circle of trusted senior men; decisions were made by him and were not up for discussion by the rank and file. Information essential to the Craft was filtered down in short bulletins, but the decision-making was kept secret within the bounds of the rulers, the centre of which was the Duke himself. This also extended to the appointment of Officers within Grand Lodge; that decision was his, and was granted to only a few individuals each year.

In 1834, Robert Crucefix was certainly not among the rulers. He had been initiated on 16th April 1829 into the Burlington Lodge No 113 (now Lodge No 96). His rise in Freemasonry was meteoric, for within three years he became the Junior Deacon in his Mother Lodge and had joined at least four other Lodges. He had also been exalted into Naval and Military Royal Arch Chapter and Installed Knight Templar in the Grand Conclave of Scotland, and was appointed a Grand Steward in 1832.

Crucefix felt that amongst the fraternity there was a general desire, not least a need, for knowledge. He commented that 'such an arrangement has long been a desideratum which the Quarterly Communications do not afford'. Not being dismayed by the hierarchy, or perhaps in ignorance, he deigned to publish, on 1st April 1834 without any official approval, a Masonic magazine entitled *The Freemasons' Quarterly Review* (*FQR*). In his words:

> *The reason behind the magazine is to create an archive of Masonic events, records, and biographies of worthy Freemasons who have advanced the interests of their art.*

The opening paragraph of the first edition explains Crucefix's objectives:

> *In the present state of our periodic literature, with the finest talent of the country engaged upon its pages, the fresh candidate who enters the arena of public opinion,*

and courts its favour, will have to contend with obstacles of no ordinary character, and should, therefore, be armed with pretension of a peculiar class.

He compares Freemasonry with other sciences, such as medicine and the military, justifying his publication by pointing out that as communication has improved the efficiency and knowledge in those sciences, so will it similarly improve the Craft.

In this first paper he outlines the style of all future editions. There would be commentaries on parliamentary debates, foreign news, particularly from the USA and Europe, theatrical news and exhibitions of fine art. Along with these were the more controversial subjects such as the Quarterly Communications and the composition of the various committees —many of which he served on — and the decisions made by them. A number of other Freemasons would also report Provincial news. Crucefix was particularly interested in the activities of those Lodges performing or practising Christian degrees. The main text would consist of various Masonic and Biblical stories. Dr Oliver, who at the time was considered the foremost authority on the history of Freemasonry, became a regular contributor. His articles would appear after the opening section entitled 'General Observations' and may be compared to a modern editorial. But it was the promise that all contributors in the future could claim anonymity that became controversial with senior Freemasons, especially those of the inner circle around the Grand Master. Its contents were not particularly controversial by today's standards and contained nothing resembling the disclosures and exposés published in the preceding centuries. However, the very fact he had dared to write on Masonic subjects was contrary to the tenets of the Duke, who continued to maintain that all Masonic information should be kept within the control of Grand Lodge and as such secret.

The core values of Crucefix's views were the principles of Truth, Knowledge and Virtue. His view of truth is elegantly expressed in a short poem in the first edition:

Truth shall yet be heard, no human power
Can stifle or corrupt her purposes;
Through superstitious gloom her voice is heard,
It pierces through the veil of barbarous ages
The prejudices of time — the venal lay
Full impotent before its god like sound
It pierces e'en the silence of the tomb,
Bursting the barriers of icy death,

And injured virtue walks triumphant forth
Free from the taint of calumny or crime.

Crucefix used the same printers, Sherwood, Gilbert & Piper of Paternoster Row in the City of London, as had published his professional volumes such as *Time versus Life*. This was a well-known and respectable publishing house that printed a wide range of books and articles, including anatomical and medical texts. However, the publication of illustrated anatomical books was considered by some as, if not pornographic, not the thing polite society would read. This factor was to be later used to vilify him.

The July issue of 1834 included the first reference to a benevolent project to erect and endow an Asylum for Aged and Decayed Freemasons of good character. There was a general acceptance by the middle classes of the need for the various Reform Acts introduced throughout the 1820s and 1830s. Even the Poor Law Amendment Act was seen by most as essential, otherwise the country would be overrun and bankrupted by the countless paupers migrating from the country into the towns. Members of affluent society generally thought that this particular law was unlikely to affect them, but a few enlightened individuals could see that under certain circumstances some could, and would, inevitably fall into the entrapment of the workhouse. It would only need a few financial mishaps, disinheritance or a sudden death to reduce a rich man or his family to penury. If these individuals just happened to be Freemasons, who was to look after them, especially if they were old and infirm?

The original concept of a care home had been suggested by the Rev Gilbert Gilbert of the Harmony Lodge No 255 in March 1831, but it did not stimulate any necessity to do anything. Four years were to elapse before Crucefix picked up the baton and ran with it. He wrote in the March 1836 edition of the *FQR*:

The new code of poor laws varies from the former; and without making one illusion to its propriety or otherwise, it teaches us this: that it will argue a cold and callous heart to wish, much less allow, a deserving Freemason to become an inmate of any other asylum than that which the Fraternity shall accord to him as the reward of his conduct ... Shall Freemasonry exhibit the monstrous exception! We dare reply, No, and dismayed by delay, and unshaken in our confidence, we reiterate our hope.

In 1842, Sir Edwin Chadwick delivered a report to

Parliament on death and disease amongst the labouring population within industrial towns, for it had suddenly come to their attention that the poor living in conurbations died much younger than their rural counterparts, especially from those infectious diseases that ravaged the crowded inner cities. This obvious phenomenon he blamed on bad ventilation or miasma, a popular but erroneous theory common in the mid-19th century that disease was spread by bad, stinking air. He was also aware that poor sanitation contributed to the high mortality rate. When Charles Dickens visited a workhouse in 1850, he wrote:

It was inhabited by a population of some fifteen hundred or two thousand paupers, ranging from the infant newly born or not yet come into the pauper world to the old man dying on his bed ... some old people were bedridden, and had been for a long time; some were sitting on their beds half naked; some dying in their beds; some out of bed; and sitting at a table near the fire. A sullen and lethargic indifference to what was asked, a blunted sensibility to everything but warmth and food, a resentful desire to be left alone again.

The state of the conditions in Union Workhouses finally called for the formation of a medically led Commission, which eventually published its findings in *The Lancet* in 1866. The St Pancras Workhouse was probably one of the largest in London and would have been well known to Crucefix and his associates. It had a range of inmates, from basic paupers, the insane, the sick, who could not afford medicine or care from a physician, and the elderly; all were expected to work if physically possible. Invariably both men and women would be separately housed, even if they were husband and wife. On 26th January 1865, there were 232 in the infirmary, 746 in the infirm wards and 116 insane — a total of 1,094 individuals in the St Pancras Workhouse. There were only two residential physicians and most of the medical assistants came from the untrained residents within the institution. It is not surprising that

as a consequence of the crowded conditions, individuals succumbed to infectious diseases such as measles, typhus, tuberculosis and gastrointestinal diseases. Death rates were substantially higher than amongst the general public.

In this second issue of the *FQR*, Crucefix proposed that his new project for aged Freemasons be combined with the existing Masonic charities for orphans. He was, at this time, on the Board of the Royal Freemasons' Charity for Female Children, currently chaired by Lord John Winston Spencer Churchill, and was well placed to understand the practicalities of a charity. He estimated that the combined cost would be around £5,000. Although well received, it was felt that it had not been properly thought through. It was, however, deemed worthy enough to be raised at the Quarterly Communications held on 4th June as one of the 'Subjects under consideration':

The aged Masons' Asylum, with a plan for its erection, suggestions on raising the funds necessary for that purpose, and suggestions for its further endowment, in connection with a Masonic Orphans and Children of deceased and indigent Freemason.

Crucefix was in his element and enthusiastically supported the cause for the elderly, so that by the time of the October 1834 edition of the *FQR* he stated:

That the aged Mason, whose earlier years have passed in the active cheerful exercise of his avocation, whose summer has been warmed by friendship and cherished in hope, should, in the winter of life, find no haven to receive him, is neglect in the Order itself. The pure and blessed spirit of Masonry will readily cast a veil over the frailties of many, but oh! Let her enshrine the few choicer but aged veterans, when no longer able to work, even for a morsel of bread.

LEFT **Dr Robert Thomas Crucefix by Bro Mosely.** *Royal Masonic Benevolent Institute*

A common fear of the middle classes was that one small financial mistake could render their final years confined to a workhouse. Many Freemasons, convinced of the virtue of their cause, wished to draw in the Grand Master and suggested that his birthday, 27th January, would be the day to celebrate the concept of the Aged Masons' Asylum. It was suggested that a building subscription should be started to pay for the upkeep of the girls' school and the new Home for the Aged. That December, Robert Crucefix had the honour of seconding the proposition in Grand Lodge, formerly proposed by Bro Palmer, that the Duke of Sussex should continue as the Grand Master and at the following meeting of the Quarterly Communications, Crucefix was appointed the Grand Junior Deacon.

Support for a Home now began to gather momentum and soon the editorial desk of the *FQR* was covered with letters from enthusiastic but anxious supporters. On 31st March 1835, Henry Rowe, the Master of the Neptune Lodge, wrote:

> Your Powerful advocacy in favour of an asylum for the aged and infirmed mason attracted our serious attention, and we at length considered that the fraternity only waited for someone to begin so laudable a works, but we were fearful that if we waited for each other it might never be accomplished, and have resolved that each member of the Neptune Lodge shall pay a third subscription of two shillings per annum, and that the Lodge shall set apart one guinea out of every initiation fee; ... until the erection and endowment of the Masonic Asylum can be carried into execution.

Crucefix's response was as follows:

> This is something like working for good cause — it is hitting the nail right on the head and ultimately must succeed. The example of the Worshipful Master of the Neptune Lodge will not be lost upon the fraternity.

Support for an institution for the elderly was now spreading beyond the metropolis. The *Sherborne Mercury* published a letter in the edition issued on 16th April supporting the cause:

> Merit and Virtue in distress; persons who are incapable of extracting themselves from misfortune in their journey through life; industrious men, who, from inevitable accidents and acts of providence have fallen into ruin, widows left survivors of their husband, by whose labours they subsisted, orphans in tender years left naked to the world; and the aged, whose spirits are exhausted, whose arms are embraced by time, and thereby rendered unable to procure from themselves that sustenance they could accomplish in their youthful day.
>
> This is charity, the keystone of our mystical fabric.

It was now considered the appropriate time to approach officially the Grand Master. Joseph Copeland Bell wrote to the Duke of Sussex informing him that several of the Brethren were keen to establish a home for elderly Freemasons and as such were planning to raise funds, initially by staging a theatrical event, and they would be grateful for any help and advice he might suggest. The response from Kensington Palace was immediate. The Grand Secretary, William White, writing on behalf of the Grand Master, replied that the Duke was interested and would meet with a representative group at some time, but would like to understand what their aims and objectives were and how the establishment of the Institution was to be achieved. A series of correspondence flowed backward and forward between the Grand Secretary and Joseph Bell to clarify matters, and in the meantime the proposed theatrical entertainment was held on 29th May 1835 at the Theatre Royal (English Opera House) — a production of *La Sonnambula* by Vincenzo Bellini. This was something of a coup, as the opera had premiered in Italy only three years previously. The house was packed full and the opera was a great social event, crowned by an address on the virtues of such an asylum delivered by Bro Douglas Jerrold of the Bank of England Lodge. The event raised £100 towards the charity.

Crucefix, confident enough to comment on the rapid progress that now appeared unstoppable, wrote in June's *FQR*:

> But shall we trust ourselves to speak of the Asylum for the aged and decayed Freemason: we can hardly claim our feeling in announcing that this splendid offering is no longer doubtful. Lodges have been appealed to, and nobly have they acted. Brethren unsolicited have rallied around the 'Poor old Mason's Cause' — his sufferings have been made known — the standard of his hopes has at length been unfurled, and if, till now, many have 'unaided, unremembered, died' — joy — joy to the hope which pronounces that:
>
>   'This stone is laid — the temple is begun —
>   Help! — and its walls will glitter in the sun.'

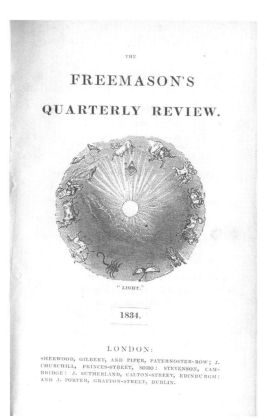

THE

FREEMASON'S QUARTERLY REVIEW.

" LIGHT."

1834.

LONDON:

SHERWOOD, GILBERT, AND PIPER, PATERNOSTER-ROW; J. CHURCHILL, PRINCES-STREET, SOHO: STEVENSON, CAMBRIDGE: J. SUTHERLAND, CALTON-STREET, EDINBURGH: AND J. PORTER, GRAFTON-STREET, DUBLIN.

A series of resolutions were passed by the subscribers at the meeting held on 22nd June, at Radley's Hotel, Bridge Street, Blackfriars, the most important being that 'it is expedient to provide for the wants of the meritorious and decayed Freemason by the erection of an asylum to receive him within its sanctuary'. It was suggested that each member of the London Lodges, as well as interested Provincial Lodges, should voluntarily subscribe 16s a year; within three years there would be £10,000 — sufficient to build and equip a house for 20 residents.

Crucefix informed those gathered that he had approached both the Earl of Durham (the newly installed Deputy Grand Master) and W. W. Prescott (the Grand Treasurer) and was now pleased to note that both had consented to become trustees and that a Festival was to be held on 31st July to launch this great crusade. The Earl of Durham had also agreed to address the assembly on the occasion. A working committee was duly constituted to support these eminent trustees, and in the meantime Bros J. C. Bell and J. Palmer were tasked to prepare a formal letter humbly soliciting HRH the Duke of Sussex if he would be prepared to become the first President of the Institution. This was to be presented at the centenary celebrations of Grand Stewards on 9th December. Everything was going smoothly when suddenly and surprisingly a letter dated 9th July was received from the DGM, the Earl of Durham, written from Cowes on the Isle of Wight:

Dear Sir and Brother
When I consented to become Trustee of the new Masonic charity, and to preside at the dinner, I, of course, presumed that the whole proceedings had received the sanctions and approbation of His Royal Highness the Grand Master. It is therefore with great surprise and regret that I find, from a communication

with His Royal Highness, that such is not the case. You will see the impropriety — nay, the impossibility — of my interfering at all in the matter. As His Royal Highness's Deputy, I am bound to obey his commands, and as such His Royal Highness's attached servant, to respect his feelings and attend to his wishes.

As I am in daily expectation of the arrival here of the ship of war which is to take me from this country on the embassy to which I have been appointed, I shall have no opportunity of corresponding with you on the subject; but I earnestly recommend you, and all who are engaged with you on the laudable object of charity, to take no steps without the full approval of the Grand Master.

With the best wishes for the welfare and prosperity of the Craft,

I remain, dear Sir and Brother,
Yours truly
Durham DGM

That same week, Crucefix received a letter from the Grand Secretary clearly indicating the suspicion that the Duke held for the group. He goes on to write:

When the subject was first introduced to the notice of the Grand Master by Bro J. C. Bell, His Royal Highness requested to be furnished with such particulars of the proposed plan of the contemplated or expected means as would enable him, before offering an opinion, to give the subject a full and fair consideration preparatory to any interview with that brother, so that His Royal Highness might be prepared to discuss the matter.

Bro Bell immediately forwarded a brief and hasty sketch (probably all that the shortness of time enabled him to offer) not however sufficient for the purpose, and His Royal Highness consequently requested something more in detail, but no further statement was received until the arrival of the memorial and other papers sent by you. And here His Royal Highness remarks, not in the way of conveying an expression of displeasure or imputing an intentional irregularity, that the convening of a meeting of a number of Brethren to appoint officers and make laws and regulations for the intended Institution was altogether irregular, while seeking to obtain the approval of the Grand Master and ultimately the sanction of the Grand Lodge; because, by such a proceeding the meeting predetermines important preliminary points, and it must be evident upon reflection that His Royal Highness cannot as Grand Master enter into communication with a body of Masons not known to the Grand Lodge, nor acting under any recognised authority. If the Brethren think fit to meet and carry out their plans as individuals, not seeking the countenance of the Grand Master or the Grand Lodge, they are certainly at liberty so to do; but they cannot, under such circumstances, be permitted to correspond as a body with the various Lodges. His Royal Highness was ready, and is still willing, to receive from Bro Bell any suggestions or information which the friends of the plan may desire to submit, to enable His Royal Highness to form a judgement on the matter, and to determine on the propriety of bringing it to the notice of Grand Lodge, without concurrence of which body a business of so much importance involving so many interests, ought not to proceed with hastily, neither could any beneficial result be expected.

The M.W. Grand Master is much surprised to observe amongst the resolutions passed at the meeting on the 22nd June one fixing an 'Inaugural Dinner' for the 31st inst., under the direction of certain Stewards; and still more at having been shown a printed circular announcing the dinner, in which the Brethren attending are requested to appear in Masonic clothing. Upon this latter point the Grand Master observes that the proceeding is most irregular and contrary to the laws of the Craft, and he therefore trusts that part of the plan will be immediately abandoned.

It was now self-evident that the group had infringed on the Duke's sensitivities relating to the management of the Craft. How dare they make decisions and pass rules that he was not specifically central to? This clearly was not to be permitted. The mystique and secrecy that he tried to maintain were being eroded, and this must not be allowed to happen.

When the subscribers reconvened at Radley's Hotel on 15th July 1835, it was agreed to defer the inaugural dinner; instead a small private dinner of 40 Stewards would take place. Conscious that the pro-Asylum party had exceeded their position within the Craft and as a consequence had potentially put the whole project into jeopardy, to repair the damage and to improve relationships between the two factions Bros Crucefix, Bell and Palmer were to form a sub-committee to continue the dialogue with the Grand Master, and so a letter was sent to the Duke on 21st July 1835 stating:

We, the undersigned, in pursuance of a resolution passed at a meeting of subscribers to the intended Asylum for Aged and Decayed Masons, held on the 15th instant, humbly beg to lay before your Royal Highness a copy of the resolutions passed at that meeting.

Your memorialists with perfect confidence venture to assure your Royal Highness that, in taking measures which they consider merely preliminary, they were anxious to avoid any steps which could be considered as wanting in respect to your Royal Highness as regards your exalted rank or in your character as M.W. Grand Master of the Masonic Craft, which, under your Royal Highness's government, has flourished in this country beyond example.

Your memorialists beg also to state that their proceedings on behalf of the intended Asylum now await your Royal Highness's commands, and with which your memorialists humbly yet earnestly hope to be favoured.

Your memorialists beg to subscribe themselves, &c., &c.

Robert T. Crucefix
Joseph C. Bell
James Palmer
21st July 1835.

The celebrations for the centenary of Grand Stewards Lodge were held in the December of 1835, and Robert Crucefix gave a short address to the Grand Master during which he suggested that the Duke's birthday, 27th January, should still be a Festival but made no reference to the Asylum. Crucefix was now invited to propose the re-election of the Duke of Sussex as Grand Master at the next Quarterly Communications of Grand Lodge and, as is customary, the Grand Master invested Robert Thomas Crucefix as the Grand Senior Deacon in June 1836. It would appear that a temporary peace had been declared and at this precise moment the Grand Master appeared to be the victor.

Meanwhile another theatrical presentation was held, this time at the Royal Pavilion Theatre in Whitechapel. The reviews, published the following day, commented that it had been to a full house comprising a most fashionable audience, which was an unusual occurrence in this dilapidated area of town. The various sketches were enjoyed by all, and the tale of the Bankrupt Mason was said to have brought the house down. During the performance an address was given by a member of Lodge No 78, and the evening concluded with the announcement that £50 had been raised for the charity.

Crucefix presented the state of the finances at the subscribers' meeting on 9th May 1836. Donations had been generous, especially from the Neptune Lodge and the Lodge of Peace and Harmony. Crucefix was particularly effusive when thanking the ladies for their generosity. The Sub-Committee had now opened an account at Grote, Prescott & Co, a reputable bank situated in Threadneedle Street in the City, and trustees were proposed and appointed to manage the accounts in their name.

A Festival, co-ordinated by 21 Stewards, was to be held on 22nd July 1836 in support of the Asylum. The chosen venue was the West India Arms Tavern, situated in Blackwall and owned by Bro Lovegrove, and the cost was to be 15s per head. The Grand Master was informed of this forthcoming event in a letter stating that a Board of Stewards was to be used in the benevolent cause for aged Masons. The letter also courteously congratulated him on regaining his sight after a recent successful cataract operation.

The Festival was a success, raising a sum of £700. A number of eminent Freemasons had been invited to chair the dinner, several of whom donated money, but all politely declined, citing other commitments. Altogether 116 attended, predominantly Freemasons, although some guests were also invited and, with respect to the Grand Master's request, Masonic regalia was therefore not worn. Joseph Copeland Bell chaired the Festival, which opened with a chorus of *Non Nobis Domine* chanted by Bros Collier and Atkins along with Mr Turner. Dr Crucefix then addressed those assembled with a long and emotional report on the Aged and Decayed Mason and announced that the total cost of the project would now be in the region of £7,000.

This was followed by various boisterous toasts to distinguished people, present and absent, especially the Grand Master. Comment was also recorded on the snuffbox presented to the Doctor, which was beautifully constructed and engraved with the inscription 'Do not forget the Aged Masons Asylum at a pinch'.

A resolution was passed at the next committee meeting, convened on 29th August:

expressive of the pleasurable prospect of success that was

ABOVE **New Bridge Street — the site of Radley's Hotel by W. Thornbury.** *Author's Collection*

now presented, and which nothing but a want of energy and perseverance can defeat.

The committee agreed that the popularity of the movement within the Craft justified setting up an award scheme whereby members could qualify for various levels, depending on the size of their donation. The membership agreed that all future meetings should be held at Radley's Hotel at 7pm on every second Wednesday of the month. They also agreed that the patronage or presidency of the charity should be offered to the Grand Master, the Duke of Sussex. However, sadly this was to be rejected in a letter written by John Spencer Churchill, the DGM, on behalf of the Duke on 10th September 1836 from Kensington Palace:

W. Brother, — Having laid before the M.W. Grand Master, the Duke of Sussex, the address signed by yourself and some other Brethren on behalf of the Stewards for the anniversary meeting of the suggested Asylum for Aged Masons, I am commanded by His Royal Highness to convey to you his thanks for the expressions of congratulation and kind feeling towards his person, and which His Royal Highness is happy to acknowledge as coming from the individual Brethren; but the proposed Institution not having received the sanction of the Grand Lodge, you will see the impossibility of the Grand Master admitting the address in any other than its individual character.

When the subscribers met on 11th November they were

informed that a very generous offer had been received from two of the theatrical members of the Bank of England Lodge, namely Bros Hammond and Jerrold. They had placed the New Strand Theatre at the Institution's disposal for a new production of John Tobin's comedy *The Honeymoon*. The performance would take place on 16th December 1836 and would include a number of new songs and reviews.

The New Strand Theatre which was on the site now occupied by Aldwych Underground Station had recently reopened, having previously been closed for various licensing infringements. Now, on 25th April 1836, it reopened under the combined management of Douglas William Jerrold and William John Hammond. Jerrold had been born in London but had lived in Cranbrook, Kent, and in 1813 became a midshipman serving on a guard ship off Sheerness. When peace returned in 1815, he trained as a printer before progressing to writing sketches and plays. He published in a range of magazines, including *Punch*, and made innumerable contributions to the *FQR*.

Hammond was a well-known comedian from Liverpool, a close friend of Charles Dickens and the brother-in-law of Jerrold. His most famous roles were performed at the New Strand Theatre in the late 1830s.

The eventual Masonic production was performed on Monday 13th February 1837. Staged that evening were two favourite Burlettas, a form of burlesque parodying opera, interspersed with addresses in support of the Aged and Decayed Freemasons. The cast included Brethren employed from within the theatre and the performance ran over two nights, raising a sum of upwards of 50 guineas.

January 1837 saw the first elements of doubt begin to creep into the Doctor's mind. Although the cause of the Aged and Decayed Freemason had been gathering momentum, barriers always seemed to appear in one form or another. In the January edition of the *FQR*, although still certain that he would ultimately succeed, he wrote that 'the prejudices of some, and doubts and fears of others, were yielding a more enlarged and liberal consideration of the subject'.

His morale would always be uplifted by some of the more erudite and educated Freemasons, the most important being Dr George Oliver (1782-1867), a priest living in Lincolnshire. Dr Oliver had a passion for Freemasonry, especially its history, and had been a regular contributor to the *FQR* since its conception. His writings were exactly what Crucefix needed: the Brethren should understand the origins and philosophy of the Craft, and Oliver's reputation as an authority on all things Masonic provided precisely that. One particular article of Oliver's, published in June that year, was

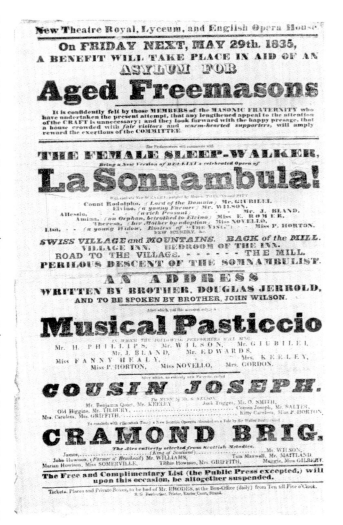

ABOVE **Play bill of an entertainment 1835.** *Library and Museum of Freemasonry*

entitled *The Practical Benevolence of Freemasonry*. This specifically concentrated on current events relating to elderly Masons:

We are informed that, an Asylum of the same nature is in progress amongst the members of our Society. I know not — I care not — by whom the idea was first suggested but I hail the project with every determination of joy, as being in strict accordance with the best principles of the Order ... I am a friend to the Asylum on its simple intrinsic merits. It deserves to be popular; and it will undoubtedly meet with the support which its importance so imperiously demands.

The New Year brought further support when Crucefix received a letter from Bro Eales Smith, a member of the Lodge of Unanimity and Sincerity meeting in Taunton, containing the sum of £50 together with the promise of an annual sum of two guineas to be received after the laying of the foundation stone. He also offered his services as the Collector for the western division of the country.

On 8th February 1837, a letter was read to the membership from W. Halton of the Burlington Lodge:

9, Charles Street, St James's Square,
7th February 1837.
Dear Sirs and Brethren,
The interest which the Craft have felt in the success which has attended our laudable exertions for the erection of an Asylum for Aged Freemasons has been approved by all who are desirous that the principles of our Order shall be fully exemplified and made manifest to the world. I consider the object of our solicitude and prayers is now beyond the possibility of failure. Our deep and lasting gratitude is due to many Brethren who have toiled hard in this truly Masonic cause, but more particularly so to my friend Bro Dr Crucefix, who has, night and day, through evil and good report (without dismay), so fought the battles and defended the interests of this Asylum as to demand a more lasting token of our thanks than mere words. I have, therefore, the pleasure to inform you that our present Treasurer, Dr Crucefix, has thus sat for his portrait to Bro Mosely, who has, I think, succeeded in giving a very good likeness of our friend upon canvas highly creditable to him as an artist.

The portrait I humbly venture to beg the Governors of the Asylum to accept as a memorial of my personal respect and Masonic gratitude. I have entrusted it to the custody of my mother lodge [the Burlington No 113], who will deliver it up as soon as the Board room of our Institution shall be in a state to receive it.
I am, &c.,
W. Halton PM

The picture was thankfully received, and all hoped that it would set an example to other Freemasons.

The principal item on the agenda at the next meeting of the subscribers, on 24th February, related to the appropriate measures that should be taken to secure the charity's future prosperity. It was also decided that they should hold another Festival, on 21st June, and Bro James Pattison MP, the Governor of the Bank of England, would preside on that occasion. Subsequently, at the June meeting, it was unanimously agreed that the time had come when the whole question of the future of the Aged Masons' Asylum should be brought before Grand Lodge. This should be done as soon as possible, but they were conscious that the June agenda for the Quarterly Communications was full and as a consequence it would have to be postponed until the September meeting.

Disappointingly, a letter was sent from James Pattison, declining with regret the opportunity to chair the forthcoming Festival; his reasoning was that he had received a letter from Lord John Spencer Churchill, the DGM, expressing the Duke of Sussex's opinions:

His Highness still thinking that such Asylum thinking will tend to hold out an inducement for an improper class of individuals to enter the Fraternity, as also run counter to the interest of the two charities, viz Boys' and Girls' Schools ...

E. R. Moran, the Secretary to the charity, wrote to Lord John Spencer Churchill with a copy to Mr Pattison, stating there was no way that the Aged and Decayed Freemasons' Charity would induce improper classes of people to join the Craft. However, it was to no avail — the Grand Master was adamant and reaffirmed his previous stance that he could not recognise an unconstitutional body of Freemasons and that this had been discussed and agreed with Crucefix at the meeting they had held the previous year.

Dr Crucefix, who always kept scrupulous notes of meetings, denied that he had made any such statement and could vouchsafe that the subject of the Aged and Decayed Masons was never raised at that meeting, but he would seek another meeting with the Duke to clarify the situation. This meeting eventually took place, after repeated last-minute cancellations, on 9th June, during which the Duke affirmed to the Doctor that he had not been, and was not now, in any manner either directly or indirectly opposed to the contemplated Asylum.

The nation was shocked to receive the news that King William IV had died on 20th June 1837. His late Majesty had sired numerous children, 10 in total, all illegitimate, from his relationship with Mrs Dorothea Jordan, an Irish actress and courtesan. Therefore, his legitimate successor to the Crown was his niece Victoria, the daughter of his younger brother, the late Duke of Kent. William IV and his wife Queen Adelaide had always been very fond of Victoria; however, she was very conscious of the tension that existed between the King and her mother, the Dowager Duchess of Kent. William, affectionately known to the masses as 'Sailor Bill', had enjoyed his life in the Royal Navy and had seen action at the Battle of Cape St Vincent in the recent wars. He was said to have been a friendly individual, if eccentric, and was always anxious to show favour with the young Victoria. She commented later:

He was always kind to me and he meant it well I know. I am grateful for it and shall always remember his kindness with gratitude. He was odd, very odd and singular, but his intentions were often ill interpreted.

There was little published in the *FQR* on 30th June other than obituaries of the late King, and the second Festival had to be postponed as a result of the King's death. William IV had been a Freemason for 20 years.

It was decided at the Sub-Committee's August meeting that Dr Crucefix would present two resolutions before Grand Lodge:

1. That the opinion of the Craft with regards the erection and endowment of an Asylum for Aged and Decayed Freemasons having been taken in the most public manner possible, and the result being most decidedly in favour of such Institution, that this Grand Lodge recommend the same to the protection and support of all lodges within the Constitution of England.

2. That with a view to the more considerate attention of Grand Lodge to the subject of an Asylum, a committee of Inquiry be appointed, who shall examine and report thereon.

The September edition of the *FQR* reported on the second Festival, held in July that year at the Freemasons' Tavern, Great Queen Street, London, and chaired by the distinguished barrister Joseph Copeland Bell:

Never did a Masonic Festival pass with such satisfaction. The Stewards were indefatigable — Mason's wives, daughters, and friends witnessed with approving smile — all noble subscription rewarded the labourer's toil.

Crucefix considered that he was now in a position of strength. He had the support of a large part of the Craft behind him and as a consequence of his recent meeting with the Duke nothing could go wrong. He would propose the resolutions before Grand Lodge at the next Quarterly Communications.

The day came — 6th September 1837 — and Freemasons' Hall was packed with all parties. It was announced that the Duke, who was to have chaired the occasion, was absent from the meeting. The excuse was that his brother, the Duke of Cambridge, had suddenly arrived in London. The meeting continued and an initial vote was taken by those present in the hall, at which five out of six members were in favour of the motion about to be submitted, but strangely and at the last moment Crucefix himself postponed it. Two days later, he wrote to the Duke of Sussex again to try and clarify the Grand Master's intentions:

These glad tidings were delivered with that simplicity which characterises the language of your Royal Highness, and which rendered it impossible for the most homespun mind to mistake its purport, and left me, as I rejoice to feel, at full liberty to bring the important subject of the contemplated Asylum before the Grand Lodge on Wednesday last. Animated by this assurance on the part of your Royal Highness, I was about to enter the Grand Lodge to fulfil what I deem a sacred duty — a duty — I must ever feel to be associated with my Masonic existence — when to my dismay, and to my sorrow (and I may add to the subsequent sorrow of a great majority of the assembled Brethren) I was abruptly informed that your Royal Highness was opposed to the measure.

I was not actually commanded to withdraw the motion, but the terms in which the message was conveyed left me no alternative between postponing or pressing the motion; to have withdrawn it would have been disgraceful. With the words of your Royal Highness — a Prince's word — still beating in my mind, I nevertheless bowed to the imperative suggestion of the Deputy Grand Master (if I may use the term suggestion, wanting one to explain the anomalous nature of things), for I could not believe that such suggestion must have proceeded from some extraordinary error, some unhappy misrepresentation, which it is my present object, with the gracious permission of your Royal Highness, to endeavour to explain and remove, to the end that I may in December next be enabled to redeem

ABOVE **The Duke of Marlborough taken from *Earl of Beaconsfield* by A. E. Ewald (1883) and engraved by G. I. Stodart.** *Author's Collection*

widows. An officer was to be appointed to look after their welfare as well as attending to their morals, having the power to expel any miscreant. This document was designed to strengthen Crucefix's argument when he next attended the Quarterly Communications in December.

The Doctor also sought to solicit the ideas of others to bolster his case for the coming meeting, and so he offered a prize for an essay to be entitled *Objections to the contemplated Asylum, for the worthy but indigent and aged Masons, founded upon facts, and proving that such an Institution will endanger the principles of Masonry.* The prize was four volumes of the *FQR* Masonically bound.

The next Quarterly Communications was held on 6th December 1837 before a packed Freemasons' Hall. Again the Grand Master did not attend, and the DGM, Lord John Spencer Churchill, presided. Robert Crucefix was called to present his resolution, but before this could take place the DGM read an address from the Duke of Sussex as follows:

> *An explanation formerly made to the Grand Lodge by the Grand Master on a motion somewhat similar, and intimating that it would be necessary to collect a sufficient sum for the erection and endowment of the proposed institution. That when existing charities should attain permanent means to equal their expenditure, such assurance would facilitate measures favourable to the proposed Institution.*

the pledge which hundreds of my Brethren consider that I have in a great measure disregarded, and which nothing but a desire to prevent a too ardent expression of their feelings justified me in encountering so severe a trial as the disappointment at such a moment (however only for a time) of their honest and long cherished hopes.

In the meantime, with the charity's coffers getting bigger by the day and with its reputation now spreading throughout the Masonic world, a group of individuals from within the Committee were requested to prepare a document on precisely what was required. The interim conclusion was the erection of a purpose-built building or a series of designed cottages for the Aged and Decayed Freemasons and their

The Duke's concern was that the new Institution should not denigrate nor harm the current charities, but Crucefix pleaded that the Craft now had a duty to form this new charity. The proposed resolution was then read and seconded by Bro Rowe:

> *That the Grand Lodge recommend the contemplated Asylum for the Aged and decayed Freemason to the favourable consideration of the Craft.*

There was a general discussion before the ballot was held, with the result that the resolution was unanimously accepted. The new charity was now part of the Masonic Constitution.

CHAPTER 5

DIVERGING FORCES

By 1838 the funds had reached £2,000 and, with success in sight, plans were made for further theatrical events as well as the third Festival in June under the presidency of Bro Alderman Thomas Wood of the Tuscan Lodge, a solicitor with ambitions to become the Lord Mayor of London.

The curtain was raised on 26th June 1839 at the Theatre Royal to reveal His Grace Augustus Frederick FitzGerald, 3rd Duke of Leinster, and Grand Master of Ireland, seated on a throne surrounded by Freemasons all in their full regalia. He was escorted by Bros Joseph White and Edward Tandy, both supporting his heraldic banners. This colourful extravaganza was followed by a production of *The White Horse of the Peppers*, a two-act comedy by Samuel Lover, followed by *Teddy the Tiler*, a highly popular farce in which Mr Powers, a celebrated Irish comedian, played the leading roles.

That same month, conscious of the Duke's concerns of the new charity's effects on the existing Masonic charities, Crucefix wrote:

The committee do not wish to conceal that our illustrious Most Worshipful Grand Master who has ever been at the head of numerous institutions for Charity, has doubted whether the Craft possesses sufficient resources to carry the plan into effect. It is for us, Brethren, to prove that he has not sufficiently calculated the liberality and perseverance of Masons. It is for us to exert ourselves, and by one simultaneous effort to raise such a sum as will enable the Committee to enter into immediate arrangement for selecting a plot of ground, and commissioning an Asylum.

Three days before Christmas the subscribers met to discuss the practicalities relating to the annuities for Worthy, Aged and Decayed Freemasons. The agreed criteria recommended that each recipient must have reached the age of 60, or, in the case of total blindness, 50 years of age, and have no annual income over £20. He must have been an Installed Master for at least seven years, as well as being a subscribing member of a Lodge or Lodges for at least ten years. Each candidate was to be supported by a petition, birth or baptism certificate and written recommendations from his Lodge or Lodges.

The first six completed nominations were presented to the subscribers on 6th May 1839. Three were immediately approved and a subsequent two were later accepted; one from an 'out' pensioner from the Chelsea Hospital was rejected. Chelsea Pensioners fell into two groups: those who lived in the Hospital and were designated 'in pensioners', and those who received an annuity and lived in private accommodation and were denominated 'out pensioners'.

The business completed, John Lee Stevens commented on the pleasing remarks made by the Duke at the Grand Festival of 1838. His Royal Highness had let it be known that he would be willing to patronise the Institution for Aged and Decayed Masons provided it was regulated and controlled by the individuals who had set up the charity related to annuities. This was a reference to the interim suggestions passed by the General Committee the previous December when the Duke gave his approval for an Annuity Institution for the relief of the Aged and Decayed. He continued by stating that all further matters relating to the construction of a building for housing the elderly should be deferred until a sum of £7,000 had been collected and invested. The interest from this sum would be used to fund the annuitants, whilst any further monies could then, and only then, be collected and used towards the construction and endowment fund. This caused a dilemma: how to resolve or merge the original resolutions to create a Home with the Duke's desire for annuities.

By the time the AGM was held on 31st July, Dr Crucefix thought they had found the compromise and presented the following resolutions:

1st. That the said sum of £2000 already invested shall remain intact without diminution or increase, as the nucleus of a fund for the erection and endowment of the Asylum, until a subsequent sum of £7000 has been

raised.

2nd. That the interest on the said sum of £2000, together with all receipts beyond that sum, shall be applied in making good the annuities to be granted and in accumulating the said sum of £7000.

3rd. That until the said sum of £7000, clear of the said sum of £2000, shall have been accumulated, the erection of the Asylum shall be deferred, and that the interest only of the said sum of £7000 shall be applicable to the purposes of the Annuities.

4th. That in and from the accumulation of the said sum of £7000, the said sum of £2000, together with all other moneys received by this Institution, and all accumulations of interest respectively, shall be applied as a fund for the erection and endowment of the Asylum.

The five annuitants selected were also approved during the meeting and were now entitled to receive an annual allowance of £10 which would be paid quarterly. The election of permanent trustees, to replace those acting in a provisional capacity, was decided and a deputation was selected to communicate the result to the Duke, which they were confident he would approve as it clarified the status of the charity.

Sussex had a severe attack of asthma that spring, which left him seriously debilitated, and whilst recuperating at his friend's (Mr Thistlethwayte) estate at Southwick Park near Fareham in Hampshire he wrote to Crucefix, Bell, Watkins and McMullen expressing his disappointment at what he perceived as their deliberate misinterpretations of his previous statements:

26th August 1839.
Gentlemen and Brothers,
Having received from Brother Crucefix a note communicating to me various resolutions which had been passed at different meetings by several Brethren who have at heart the establishment of some Institution calculated to relieve Decayed and Aged Masons, I feel it incumbent on me to repeat the statement which I first made upon that subject at the Grand Festival in the present year. On that occasion I stated that as to an Asylum Building I could not and never would lend

ABOVE LEFT **Dr Robert Thomas Crucefix by an unknown artist.**
Library and Museum of Freemasonry

LEFT **HRH the Duke of Sussex (1773-1843) by Samuel Drummond.**
Library and Museum of Freemasonry

either the sanction of my name or my pecuniary assistance, inasmuch as I was convinced that it would be a useless expenditure, a waste of money, without the slightest chance of any profitable or beneficial result therefrom, but that if such a project were given up and then the Brethren were disposed to form a plan for granting Annuities which were to be taken solely from the interest of moneys collected, and not break upon the capital, that to such a proposition I would listen.

Since the time a proposition was made to me to receive a deputation on the subject, which I left unanswered in consequence of seeing a circular which the Committee had in the interim circulated, and which had misrepresented the statement I have here made, without and communication to me.

In the paper now communicated to me it is stated 'that the sum of £2000 shall be the nucleus of a Fund for the erection of an Asylum'. This I have no hesitation in saying is completely at variance with my statement.

From the whole tenor of the paper it is clear the same disposition and inclination on the part of some individuals as to the erection of an Asylum still remains. Now, without imputing motives to anyone, there can be no doubt the Craft will be misled in supposing that I have given a silent consent to such a plan, which I am equally determined, as before, to resist; therefore unless it is clearly understood that the intention of erecting an Asylum is totally abandoned I feel myself under the necessity of declining any communication upon the subject. I hope this will be deemed a fair answer to the application made to me, and as such I wish it to be communicated to those Brethren who framed the resolution upon which the request of an interview with me has been grounded and which I consequently decline; but to show that this determination has been taken in conformity with those opinions which have actuated the whole of my conduct in this transaction. I will further add, that until next April, if it please God to spare my life, I will take no further step; but should the Brethren at that time have made no advance in the matter, I shall think myself at liberty to state my own plan, when I have no doubt the Brethren will see which is most feasible, and when I shall call upon the Fraternity for that assistance which I have never found them unwilling to afford when useful objects are proposed for their consideration.

The Duke now recognised that his opposition to Crucefix's

ABOVE **Douglas Jerrold.** *Author's Collection*

BELOW **William Farnfield.** *Library and Museum of Freemasonry*

charity just seemed to increase its popularity, and the only solution he had was the immediate implementation of his own Annuitants' Charity.

Crucefix and his acquaintants, realising that their attempt at a compromise had failed, were now confused over the Duke's real intentions. They therefore agreed to present Sussex's letter at their next meeting on 9th October in the hope that some solution might be found. They were adamant that as they could not accept the Grand Master's argument, they had no alternative but to continue down the path of building a Home for the elderly. They were ever conscious that some elderly Freemasons were so frail they were unable to look after themselves and that the Duke's annuity would be of little relief. There was no doubting that the letter did contain some valuable suggestions and, on reflection, they could understand his suggestion that it was unwise to start building until funds were sufficient. They would, therefore, recommend a delay in the building until such time when there would be sufficient funds to complete the project.

The Special General Meeting to debate the letter was called in the November, when the charity's Secretary, William Farnfield, read the letter to those assembled and concluded by stating that it was now obvious and beyond doubt that they were at odds with the Grand Master. Farnfield worked in the Grand Secretary's office and now considered himself at variance as it could be perceived he had a conflict of interest. Whilst his support for the Asylum had not changed, he could not afford to lose his stipendiary post and so reluctantly proffered his resignation.

William Farnfield had a long and distinguished life in Freemasonry. He worked in the Grand Secretary's office for upwards of 40 years. He was appointed as Assistant Grand Secretary in 1845 and remained in post until he retired on a well-deserved pension of £250 per annum in 1866. He was initially made Secretary of the Royal Masonic Benevolent Annuity Fund in 1842, and at the unification of both charities continued in that role until 1872, again receiving a substantial and deserved pension of £200 per annum. He died on 27th February 1876 at the age of 79 and was interred in Tooting Cemetery.

Those present at this meeting were conscious that prior to the meeting an anonymous letter had been circulated by one of the porters at Radley's Hotel. When its contents became known there was an outcry. Mr Radley was summoned and questioned on what he knew of its distribution. Declaring his own innocence, he defended his porter who had only co-operated on behalf of an individual attending the meeting. The contents of the paper were then read aloud:

The Scurrilous Paper
The Asylum for Worthy and Decayed Freemasons alias the Workhouse Question.

Brethren,
Are we to have a Workhouse or not? Are we to have an Institution calculated to relieve worthy, aged and decayed freemasons or not? These are important antagonistic questions, which the Brethren must decide.

When we look for persons most forward in proposing and maintaining these questions, the mind hardly hesitates one instant in its decision.

His Royal Highness the Duke of Sussex, our Worshipful Grand Master, proposes and maintains that we ought to have an Institution 'calculated to relieve' worthy, aged and decayed freemasons. And is His Royal Highness an adventurer, seeking or calculating any personal profit in the matter? No. Whatever he proposes is solely for the benefit of the Craft.

But if we consider the question of a Workhouse, and look at the proposition practically in the face, we constantly see Job Humbug and Co in a long train of surveyors, builders, bricklayers, carpenters, plumbers, painters, glaziers, upholders, tailors, butchers, bakers, tallow-chandlers, doctors and lawyers — every man Jack of them seeking a Masonic charitable contract that will put solid pudding into their own hungry stomachs and send the real claimants — the worthy aged and decayed freemasons — empty away. For will it be maintained that they will buy ground for nothing; build the Workhouse for nothing; furnish it for nothing; clothe the paupers for nothing; feed them for nothing; and physic them for nothing? And when these somethings are put together, will the remainder be like an Irishman's stockings — no feet without any legs.

Let not Brethren be offended by the word Pauper: for surely the Workhouse proposition is a recruiting for Paupers; as they declare that they only want to help and relieve those who are 'destitute of all resources, except what charity supplied'. God bless those poor destitute! Their best self styled friends say, 'Good people, we have a sum of money in hand, but we cannot relieve you; it is devoted to a building fund; our Brother Turnstyle has got a contract, and he must be paid.' Which is, properly speaking, giving a Brother a stone when he asks for bread; and inclines us to believe that when certain persons relieve Paupers they 'cry for pleasure'. That themselves will have relief without appearing to claim charity.

Thus far even a comparison of the persons proposing these two questions ought at once to decide the matter with any reasonable mind. Shall His Royal Highness's advice be followed, who seeks to benefit the real claimants for charity, without personal profit; or the advice of some smooth-tongued adventurers, who speak of paupers and mean themselves? As for 'happy go lucky' we will have nothing to do with them.

But then, again, the thing proposed. The Workhouse people say 'we will have a workhouse'. And why?

1. Because it will be a job for ourselves;

2. The Grand Master sanctions it;

3. The subscribers have given their money upon the faith of it;

4. The Annuities granted prove their utility;

5. We will have a Workhouse, because we will have a Workhouse; and

6. O lovers of truth! Because an Annuity scheme would peril the other Charities;

To which we answer —

1. Your first reason is enough to disgust us;

2. The Grand Master never did sanction it;

3. Many subscribers never did, and never would have put down a farthing for a brick- and-mortar-Workhouse job had thy known it;

4. The utility of the Annuities only prove the correctness of His Royal Highness's views;

5. We do not believe that you will have a Workhouse, for the Craft will never support it; and

6. A judicious Annuity scheme, so far from periling, will rather relieve and promote the other Charities.

So there is no sense in selfishness in all those cunningly devised resolutions which give the lie direct to our Worshipful Grand Master and seem to have been drawn up with a sly view of insulting him out of the Craft. And really when we compare those direct insults with the affected adulation and reverence sometimes paid to His Royal Highness, and mockery of being 'desirous of deferring to His Royal Highness, and to the opinion of the Grand Lodge', we scarcely know which to admire most, the insolence of the insult, the degradation of their fulsomeness, the impudence of their affected reverence, or the apathy of the Brethren who are thus led by the nose.

His Royal Highness has, with prophetic view, fully described the adverse position as 'useless expenditure'

— 'a waste of money' — and his own proposition of granting Annuities will be the amplest, best, and most satisfactory method of relieving worthy, aged, and decayed Masons, because:

It will have instant operation, and not a hope deferred.

It will be most extensive in its application.

It will be most easy in practice.

It will be least expensive in practice.

It will curtail jobbing.

It will not degrade the Annuitant.

It will be well and nobly supported.

So then, we say, Hurrah for the Annuities, and no Workhouse!

In conclusion, Brethren, we have a strong suspicion that this Workhouse Question is to be made use of for political purposes. We know the peculiarity of our Masonic organisation; we know how important an instrument that organisation would be for a political adventurer seeking admission to the highest power in the Government; and surely the deposition or resignation of His Royal Highness would (apparently undersignedly) make way for that adventurer. The question then is, will you be such mean and despicable animals as to pander to any man's personal ambition? Perish the thought!

There remains but one course for right-minded and honourable Masons, viz., to move and carry the following resolutions:

That, having misunderstood the gracious intentions of His Royal Highness, all Resolutions founded on such misunderstandings are, and shall be, null and void.

That this meeting agrees with His Royal Highness that the erection of an Asylum will be wasteful and useless expenditure.

That His Royal Highness be respectfully requested to develop his plan granting Annuities to worthy, aged, and decayed Masons.

CAVEAC 205

The atmosphere became explosive and many demanded the name of the author. William Jackson, a Freemason of six months' standing, arose and admitted ownership of the document. Alderman Thomas Wood, along with John Lee Stevens, began by verbally assaulting the character of the Grand Master, declaring:

That His Royal Highness is a grossly selfish man, and an enemy of the Craft;

LEFT **Feast in Freemasons'
Tavern in 1843.** *Author's
Collection*

BELOW **A watercolour of the
Freemasons' Tavern c1800 by
Nixon.** *Library and Museum of
Freemasonry*

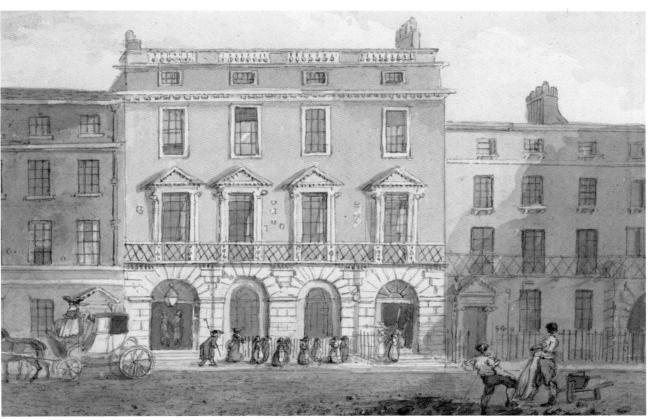

That His Royal Highness always endeavoured to destroy every plan proposed for the good of Masonry unless it emanated from himself;

That His Royal Highness is a tyrant, wanting to ride roughshod over the Craft;

That His Royal Highness would if he could crush the building scheme, but he defied him, and would defy him to his face;

That His Royal Highness might be King of the Craft, but personally he owed him no respect and implied His Royal Highness never paid his subscriptions; nor his aprons and jewels, and was altogether a most contemptible person;

That His Royal Highness often said one thing at one time, and contrary at another;

That His Royal Highness had often eaten his words, so he expected him to repeat that feat in this matter;

That His Royal Highness had, in fact, said and done that which His Royal Highness has declared NEVER did say or do; viz., gave his consent to the building of the Asylum or Workhouse.

Throughout this outburst the Chairman, Robert Crucefix, was seen to occasionally nod in approval at these accusations. Because this paper had been presented as a resolution, as a consequence another resolution was tabled, this time condemning the scurrilous letter and the manner of its circulation. Without mentioning the name of the author, it was phrased as follows:

That Bro x x having circulated an anonymous paper, relative to the Aged Masons Asylum — This meeting is of the opinion, that such a paper is false and scurrilous, and deserving the severe censure of this meeting.

The meeting continued late into the night before eventually being brought to a close.

Prior to the December's Quarterly Communications, William Jackson had been seen distributing the 'scurrilous letter' to those assembled, along with an additional paper which stated:

Gentlemen and Brethren,
Being for the most part a stranger amongst you, and as a very young Freemason, I feel the great diffidence in intruding upon your notice. But have I not a solemn

duty to perform towards the poor, our Brethren, and our Most Worshipful Grand Master? Towards the poor worthy aged, and decayed Freemason, in urging his just claim; towards our Brethren who are likely to be misled, and whose best interests as a society are greatly endangered, and towards our Most Worshipful Grand Master, in boldly repelling the revilers of his good name? Such being the case, and with the knowledge that 'the good I stand on is my truth and honesty,' I most respectfully entreat your attention to the following statement of facts.

On the 13th of November a public meeting of the Governors and Subscribers to the Aged Masons' Asylum, was held at Radley's Hotel, Bridge Street, Blackfriars, in pursuance of a circular notice, and for the purpose of confirming certain resolutions passed at a former meeting, and for general business. Having perused that circular notice, and being a subscriber, I attended and before the commencement of business, caused the following printed letter to be in the hands of every person present ...

The letter closed with a detailed description of the events at the meeting of the subscribers and concluded with the signature of William Jackson, residing at No 14 Bucklersbury and dated 26th November 1839.

The subscribers reconvened on the evening of 11th December 1839, to receive and accept Bro Farnfield's written resignation. His retirement was accepted with regret, for he had been a popular and conscientious servant of the charity. He was replaced by Bro Robert Field. The circumstances of the previous meeting and those at Grand Lodge dominated the meeting, and it was unanimously resolved:

that the statement in the former part of this paper, distributed at the last general meeting of this Institution, has been already resolved to be false and scurrilous, in which this Committee fully concurs: and that the pretended report of the proceedings of that meeting is a wickedly distorted, false, illiberal, and scurrilous statement.

Crucefix was still optimistic and convinced that the Duke could be converted to his way of thinking, and in the last edition of the *FQR* for that year he wrote:

LEFT **Rev Dr George Oliver by an unknown artist.** *Library and Museum of Freemasonry*

RIGHT **Pavilion Theatre.** *Matthew Lloyd*

BELOW LEFT **Peter Thompson (1779-1851) by Robert Frain.** *Library and Museum of Freemasonry*

In the general report of this Institution there is much to be regretted, but more, abundantly more, room for congratulation. That the Misconception of the great principle has prevented a more speedy development of the means necessary to prove the extreme liberality of many who were disposed to join the Institution is too true, but time, and a proper sense of public duty, will gradually disperse the mists and the true beauty of the subject will be clear to those who now either doubt because of fear — or withhold because they feel compelled.

To such as have apostatized from principle it were a waste of words to say anything; their loss is a moral gain, and their adhesion to any new system, we are convinced, will only entangle others, as their withdrawal will relieve the Asylum from dangerous friendship.

But the cause for congratulation is in the consolidated moral power which has grown out of the severest examination of the principle of the Asylum; and we unresistingly court the strictest scrutiny into its 'manifesto', which is logically drawn up, is creditable to the cause it espouses, and above all, is most respectfully addressed under circumstances trying to the judgment and to the feelings of Brethren, who have no other object in view than the furtherance of

ABOVE LEFT **King William IV (1765-1837) by Joyce Aris.** *Library and Museum of Freemasonry*

ABOVE **Benjamin Bond Cabbell.** *Library and Museum of Freemasonry*

sound Masonic principles.

In the recent reply of the Grand Master to the Lenox Lodge, Richmond, he graciously repeated his sentiments delivered at the Especial Grand Lodge in April last, as follows:

'While I am aware that it is impossible to satisfy the wishes of every Brother, still I have the consolation to think that whenever it has been my misfortune to differ with anyone, I have always stated my objections tamely: I have argued the case calmly, and have taken my determination disinterestedly, upon the firm conviction that the welfare of the body at large required such a decision which prescribes to us the golden rule of PEACE ON EARTH AND GOODWILL TOWARDS MAN!

'These are truly Masonic Sentiments and in their adoption we shall have much cause to rejoice.

William Jackson unashamedly appeared at the AGM held on 8th January 1840 and was again observed taking notes on the various conversations and comments. This was considered to be in bad taste and he was ordered to stop, but he remonstrated at such length that it became necessary to pass a motion that the only person allowed to take notes was the Secretary. It was generally felt that Jackson was a spy, which was confirmed when his notes taken at the previous meeting were later responsible for the charges laid before the Board of General Purposes against Bros Crucefix, Alderman John Wood and John Lee Stevens.

In spite of these problems the fund-raising activities continued, with a ball held on Tuesday 14th January 1840 at the Freemasons' Tavern. Tickets could be purchased from Bro Acklam, a well-known Masonic jewel, furniture and clothing manufacturer, at his premises at 138 Strand; the price was 7s 6d for ladies and 12s 6d for gentlemen. The evening's entertainment was provided by Musard's Band accompanied by many famous contemporary artists including Messrs Baumann, Lazarus, Laurent, Keating and Champion. Edgar and Jarred sang songs and recited soliloquies. Musard's Band was better known as the Concert à la Musard of the English Opera House, the Quadrille Institute, etc, and performed regularly at the Theatre Royal. The ball was a success and raised the sum of £53.

Throughout January the corridors of power in Freemasons'

Hall resounded with rumours, intrigues and discussions concerning the 'scurrilous letter' and, as expected, the Board of General Purposes was convened to enquire into what actually did happen at that November meeting of the subscribers. Robert Crucefix, Alderman John Wood and John Lee Stevens were each summoned by a letter signed by Bros Peter Thomson PM 227, Laurence Thompson PM 66, William Bond PM 66 and John B. King WM 66, charging them and demanding that they attend a meeting at Grand Lodge at three o'clock on 28th January 1840:

> The three Brothers against whose conduct we complain are Past Masters of Lodges; we therefore charge them with having, by such language and conduct, endeavoured to subvert the grand principles on which our Order is based, with breach of allegiance to our Grand Master, and with violation of their solemn pledge given as Master Masons, and also of the promise made by them upon their installation into the chairs of their Lodges ...

These signatories were not ordinary Freemasons. Peter Thomson was probably the most well known and well loved. The first act after the Union of the Antients and Moderns in 1813 had been to form the Lodge of Reconciliation, and its final undertaking was formulating the idea of standardising the ritual. Accordingly, in 1817, the Stability Lodge of Improvement had been created, and Peter Thomson was its Preceptor and played a pivotal role in its formation. His conscientious enthusiasm for the task was rewarded at the 20th anniversary of the Lodge by the presentation of a gold watch.

The second, Laurence Thompson, was the last surviving pupil of William Preston, the author of *Illustrations of Masonry*. Preston bequeathed the sum of £300 to fund an annual lecture in his name, and Laurence Thompson was awarded the honour of being the first Prestonian lecturer, a title he proudly boasted until his death in 1857.

The stated day arrived, and each was to be interrogated separately, but Crucefix was allowed to witness the interview with Alderman John Wood who was the principal defendant, having been on the occasion the most outspoken. The President of the Court was Bro B. Bond Cabbell, and the Vice President was Bro Henderson. The charges were read by Bro Dobie, the Grand Registrar and Provincial Grand Master of Surrey.

Crucefix immediately objected that two of the Brethren present were biased: Bros Bossy and McMullen had already made their opinions clear before the hearing, and as such should not be present to pass judgement on the proceedings. Fearing that he was not going to get a fair hearing, he naively wrote to the Duke of Sussex, asking for his intervention. However, the Duke protested that he could not get involved as he was the slandered individual.

Farnfield was called as a witness and asked to give his version of the incident. He initially intimated that he could not recall much, but on further questioning had to declare that he thought Alderman Wood had been disrespectful to the Grand Master. A week later, Bro Stracey Wood was called to give evidence and confirmed that the account written by Jackson was a true record.

On 26th February, the Committee of Masters concluded that they had heard sufficient to announce their verdict, but just prior to their announcement Crucefix rose to propose two motions. Each was designed to show his utter contempt towards the Board of General Purposes, for he was now fully aware that this had not been a fair trial, especially in his case; all he had done on that evening was to chair the meeting. His motions were:

BELOW **The Funeral Procession of the Duke of Sussex to Kensal Rise Cemetery.** *Author's Collection*

1. That the evidence already taken by Bro R. J. Jennings, and all future evidence that may be taken by him, or any other person authorized by the Board of General Purposes in the case of Bro. Alderman John Wood and others, be printed for the information of Grand Lodge.

2. That a committee be appointed to draw up a code of regulation for the government of the Board of General Purpose, and that if carried be submitted for the approval of Grand Lodge.

Crucefix's intentions were to open this debate to the whole Masonic community, contrary to the wishes of both the Board of General Purposes and the Grand Master. Not surprisingly, both motions were rejected.

The decision of the Board was delivered on 29th February. William White, the Grand Secretary, wrote to each informing them that they had been found guilty. This was later confirmed and endorsed, and sentence was passed at the Board of General Purposes on 10th March 1840. The Board declared that Alderman Thomas Wood, John Lee Stevens and Robert Thomas Crucefix had spoken words deficient in respect to the Grand Master at a public meeting of Aged and Decayed Masons, and that this had been proved. Wood was suspended from all Masonic functions and privileges for six months, John Lee Stevens for three months, and Crucefix for six months.

CHAPTER 6

BITTER RECRIMINATIONS

Crucefix, Wood and Lee Stevens immediately appealed against the legality of their sentence. They had been given no information on the date their suspension would begin and decided to seek the guidance of a fellow Lodge member, Sir Frederick Pollock, at his law practice in the Temple. Sir Frederick was an influential barrister who was born in London in 1783, and educated at St Paul's School and Trinity College, Cambridge. He was a Fellow of the Royal Society and the MP for Huntingdon and served as the Attorney General under the Tory administration of Robert Peel. His advice to them was that, as their appeal had just been submitted, the sentence could not commence until after the hearing.

Crucefix thought it prudent to resign from the Asylum Committee, but after much discussion the membership refused to accept it and immediately re-elected him with a vote of confidence. There was no doubt that he was a stubborn man, but this continual confrontation along with his progressive illness was affecting his mental state. He expressed his feelings in the March edition of the *FQR*:

> *Much sadness about the current state and clearly put down to a misunderstanding. The Treasurer of the Asylum is among those who have fallen under 'displeasure', his crime attributed to his not having interrupted two Brethren in their remarks at a meeting of the Institution, at which he presided as Chairman.*

As the editor of the *FQR*, he tried to take a neutral stance with both his critics and supporters, and although most letters were supportive, some expressed vehement opposition. One such letter was sent by someone calling himself 'One of the Old School' whose views could have been penned by William Jackson. Although there was no evidence that this was the case, Crucefix was, however, clearly sure of the author's identity. The writer expressed his disgust by vehemently attacking the *FQR*, blaming it for this dispute. In his view this new charity was unnecessary and nothing more than a workhouse or an alms-house. He continued:

> *I have called the proposed Asylum a Workhouse, and I did so advisedly, because the term workhouse is known to be unpopular, and the giving a nickname is sometimes the best argument that can be used. I grant that a workhouse itself is a charitable provision, and saves the life of many who would starve; but still it is forced charity, which men only pay for because they are obliged, as is proved by the fact, that the paupers are not much better fed and clothed than by many of the rate payers.*

The next confrontation occurred on 29th April 1840. A Grand Festival was to be held, tickets for which could be purchased from the Treasurer of the Grand Officers' Club. When Crucefix endeavoured to buy one, to his surprise he was refused by the Treasurer on the grounds that as he had been suspended he could not take part in any Masonic activity. Crucefix objected, quoting Sir Frederick Pollock's advice that as his appeal had not been heard he was still an active member. The Grand Master was conveniently in a nearby office and on hearing the commotion stormed out in an excited manner, exclaiming that he was surprised at the Doctor's behaviour; he had been sentenced and as such he should endure it. Crucefix had grossly misconducted himself and was a disgrace to Masonry.

The appeal was set for 3rd June at the Quarterly Communications and would be presided over by the Grand Master. The three facing suspension duly entered the Lodge, but before they could take their seats they were told to leave. The three were escorted out to wait in the ante-room until the subject of their expulsion came up on the agenda. In their absence, three empty chairs were placed in the centre of the Lodge, and when they were readmitted they were instructed to sit on those seats to hear the outcome of their appeal. Altogether 26 Brethren were entitled to vote, but only eight were present; of these, six upheld the sentence and two opposed it. Wood, the main protagonist, immediately apologised, which was happily accepted and he was forgiven. Lee Stevens, however, showed no remorse and his suspension was upheld. Crucefix, who had played no part other than to chair the original meeting, was told his appeal was invalid and specified no grounds. Furious at this denial of justice, and conscious of the pleasure shown by the Duke of Sussex, he foolishly published in the June edition of the *FQR*:

There have been two great questions before the Masonic world: the one arising out of the report of a General Meeting of the Asylum, wherein three Brethren were charged with disloyalty to the Grand Master; which pretended report states that persons not Masons were present. Now that being the case, it could not be a Masonic meeting, and therefore its proceedings were not amenable to Masonic jurisdiction — this object is honestly taken. But presuming the exception to be rejected, should there not have been the semblance of justice in the course of the prosecution? We refer the reader to the proceeding, wherein Masonic justice became deaf, blind, and lame. And, in the Grand Lodge, where the case was ridiculously pretended to be re-heard, this curious result was arrived at: the principal party against whom the charges pointed with the most unnecessary severity, simply exposed his regret that any observation he made should have borne a construction he himself never attended; scarce had a word passed his lips, than the Grand Master evinced his joy and calling him to him, shook hands and with that showed how glad he was to release himself from difficulty. Hey! — presto! — Grand Lodge unanimously voted, that in case of that Brother all should be buried in oblivion! Mark, reader, this case was the only one upon which one iota of blame could possibly rest. Hands were shaken — aye, and heads were also shaken! ... On 19th March, the Grand Master of Masons, in vast assembly, where perhaps not twenty Masons were present, very coolly and deliberately pledged the whole Craft to certain views of religious and political nature. Now we by our ancient charges being 'resolved against all politics', and being desirous to present all dissension upon the important question of religion, declare that no such topics shall under any circumstances be entrusted; consequently this declaration of the Grand Master was totally at variance with his obligation, and the deliverance of such sentiment by him was likely to subvert the existence of the Order himself.

ABOVE **Dr Robert Thomas Crucefix by R. Martin.** *Library and Museum of Freemasonry*

Has he not abused his power, and rendered himself unworthy of obedience?

This publication gave the Duke of Sussex the evidence he needed, and later that year he would use it to further humiliate Crucefix to get him excluded from the Craft. Crucefix now felt that he had no other option but to resign from English Freemasonry, and wrote to both His Royal Highness and the Grand Secretary tendering his resignation forthwith.

Now Crucefix was free to publish the events leading to his suspension, starting with the Grand Master's letter of 26th August 1839 to his own personal resignation; now everyone could read the injustice and vindictiveness of the Grand Master. He received many letters of support, and one particular letter, from a gentleman using the pseudonym

ABOVE **The Rev Dr George Oliver at Witham Lodge.** *Province of Lincolnshire*

the customary removal of the cloth followed by a rendition of the *Sanctus* sung by the gentlemen and choristers of the Chapel Royal. The main concert was admirably directed by Bro Hawes. Signor Negri conducted the orchestra of the Theatre Royal, whilst Signor Giubelei, the noted opera composer, directed the performances of H. Soguin, Lane Lloyd and Miss Turner. There followed innumerable toasts to Royal and Masonic celebrities, the highlight being to Queen Victoria and her new husband Prince Albert.

Crucefix still chaired the Quarterly General Meeting of the Asylum on 8th July 1840, and donations continued to increase from all quarters of society including Adelaide, the Queen Dowager. The Doctor was re-elected Treasurer along with Bro Field as Secretary and Bro Nichols as the Collector. Crucefix informed those present:

> *The high moral evidence of the ability of this Institution stands so clear and distinct that we are much mistaken if before another year is passed this Charity does not stand in the proud station of parentage to others. For it is already in agitation to commence similar Institutions in India and elsewhere. These happy circumstances may affect us a little in point of finance, but they abundantly prove the high character of the Institution.*

He continued:

> *... drawback on this otherwise successful statement is only to be discovered in that misunderstanding which has arisen out of falsehood, the effect of which no exertion could prevent, but which effects your Committee have left no means unattempted to remove.*

Pythagoras, delivered a review on what he considered the Grand Master's wrongdoings:

> *When evil counsel prevails, the post of honour is the private station. Dr Crucefix, we observe, has resigned his connections with English Craft Lodges, under the eighth Constitution, and has resigned into the hands of the Grand Master his distinction as a Grand Officer.*

The Asylum's fifth Festival, held on 24th June 1840, raised £701 7s 4d and was attended by 160 gentlemen. The current Senior Grand Warden, Bro the Hon Henry Fitzroy MP, presided. He was the second son of Lt-Gen George Fitzroy, the 2nd Lord Southampton, and was MP for Lewes in Sussex. He had recently married Hannah, the daughter of the wealthy Nathan Rothschild. The Festival commenced with

A special meeting of Grand Lodge was held at Kensington Palace on the morning of 13th October, primarily to obligate the Most Honourable and Right Worshipful James Gascoyne-Cecil, the Marquess of Salisbury, as Deputy Grand Master of England. Salisbury had served in Lord Derby's cabinet and was a Privy Councillor, for which purpose he would be made a Knight of the Garter in 1842. When the investiture was completed, the subject turned to Dr Crucefix's potential expulsion. Crucefix, deliberately being awkward, entered clad in his Scottish regalia. (He was entitled to do so as an honorary member of the Lodge Canongate Kilwinning of Edinburgh.) Salisbury, who was at that moment presiding, politely requested the Doctor to retire to clothe himself as Grand Officer of the United Grand Lodge of England, thereby restoring some dignity to the proceedings. Crucefix initially declined, declaring he had resigned from English Freemasonry, but out of respect to Grand Lodge he did retire and put on his Past Grand Deacon's apron. He was then warmly welcomed back into the room.

It did occur to Crucefix that his expulsion from the Craft would leave him and, more importantly the future of the Asylum, in a precarious state. The Deputy Grand Master regretted that he had to preside over such an occasion and asked the Doctor if he wished to have the charge, namely why he should be expelled from the Craft, read out. Crucefix justified his stance but regretted the vendetta against himself and his colleagues, and realised the future of the Asylum would be in jeopardy if he continued. He accepted he had lost this round; now he should leave it to his friends and allies to negotiate an apology. He therefore retired, leaving his friends to work out some form of an apology that would be acceptable to all. Crucefix was now resigned to take his punishment and so in the end Bro Joseph Copeland Bell came up with a compromise:

> *That Bro. Dr Robert Crucefix having written the letter to H.R.H. the Grand Master, and published the proceedings of Grand Lodge in June under great excitement, and believing himself to be innocent of the charges which had been made against him and he having apologised for so doing, it is not expedient that Grand Lodge should proceed any further in the matter.*

This, with minor alterations, was eventually accepted by those assembled, with 145 in favour, 127 against, and 18 abstaining. Crucefix's humiliation was complete. He signed the apology and was readmitted into the Lodge with cheers from his supporters. Neither party had won: the Duke of Sussex was seen as a bigoted bully and the establishment that surrounded him as a group of sycophantic aristocrats, whilst Crucefix's party was shown to be insensitive to the Duke's feelings.

However, this did not end the matter, for at the annual election of the Grand Master during the Quarterly Communications held on 2nd December 1840, Bro Lee Stevens, often referred to by Crucefix as his Lance Corporal, stood up, contrary to protocol, and opposed the Duke of Sussex's re-election, giving four reasons.

The first was the discourtesy shown by the Grand Master to Crucefix, Wood and himself over the past year because at no time had he personally interviewed the three individuals and therefore his accusations must have been based on

ABOVE **Grand Secretary William White.** *Library and Museum of Freemasonry*

statements of others.

Secondly, the Grand Master was vehemently against the Asylum and would not countenance any argument expressed by the supporters to allay his concerns. Thirdly, did the Duke's statement that the supporters of the Asylum where 'nothing but jobbers and penniless speculators' mean that he included the Queen Dowager, who was a supporter, in this category? Finally, he believed it was unconstitutional that the Grand Master should be elected by Grand Officers he had appointed and who therefore showed fealty only to him. This was not necessary for the good of the Craft, but rather to the contrary. No sooner had Lee Stevens sat down than Bro Fraser arose and not only agreed with him but seconded the proposition.

The Duke then declared:

detriment of the other Masonic charities.

Lee Stevens again requested to be heard, revealing that he had been a parliamentary reporter for the *Morning Post* since 1838 and as such could never have reported anything detrimental to the Grand Master. At this stage Salisbury intervened and now proposed the Duke himself. Lee Stevens, realising that he could not possibly win, withdrew his opposition and the election was completed unopposed.

Dr Crucefix composed his valedictory address before resigning as editor of the *FQR* in the December issue:

> *That change grows out of the anomalous state of the English Masonic Law, which punishes the publication of transactions that require general dissemination in proportion to their relative importance to the Craft at large, by the severest personal penalty; whilst it permits the parole expression of adverse opinion, and the too easy distortion of facts, with the laxity wholly subversive of Masonic Principle.*

In March 1841, the Grand Secretary dispatched two letters to be read in every Lodge. In turn, every Secretary had to reply to the Grand Secretary, confirming that it had been carried out. The first letter was to remind every Freemason of his solemn obligation to obey certain Charges and Regulations, whilst Masters were reminded of their obligation taken when installed, thereby reinforcing the Grand Master's position as ruler of the Craft. The second letter was more specific, a copy of the Grand Master's address given at the Quarterly Communications on 3rd March 1841, designed to prevent any recurrence of events that had created the recent controversies. It resolved:

> *1st. That it is the primary duty of Grand Lodge to view with the greatest jealousy any breach of the privileges secured to the Masonic body of the legislative.*
> *2nd. That one of the most valuable of those privileges, and that which constitutes the very essence of the spirit of the Order, is the secrecy with respect to the proceedings and concerns of Masonry, which is enjoyed in the ancient charges inculcated by the strongest obligations in every stage of Masonic degree, and rigidly laid down by the laws and constitution.*
> *3rd. That the publications by Masons of the proceedings and concerns of Masonry, or furnishing materials for each publication, are traitorous violations of this most important privilege, and deserving of the highest punishment denounced against such offences by the*

ABOVE **HRH the Duke of Sussex (1773-1843).** *Library and Museum of Freemasonry*

> *Now, I'll let the Brother see, and I'll let Grand Lodge see, too, that I know all about him. I know, as well as he, that he is connected to the* Morning Post *newspaper and that he has most unfairly attacked me in that paper and in the Devonport paper. But I don't want him to commit himself; he need not make any acknowledgement or apology; he has had his say, and so will I have mine, and I pledge my Masonic honour that I can prove what I have said.*

He continued by implying that he knew how the Queen Dowager and various nobles and gentlemen had been persuaded to donate money towards the Institution, and again expressed his view that the Asylum would be to the laws and constitutions, as such publications, if not discouraged and suppressed, must ultimately destroy the respectability, and may even hazard the existence of the Craft.

4th. That with a view of checking the evil, the Grand Lodge call on all Masonic Authorities and Masters of Lodges on their Masonic allegiance to use their utmost endeavours to cause all Brothers who may violate this privilege by engaging in such publications as the late Freemasons' Quarterly Review, or by furnishing material for such publication by any disclosure without due sanction of the proceedings or concerns of Masonry, to be brought before the proper tribunal, to be dealt with according to the laws and constitutions of the Order.

5th. That the resolutions be forthwith transmitted by the Grand Secretary to all Lodges under the jurisdiction of the United Grand Lodge of England.

6th. That the Most Worshipful Grand Master be requested to communicate the same, in whatever manner he may deem fit, to the Grand Master of Masons in Scotland and Ireland, and of other Grand Lodges.

7th. That the Master of every Lodge under the jurisdiction of United Grand Lodge of England shall cause these resolutions to be read in open Lodge at the next meeting of the receipt thereof, and to be entered on the minutes of such Lodge, and that he shall immediately after such meeting report to the Grand Secretary the compliance with the resolution.

Extracted from the Minute
William H. White GS

ABOVE **Her Majesty the Queen Dowager, Adelaide by H. Cook.**
Author's Collection

Freemasonry was to revert to strict secrecy controlled by the inner circle of the Duke's: all the gains made by Crucefix and his associates to enlighten and democratise the Craft had come to nothing. In addition, the charities could likewise be tailored to the Grand Master's wishes.

Initially Grand Lodge's approach did appear to modify. It was as if they believed they had pushed the membership as far as they could and now was the time for reconciliation. The charity continued to flourish and gain momentum. However, the *FQR* became noticeably less informative, and transactions from Grand Lodge were not reported. Crucefix and Oliver were permitted to contribute the occasional article on historical matters, and the new editor did admit that Crucefix had committed editorial martyrdom and had been unfairly treated. The September edition of the *FQR* reported that both sides were attempting to find a peaceful solution:

Our readers, especially those who reside at a distance from the seat of Masonic Rule, will be gratified, indeed, to learn that all differences of opinion appear to be merged in a general desire to establish the Third Masonic Charity in the most permanent and extensive basis; and that the decision of Grand Lodge on the 1st of September, 1841, is so far in unison with that of the 6th of December, 1837, that the wishes of all may be attained, without doing violence to the feelings of any. The first resolution of Grand Lodge contemplated the erection of an Asylum; the second supports a System of Annuities; and both these, complying within the provisions of the existing Institution, one may be therefore carried out just in proportion to the feeling in favour of either. Those who would provide generally a regular stipend for the distressed may subscribe to the Annuity Fund; those who would provide a home for the absolute destitute may contribute to the Building Fund, and the most zealous may add both.

In the meantime the Committee for the charity continued planning fund-raising events. The next Festival arranged by the Board of Stewards was held on 14th April but was boycotted by the senior membership, leading to the comment in the *FQR*:

In the absence of the aristocratic patronage, which so seldom adds any real pleasure to the scene, the utmost sociality and good nature prevailed.

The sixth Festival for the Aged and Decayed Freemasons was held on 15th June 1841. Benjamin Wood should have presided, but his workload, as a consequence of his recent victory in gaining the parliamentary seat of Southwark, was becoming arduous and so he tactfully declined the Presidency. That honour was now offered to Joseph Copeland Bell. The entertainment was organised as usual by Mr Hawes, who produced a bevy of the most celebrated performers in the London theatrical circle. The gallery was filled to capacity with the ladies, and the formal proceedings were followed by many toasts to the Queen and to Masonic nobility. Finally Miss Turner sang one of Lee Stevens' songs to rapturous applause. The evening was complete when Dr Crucefix rose to announce that the charity's account had now reached £3,445.

However, the attempted harmony between the two camps was short-lived, for at Radley's Hotel on Wednesday 13th October at 7pm the following motion was tabled:

That the meeting acknowledge, with equal satisfaction and gratification, the declaration of His Royal Highness, the M.W. Grand Master, in favour of an Annuity Institution for the Relief of Aged and Decayed Freemasons, and most strongly recommend the adoption of His Royal Highness's suggestion by carrying out an annuity principle, that the erection of an Asylum be deferred until the sum of £7,000 shall have been received and invested, the interest only of such sum applicable to the purposes of annuities. All monies collected beyond the above sum to be set

ABOVE **The Crucefix Candelabra.** *Library and Museum of Freemasonry*

aside expressly as a Building Endowment Fund, the interest thereof to accumulate and be added to the principal. That the said sum of £2,000, already invested, shall remain intact, without diminution or increase, as a nucleus of a fund for the erection and endowment of the Asylum, and until a subsequent sum of £7,000 has been raised.

Crucefix, Bell and Lee Stevens, assisted by the Secretary, Robert Field, were asked to prepare a response to the Board of General Purposes. This was completed and sent by 6th December 1841, and demanded that:

1. That the Annuity Fund of the Institution be added to the fund proposed to be raised in accordance with the report of the Board of General Purposes provided that the annuitants now in the Institution are respectfully provided for on equal terms with the other annuitants; and the Subscribers of the Institution do return their privileges, pro rata, in that about to be formed.

2. That the Building Fund of this Institution be also placed in the hands of Grand Lodge through the Board of General Purposes, to accumulate and to be applied in accordance with the resolutions passed at the Meeting on 13th of October last, and communicated to the Board of General Purposes.

3. That once the arrangements are made, all offices held in the Institution be vacated.

The first thing that Alex Dobie, the Chairman, and the Board of General Purposes did on receipt of the address was to decline the recommendation that the building fund be continued. This was supported the following day by the Grand Secretary. Robert Field thought as a consequence that as all now agreed with the Annuity Fund it should go ahead, but the subject of the Building Fund should be temporarily postponed to maintain peace and harmony. In other words, the Building Fund would continue but firmly in the hands of the subscribers. The two charities had now separated and would remain so for the next eight years.

The function of the Annuity Fund was explained in the editorial of the *FQR* published in March 1842, with a warning that it would be a breach of faith to use monies already donated for the Building Fund for anything other than the Asylum. In a letter dated 24th May 1842, Crucefix confided to Dr Oliver his concerns relating to the legality and even the fairness of the Annuity Fund. He went on to write:

It is expected that the Grand Master will be present at the next Grand Lodge and will prevent all discussion — if so it is difficult to predict the result as I am determined to oppose the confirmation of the last minutes relative to the annuity scheme — not on the principle of a charity but in the details which are impracticable and practical unfair.

There had been rumours circulating since 1838 that the good Doctor should be rewarded with a Masonic testimonial. The proposed celebrations were repeatedly advertised in the *FQR*, and by early 1841, Lee Stevens had accrued £250 2s 6d.

The date for the testimonial was finally set for 24th November 1841, to be held at an extraordinary meeting of the Bank of England Lodge. His great friend and collaborator, W Bro the Rev George Oliver, Deputy Provincial Grand Master for the Masonic Province of Lincolnshire, was invited to preside over the occasion, and Robert Field, who appropriately was the Lodge's Secretary, planned the meeting to commence at 3pm for 4pm, followed by dinner at 6pm. The venue was again to be Radley's Hotel in Bridge Street. Lee Stevens personally delivered Crucefix's invitation, and the Doctor's acceptance was subsequently published in the December edition of the *FQR*:

18th November 1841.

My Dear Brother J. Lee Stevens, I have mentally played the improvident, by postponing, as well as I could, those thoughts which the 24th of November naturally give rise to. The kind invitation of my Brethren of the Board of Stewards has, however, awakened and gratefully affected me, and, in accepting it, I hope not to dishonour them as a guest. You will regret to know that I write from the bed-chamber; but each friend can appreciate my feelings, and will spare any attempt at expression. I pray you to offer my unaffected thanks to all, and accept them yourself, from your faithful Servant, Friend, and Brother,
R. T. Crucefix

The great day finally arrived. Lee Stevens declared Dr George Oliver an honorary member and invited him to occupy the chair. Bro Browse, Master of Old Dundee Lodge, and Bro Savage, Master of Athelstan Lodge, worked a portion of the 1st Lecture. Dr Oliver then delivered an oration founded on the 5th Antient Charge of the Constitution, followed by a rendition of Joseph Addison's famous *Ode* based on the 19th Psalm, first printed in *The Spectator* in 1712:

The spacious firmament on high,
With all the blue ethereal sky,
And spangled heavens, a shining frame,
Their great Original proclaim.
The unwearied sun, from day to day,
Does his Creator's power display,
And publishes to every land The work of an Almighty hand.

Soon as the evening shades prevail,
The moon takes up the wondrous tale,
And nightly to the listening earth

Repeats the story of her birth;
Whilst all the stars that round her burn,
And all the planets in their turn,
Confirm the tidings as they roll,
And spread the truth from pole to pole.

What though, in solemn silence, all
Move round the dark terrestrial ball?
What though no real voice nor sound,
Amid their radiant orbs be found?
In Reason's ear they all rejoice,
And utter forth a glorious voice,
Forever singing, as they shine,
'The hand that made us is Divine!'

ABOVE **Sir Frederick Pollock.** *Author's Collection*

The Lodge closed at 6pm and all moved into a large, tastefully decorated dining room. Suspended from the music gallery was the portrait of Dr Crucefix. The Rev Charles Vink said grace and the cloth was raised to a chorus of *Non Nobis* sung by Bros Fitzwilliam, Collyer and Edney. They were then treated to a gastronomic delight, followed by the Loyal Toast and various other salutes to the Grand Master and other senior Freemasons, before the Rev George Oliver delighted all present by presenting the testimonial to Robert Crucefix, which was followed by tumultuous applause.

Crucefix responded emotionally with a tear in his eye and spoke of his life and of the unfair attacks to which he had been subjected. Turning to John Lee Stevens, he said:

There is one Brother to whom I must say a word of parting grace — a fellow-sufferer with me. Side by side were we placed, a Masonic synod sitting in judgement upon us. Him no sophistry could deceive, no power appal. Day by day did we commune as to the best means of escaping the theatrical avalanche. Sentinel-like we took our turn on duty; and here we are again, I know not which the happier of the twain — he in contemplating the success of the measure in which he has been instrumental, or I in this gratefully thanking you and him. Need I name my zealous friend, Brother Lee Stevens.

He then talked lovingly of his wife:

It is true I have no Lewis to share with me the heat and burden of the day, who can hereafter look on this testimonial as a record of a sire's zeal, but there is one at home now waiting my return, as she often has with far

different feeling, in whose bosom this splendid proof of your attachment will enkindle the gentle consolation that her husband has equally gained the approbation of his friends, as he has proved deserving of her health.

Finally, he raised the subject of his failing health:

Brethren, failing strength and impaired health admonish me to limited duty; but there is honour in retirement. I feel that when I shall reflect on the transactions of this auspicious day, as if my spirits would reanimate and my health improve: in such a case, I doubt my resolution to keep from among you.

Lee Stevens then raised a glass to Dr Oliver and spoke of his life's work, which was graciously acknowledged by Oliver. Finally, other distinguished guests were toasted before the evening eventually ended with Crucefix returning home along the Strand to his wife.

On 25th January 1842, Joseph Copeland Bell presided over a ball held at Freemasons' Hall, all profits going to the Aged and Decayed Freemasons' Fund. Bell was a distinguished lawyer practising in Austin Friars, London. Born in Loughborough, Leicestershire, in 1793, he had married his wife Eliza in 1842, and had played an influential part throughout the development of the charity, having assisted Crucefix during his recent troubles. Bell later became involved with the development of the Kent Coast Railway Co, and died on 13th June 1865 at St Stephen's Terrace, Lewisham.

Crucefix's testimonial celebrations were barely concluded before the vendetta against him recommenced. This time the Grand Master attacked his friends, in particular Dr Oliver. The Provincial Grand Master of Lincolnshire, C. T. Eyncourt, wrote to Oliver on 4th March 1842, informing him that the Duke had expressed indignation over his central role during Crucefix's testimonial. This was followed, three weeks later, by Oliver's dismissal as the Deputy Provincial Grand Master.

On Wednesday 15th June 1842, the seventh Festival for Aged and Decayed Freemasons took place at the Freemasons' Hall, with William Shaw, Master of Grand Stewards Lodge No 66, acting as Chairman. The ladies assembled in the gallery to take a collation of excellent desserts and plenty of iced champagne. Some volunteered their professional talents in song, such as Miss Betts, Miss Fanny Russell and the Turner sisters accompanied by Mr T. Bishop, Mr Collyer, Mr Ransford, Mr Smith and Mr Turner under the musical directorship of Signor Brizzi, the celebrated opera singer. There was much to celebrate that evening, for the Queen had narrowly evaded assassination, a certain John Francis having taken a shot at her in St James's Park two weeks earlier. (He was apprehended and convicted of high treason, which usually carried the death penalty. However, the sentence was commuted and he was transported for life.) The Royal Family was toasted, and amid tumultuous applause, Dr Crucefix rose to announce that the fund had now reached £3,538.

It soon became clear with the sanctioning of the Annuity Fund that the subscribers would no longer be able to elect their annuitants from their funds. It was also evident that the rulers had manipulated the election to the Annuitants Committee in order to keep it firmly under their control.

CHAPTER 7

THE FINAL YEARS

Sussex was dead. Queen Victoria's favourite uncle, who had given her away at her marriage, had passed away in Kensington Palace on 21st April 1843. He had been the patron of many charities as well as President of the Society of Arts and the Royal Society and, since its union, the Most Worshipful Grand Master of the United Grand Lodge of England. He was a chronic asthmatic, but his death was due to a sudden onset of erysipelas, a particularly unpleasant condition brought about the bacterium streptococcus pyogenes. The disease presents as fever, painful red swollen blisters across the bridge of his nose giving an owl-like appearance. His general physician, Dr Holland, quickly made the diagnosis, but prior to the development of antibiotics it could often be fatal. Over the next few days the Duke appeared to make a recovery, but a sudden relapse caused his death within a few days.

Dr Chambers, Dr Holland, Sir Benjamin Brodie, Mr Keate, Mr Nussey and Mr Du Pasquier performed the post-mortem, which showed a granular diseased liver. The auricles, coronary arteries and aorta were ossified, indicative of arteriolar sclerosis or hardening of the arteries, not helped by habitual smoking. Thackeray recorded Miss Whit, the governess of Major Ponto, in his *Book of Snobs*, declaring:

> HRH such a poor dear the Duke of Sussex, such a man my dears, but alas, addicted to smoking.

Mr Bebnes, a relatively well-known sculptor, made a cast of his head, after which the body was wrapped in cerecloth (a waxed cloth for a shroud).

In his Last Will and Testament the Duke requested that he be buried in the cemetery at Kensal Green. His body, in a coffin made of Spanish mahogany and draped in a black pall, lay in state at Kensington Palace, attended by his Equerry, two Heralds of Arms and two of the Queen's Gentlemen Ushers.

The funeral took place on the morning of 4th May, escorted by Troopers of the Royal Horse Guards, the Blues.

Leading were the carriages of the Queen and the Queen Dowager accompanied by his close relations. Behind followed the carriages of the nobility, close friends, and representatives of Government and Parliament. The guard of honour was mounted by the 1st Grenadier Guards. The eight escutcheons of the Duke followed the body, which was received at Kensal Green Cemetery by the Lord Chamberlain, the Bishop of Norwich and the cemetery's Chaplain. The body was then placed in a vault in the cemetery chapel.

In the meantime a plain granite tomb was constructed as his final resting place. Two years later, in the early hours and in secret, the chapel tomb was opened. Those present could see that the pall was somewhat damaged and dusty, and the lining of the Duke's coronet had suffered from the conditions within the vault. The coffin was raised and with due ceremony transferred to its new vault.

The new tomb was plain, save for one side engraved with the words:

> *Sacred to the memory of His Royal Highness Augustus Frederick*
> *First Duke of Sussex, Sixth son of George the Third born April 21st 1773*
> *died April 21st 1843*

Sussex had been at the helm for so long that few could imagine the Craft without him. The main priority now was to find his successor. John Lee Stevens, who had for so long been a victim of his criticism, dedicated this poem to him:

> *When dies the Prince or when the Peasant dies,*
> *How seldom truth the epitaph supplies:*
> *But if of Sussex all that's true be told,*
> *Few were his faults — his virtues manifold.*

Charles Gordon, the 10th Marquess of Huntly and Earl of Aboyne, the Provincial Grand Master for Northamptonshire and Huntingdonshire, was invited to chair the Annual Festival in 1843. The Earl was a first class cricketer before entering parliament as the Tory member for East Grinstead, but following the introduction of the Reform Acts he felt he could no longer support the Tories and so crossed the floor to join the Whigs. Now he represented the constituency of Huntingdon.

The entertainment was as magnificent as ever and included the recently discovered singing prodigy Adeline Cooper who sang along with Signor Fornasari, the star of Her Majesty's Theatre, Drury Lane. The programme followed the customary pattern, but the Masonic toasts now included one to the memory of the Duke of Sussex, which was taken in silence. The Chairman addressed the audience, declaring he could not understand why there should ever have been any differences with respect to the charity. There was great applause, for everyone was conscious of the recent problems. His final remark was, 'Bygones had better be bygones.' The Secretary, Robert Field, then announced that the Asylum's fund had now reached the princely sum of £3,685 4s 6d. John Lee Stevens, poet and reporter, was then invited to recite one of his poems, appropriately dedicated to the Asylum:

> Once more we meet when oft we met before,
> In Holy Charity's behest; once more.
> We plead the AGED MASON'S claim, to share
> Whatever wealth can give or comfort spare.
> For him, domestic joys that smiled upon
> But who, alas! Hath lost them, one by one;
> For him, who ample means could once command,
> And gave with eager heart and ready hand,
> For him, once highly honoured, widely known,
> But living now — mid multitudes — alone;
> For him, who joined the Craft in early youth;
> And followed Science through the paths of Truth;
> For him, who step by step the summit gained,
> And even to the sacred fane attained;
> For him, unfriendly now, new friends we seek,
> And every generous sympathy bespeak!
> Nor shall we plead on vain! We have no fear
> For such as he, from those assembled here!
> The cause is won already, where we find
> Sincere in purpose — eloquent and kind!
> Aboyne presiding — where around we see
> Of hearty friends a goodly company;
> And where, with trustful tears of tenderness,
> Virtue and Beauty all our efforts bless!

ABOVE **Freemasons' Hall.** *Library and Museum of Freemasonry*

BELOW **Peter William Gilkes.** *Library and Museum of Freemasonry*

Come then, poor wanderer! Nor wander more:
In our Asylum there shall be a door.
Flung open to receive thee; — there shall be
Seats for the friends who come to comfort thee —
And food, and raiment; to the Asylum come,
And in its refuge find a Cheerful Home!

Rapturous applause followed, and the proceedings closed to a chorus of:

This stone is laid, the Temple is begun Help, and its walls shall glitter in the sun!

Followed by:

There, beneath Acacia groves, shall old men walk, And, calmly waiting death, with angels talk.

At the Annual General Meeting held on 12th July, Robert Crucefix announced the results of the election for officers. Not surprisingly, Crucefix retained the Treasurer's post and Robert Field continued as Secretary. There was also an enthusiastic vote of thanks for the Earl of Aboyne's chairmanship of such a successful Festival.

Thomas Dundas, the 2nd Earl of Zetland, was elected and installed as the Grand Master on 24th April 1844. It was recorded in the *FQR*:

A new aera [sic] has commenced; may it be equally propitious to the governor and the governed! ... If we glance at the past year, its history will furnish a gratifying anticipation of the future; not but it has presented a few awkward points — yet these were in some measure unavoidable.

Thomas Dundas had been born in London in 1795, and was educated at Harrow and Trinity College, Cambridge before entering parliament as the member for Richmond in Yorkshire. He was Lord Lieutenant for the North Riding, a post he held until his death in 1873. Like his predecessor, he was not well disposed to the likes of Crucefix and Oliver. George Oliver's dismissal as Deputy Grand Master for Lincolnshire was considered by many as unfair, and he had many supporters who advertised nationally for him to receive a testimonial, which came to fruition on the 9th May 1844 at a dinner held at The City Arms Hotel in Lincoln, hosted by the Witham Lodge. Crucefix was invited to propose the health of the Chairman,

the Rev J. Osmond Dakeyne MA, and of course the highlight of the evening was the presentation to George Oliver of a silver cup and five smaller ones for the members of his family.

The ninth Annual Festival was attended by 130 gentlemen and their ladies and was chaired that evening by Col the Hon George Anson, the Provincial Grand Master for Staffordshire. Anson had had a colourful career, having taken part in the Battle of Waterloo. He now held the post of Principal Storekeeper of the Ordnance. He had married the social beauty the Hon Isabella Forester and had three daughters. A keen horseracing supporter, he was also said to be addicted to whist. Politically he was a strong supporter of the Whigs and was the MP for Staffordshire South. He died of cholera during the Great Mutiny; sadly his wife died a year later.

This year's ceremony had all the glamour of previous years, and the entertainment was just as magical. Anson's address was said to have demonstrated the very best explanations of the tenets of Freemasonry. Crucefix announced that the fund had increased to £3,868 4s 9d before delivering a speech initially praising the ladies but continuing on to areas that would again prove controversial to the hierarchy of Grand Lodge:

Brethren, is it not time that we should be honest to the other sex — somewhat more unselfish in ourselves? Should we not endeavour to repay some small instalment of the great debt we owe to our best friend — whether we view her in the character of sister, wife, or above all, in that of mother? Is it not high time to remove those moral stains from our Masonic escutcheon — disregard for her interest, and selfishness for our own? For the moment may there go forth an ennobling sentiment. That shall swell into one burst of universal acclamation in favour of a fund for the widows of Masons.

At this point there was loud cheering. He continued:

I am not a young man, but I am not too old to hope that I may live to see accomplishment of what I believe to be a general desire — and which it only require moral courage to ensure — for the means to such an end are abundant.

The speeches complete, the Chairman and others retired to join their ladies in the music room, where they were lavishly entertained, culminating with a 'fire' delivered in a powerful manner by the toastmaster Mr Harker.

The success of the recent ball and Anson's speech were the principal topics at the next committee meeting. The profit, including a generous donation of 20 guineas from Col Anson, was £400. There was other good news, for Bro Benjamin Bond Cabbell, the well-known philanthropist, had agreed to chair the next Festival. Cabbell, the Tory MP for St Albans, had been educated at Westminster School and Oriel College, Oxford, where he studied Law. As High Sheriff of Norfolk, he donated a large sum of money to build a lifeboat to be based at Cromer, and there is still a lifeboat within the fleet named after him.

The union of the Asylum and the Benevolent Annuity Fund now appeared plausible, and after discussion at the next meeting of the Committee of Masters, held on 26th August 1844, they agreed that the criteria for union made by Grand Lodge had now been met. Crucefix announced:

Whereas, in the fourteenth general regulation for the government of the Craft, it is stated — That the Grand Lodge has the inherent power of investigating, regulating, and deciding all matters relative to the Craft.

And whereas, it is stated in unanimous vote of the Grand Lodge of the 6th Dec 1837 — That the Grand Lodge recommend the contemplated Asylum for Aged and Decayed Freemasons to the favourable considerations of the Craft.

A Committee shall be immediately appointed consisting of a deputation from the Grand Lodge, from the Committee of the Asylum for Aged and Decayed Freemasons and from the Committee of the Royal Masonic Benevolent Annuity Fund, with a view to the union of the two latter excellent institutions, under the patronage of the Grand Lodge; it being alike detrimental to the two Charities, and discreditable to Freemasonry, that any evidence of past disunion in the Craft should no longer be permitted to exist.

It was proposed that Bro Brewster should raise the subject at Grand Lodge, which he did on 10th August 1845. He stood, but before he could utter a word he was interrupted and reminded to stick strictly to the point. Brewster revealed that the Committee for the Asylum had now elected several well-known trustees, thereby fulfilling Grand Lodge's criteria. It was therefore now appropriate to reunite the two charities. The new permanent Board of Trustees were Bros the Earls of Aboyne and of Southampton, Col the Hon George Anson,

Benjamin Bond Cabbell and Dr R. T. Crucefix, and it was expected that those temporary trustees would relinquish their posts. Bro Cabbell, the Past Junior Warden, was unavoidably absent, and so his good friend Dr Lane seconded this motion. Initially it was well received but before it could be ratified, the Grand Secretary retired to consult the Grand Master. When he returned he pronounced that in the opinion of the latter the motion could not be entertained and must be rejected.

Crucefix later presented his motion to increase the dues for the Benefit Fund and Annuities to the Widows of Freemasons. This again was supported by the majority present, but rejected this time by the Provincial Grand Masters, who requested its postponement to allow them more time to discuss it with their membership.

In November, a committee of five subscribers was formed to meet with the representatives of the Royal Masonic Benevolent Annuity Fund to draw up plans for a union. Bros Brewster, Lane, Crucefix, Wright and Sangster were to act for the Asylum, whilst Bros Dobie, Havers, McMullen, Parkinson and W. H. White were to represent the Annuity Fund.

The new Board of Trustees had now been formed, but still there were concerns relating to a former trustee, Henry Rowe. Rowe, a member of Neptune Lodge, had managed their account held by Grote, Prescott & Co's bank, much of which derived from the estate of the late Bro Sansum and the profits from the Festivals. He now refused to relinquish his post in spite of repeated requests. The charity now had no alternative but the courts. Sadly he had previously been declared bankrupt, and nearly all the funds were lost. This was compounded by the additional legal cost. The total amount misappropriated was £620 and became public knowledge at the tenth Annual Festival held in June 1845. This year's President, Bro Cabbell, explained to those assembled that because of this one man's actions, the fund had been reduced to £3,753 12s 11d. However, an additional sum of £400 could be added as a consequence of that evening's event.

They attempted to recoup the sum by appealing to every Lodge throughout the country, advertising in the *FQR* over several editions:

The General Committee of the Asylum for the Aged and Decayed Freemasons most earnestly direct the attention of the Provincial Brethren to the state of the Funds of that excellent Institution, and Trust, that by the aid of Lodges and private Contributions, the serious expenses

to which the Charity has been subjected may be met by the kindness and liberality of the Craft.

Post Office Orders, Bankers papers, or references on London Houses, will be thankfully acknowledged by the Bankers, Messrs Prescott & Co, 62, Threadneedle Street, London; the Treasurer, Dr Crucefix, Grove, Gravesend, Kent; or the Secretary, ad interim, Mr John Whitmore, 125, Oxford Street, London.

ABOVE **Bronze plaque to commemorate Dr Crucefix at the Croydon home.** *Harriet Sandvall*

BELOW **The Stained Glass Window in the Great Hall at the Croydon home.** *Harriet Sandvall*

BELOW **10th Festival advertising bill.** *Library and Museum of Freemasonry*

MASONIC FESTIVAL & CONCERT.

Asylum for Aged Freemasons.

THE

TENTH ANNUAL FESTIVAL,

In aid of the Funds of this Institution,

WILL TAKE PLACE

ON WEDNESDAY, THE 18TH JUNE, 1845,

AT

FREEMASONS' HALL, GREAT QUEEN STREET.

Bro. B. B. CABBELL, F.R.S., P.G.W. in the Chair.

STEWARDS:

Brothers J. LANE, D.C.L. President; W. SHAW, Vice-President;
W. H. SMITH, (P.G.W.) Treasurer; R. SPENCER, Hon. Sec.;
and Twenty-four other Brethren.

Dinner on Table at Six o'Clock PUNCTUALLY. Tickets, 15s. each, may be had of the Stewards; at Freemasons' Tavern; and of Bro. R. SPENCER, 314, High Holborn.

The Brethren will NOT appear in Masonic Costume; and Gentlemen NOT of the Fraternity are respectfully invited to attend.

An Address (written by Bro. E. BREWSTER) will be distributed.

The following Ladies and Gentlemen have in the most liberal manner, consented to give their valuable services in the Concert :—

The Misses WILLIAMS.   The Misses TURNER.
Miss HILL, (Pupil of Signor NEGRI.)
Miss JULIA WARMAN, (Pupil of Mr. CROUCH,) Fantasia, Pianoforte.
Mr. FREDERICK CHATTERTON, Solo on the Harp.
Signor BRIZZI.   Mr. GENGE.
Mr. C. E. HORN.   Mr. JOLLEY (and his Pupils.)
Mr. KINGSBURY.   Signor FERRARI.
Mr. COLLYER.   Mr. F. N. CROUCH.

Signor NEGRI will preside at one of *Pape's Grand Pianofortes*, generously offered by Mr. SCOTT, from his Repository, Great Marlborough Street.

This response was so successful that by December 1845 the deficit had largely been eliminated. That same month, Robert Field announced that due to declining health he must resign. An accountant by profession, he had been a loyal and energetic Secretary, much loved by the membership, and all agreed he would be greatly missed. Sadly, not long after, aged 48 years, he passed away at his home at 25 Tibberton Square, Islington, leaving his young wife Eliza (aged 34), and several children. Bro John Whitmore agreed to act as the Secretary until a successor could be appointed.

On 3rd December 1845, Crucefix again attempted to introduce his annuities motion for the Masonic Widows but it was again rejected by the Provincial Grand Masters. The Grand Master did, however, credit his good intentions but felt obliged to support Grand Lodge's decision. A supportive letter in that edition of the *Review* stated that it was sad that the Society of Oddfellows had a fund for widows yet Freemasonry, a much bigger and more affluent organisation, continued to oppose the suggestion. The editorial in the March 1846 edition records:

> Prejudice has at length been compelled to yield to consistency. This most desirable object has attracted the attention of the Committees of both Institutions; and Sub-Committees from each are appointed to consider on what may be the most desirable means of accomplishing an end so devoutly wished for. In the present state, we purposely defer any observations, leaving the intelligent Brethren to whose cure this great question is committed, to deal with it is a 'holy one'. And may their labours be crowned with successes.

Yet again, at Grand Lodge on 22nd February 1846, Crucefix presented a Notice of Motion that a sum of £300 per annum be allotted specifically to a fund for the widows of annuitants. (Awards were given to Masonic annuitants, but terminated on the recipient's death, leaving the wife destitute.) The Grand Master presided over the next meeting, in March 1846, and Dr Crucefix was summoned to present this motion, which he did with passion, explaining to all the plight of the poor widows. Grants were often generous, he confirmed, but they were not regular, making life difficult for the widow. When he sat down the Rev W. J. Carver seconded the motion. Bro Dobie then enquired whether this had anything to do with the delay in payment of a grant to Mrs Field, the widow of the late Robert Field. Bro Pearce immediately interjected that this was not the responsibility of Grand Lodge but that of the Board of Benevolence. Bro

McMullen then declared that this was neither the time nor place for such discussions, and sadly the motion was again lost in what many considered a somewhat biased assembly.

The enmity against Mrs Field continued, for although the Board of Benevolence recommended the award of £50 to her and her family, for some unknown reason it was referred to the Board of General Purposes. There was a further delay due to a fire originating from a fractured gas pipe, necessitating the rapid evacuation of Freemasons' Hall. This unfortunately happened on 3rd June, just as Crucefix was again attempting to advance his motion for annuitants' widows.

Recorded in the Minutes of the AGM of the Annuity Fund of 15th May 1846 was the following statement:

> That it appears to both Sub Committees that it could be desirable to amalgamate the two Institutions, provided certain legal difficulties can be removed by the Asylum for Aged Freemasons, and that the Sub-Committees report to this effect to their respective constituencies.

The old veteran of Wellington's campaigns in India and the Peninsula, Field Marshal Stapleton Cotton, 1st Viscount Combermere, and Provincial Grand Master for Cheshire, was invited to preside over the eleventh Festival, but at the last moment was prevented from attending. Instead the role was taken by J. B. Byron from the Lodge of Antiquity No 2, a Vice President of the Board of Stewards. It was announced that, in spite of all the recent problems, the fund had reached £3,800 18s 4d, and that this event had raised a further £504. The concert, after the formal agenda, was under the banner of Bros Negri (father and son), and took place in the Glee Room. The greatest talents currently appearing in London volunteered their operatic skills, whilst the English musical pieces were directed by Bro F. Nicholas Crouch and the solo harpist Bro Chatterton.

Robert Crucefix was now 57 years old and his health was rapidly deteriorating. He was now continually tired and sought a cleaner environment away from stink of the River Thames. He and his wife had long thought of retiring to the country, as was evident in an unpublished letter he had written to Dr Oliver on 5th July 1842:

> I found your letter of the 27th on my return from a compulsory visit to a dear friend whom I have probably seen for the last time — a female relation — a friend of early youth.
> This visit has decided me — I have advertised my

ABOVE **Thomas Dundas (1795-1873), 2nd Earl of Zetland, by Louis William Desanges.** *Library and Museum of Freemasonry*

house for to let and furniture for sale — that object accepted — I turn my back on London for a time.

I do not retire on portence — but resignation I hope will sweeten the simplest draught for a time — and present betterment.

Wherever I am — you will be in my daily thoughts and shall be in possession of my whereabouts.

Bro John Whitmore of 125 Oxford Street was appointed as Secretary at the AGM held at the New London Hotel, as Radley's was now called, at 7pm on 8th July 1846. Bro S. Solomon, from Bevis Marks in the Jewish quarter of the City, was appointed Collector. A month later, the new Secretary mentioned that he had recently had a conversation with several friends of the charity and that now was probably the most appropriate time to begin building the Asylum. Henry Faudel, a stalwart of Jewish Freemasonry, and Lee Stevens both enthusiastically began discussing the project. The

meeting concluded with a date being set for an extraordinary meeting to begin the planning:

> *That in the opinion of this Committee it is desirable that some steps should be immediately adopted to carry out the Objects of the Charity, and they anticipate that the state of the funds is sufficient to warrant the commencement of a building or buildings as soon as sufficient information can be obtained as to the purchase of land and the cost of the building.*

Certain criteria were agreed. The Home must be within a 20-minute train journey from London and near to current Masonic centres as well as places of worship. Bros Staples, Tombleson, Wright and Crucefix were appointed to examine those shortlisted locations.

The twelfth Annual Festival for the charity was electric with the news that things were at last happening. The President, Charles Fitzroy, the 3rd Lord Southampton and a Tory peer, was suffering from a nasty cold but was adamant he was going to attend such a momentous occasion. Maj-Gen Cooke, PSGW of the USA, the Father of the United States cavalry, was an invited guest. Although he would become a supporter of Lincoln during the American Civil War, he would always be overshadowed by his more flamboyant son-in-law, J. E. B. Stuart, the Confederate cavalry commander. Cooke never again spoke to Stuart, who reflected, 'He will regret it only once, and that will be continually.' With business complete, they joined the ladies in the Glee Room where Southampton presented Crucefix with an emblazoned vote of thanks engraved with the following address:

> *As a memorial of the services rendered to the Asylum for Worthy, Aged and Decayed Freemasons, by its much esteemed and valued Treasurer, Bro. Robert Thomas Crucefix, MD, LLD Past Deacon of the Grand Lodge of England. The governors and subscribers at the Annual General Meeting held at Radley's Hotel, Bridge Street, Blackfriars, on the 8th day of July 1846 UNANIMOUSLY RESOLVED to present to him this record of their thanks for the foresight and philanthropy in suggestion of the charity, the unremitting zeal and devotion with which he has at all times watched over and protected its best interest, and for the persevering application of those talents which have mainly contributed to its progressive and permanent advancement.*

Several sites had been visited in the Croydon area, and two had been shortlisted by the July of 1847. A debate on the future naming of the established ensued. Henry Faudel suggested a more appropriate name should be the College for Aged and Decayed Freemasons rather than 'Asylum'; and that 'Decayed' was also unsuitable as it was decidedly unpleasant. Most agreed, but felt at this stage of the development that it would be inappropriate to alter things. The auditors reported that the current amount in the fund just exceeded £4,083. Lord Southampton accepted the position as the first President of the Asylum, and it was agreed that all donors of 50 guineas should be appointed as Vice Presidents.

It was finally agreed in October 1847 to purchase the plot currently owned by a Mr Morland situated adjacent to Croydon Station. The architect and Freemason Samuel Whitfield Daukes' design was accepted, which would house approximately 50 individuals in two-roomed apartments. Daukes was later appointed the Grand Superintendent of Works. He had been born in London in 1811, but had moved to York to be articled to the eminent architect James Pigott Pritchett. Daukes eventually set up his own practice in Gloucester in 1834, his most famous design being that of the Royal Agricultural College at Cirencester.

Mr Mark Patrick was awarded the building contract — not because it was the most economic but more for his reputation as a builder.

The debate on an annual donation to both widows and annuitants continued, with delays and excuses, until March 1864 when Crucefix rose to his feet and solemnly announced to all that Grand Lodge would eventually become non-existent if they did not prove themselves to be based essentially on charity.

The first sod for the new home was turned on 19th February 1849 in the north-east part of the intended structure. This was carried out by Bros Wilson, Wright, Patrick, Whitmore, Barrett and the assistant architect, and was recorded in the *FQR* as follows:

The ground having been marked out and measured accordingly to the usual system, the party gave three cheers for the success of the undertaking. Never were hearts more sensitively impressed with honesty of purpose or holiness of object. Heart gave them expression, and truth wafted them as best she could do upwards, in token of her own testimony in favour of the Aged and Decayed Freemason.

A very important meeting took place early in 1849 between Bro Dobie, Grand Registrar, the Provincial Grand Master for Surrey, and Bro R. Gardner Alston, the Deputy Provincial Grand Master for Essex, who had on two occasions been the President of the Annual Festival for the Asylum, Alston suggesting that Dobie could play an important and constructive role in the union of the charities. The outcome of this meeting came on 28th April 1849 when the two committees met and, thanks to Dobie and Alston, a series of terms were hammered out and finally agreed. This meeting became a milestone on the road to the union, but this was not the end of squabble. One such barrier came when Bro Hardwick, the Grand Superintendent of Works, along with others, sent a report suggesting the proposed site was unhealthy and altogether unfit for human habitation.

Lord Dudley Coutts Stuart MP, a passionate supporter of Polish independence, presided over the Annual Festival in 1849. Always a Whig supporter, he had married Princess Christine Bonaparte, daughter of Lucien Bonaparte, the younger brother of Napoleon. Some 150 people accompanied a very frail Dr Crucefix that evening, and the gallery was packed as usual with the ladies in their resplendent ball gowns. Following the formal meeting the President addressed those present and referred to the current rumours circulating within certain sectors of the Craft relating to the unhealthy nature of the site chosen for the Asylum. Crucefix attempted to make a response but was so ill that he was obliged to sit and Bro Whitmore had to finish.

External surveyors were employed to evaluate the various problems raised by the Grand Superintendent of Works, and eventually both parties agreed that with suitable drainage the building work could go ahead.

The date set for the Grand Master to lay the foundation stone was 31st May 1849, but it had to be postponed because:

... after the preliminaries for a union were arranged, a report was made to the Grand Master that the site selected was an un-drainable swamp, the locality insalubrious, and the design unworthy of the honour and dignity of the Craft.

Bro Whitmore maintained that this taunt against the professionalism of the architect and the judgement of the Committee had to be strongly refuted. The Doctor, having slightly recovered, was helped from his seat by his companions to warn that there were still some at the very top in Freemasonry who objected to the project, concluding:

Brethren, this will, in all probability, be the last time that I shall address you here on the subject. I will not sully the happiness of the social hour by explanation — it must be so. After so many years' service, I have earned a title to retirement, in which there is no dishonour. My heart yearns to thank you, were I able to do so, in most glowing terms, for increasing confidence and affectionate support. Before I conclude, permit me to hope that, aided by the inspiriting influence — and may I not add the moral direction — of the better sex, you will cheer my retiring effort by such a subscription as may render my night's slumber as refreshing as my heart will be grateful.

The chair for the AGM was taken by Bro W. L. Wright for the first time on 11th July 1849. Crucefix was too ill to attend. A resolution thereon was moved by Bro John Lee Stevens and seconded by Bro Barrett:

That the meeting having heard with deep regret of the serious illness of Bro R. T. Crucefix, the Treasurer, and feeling the impossibility of forgoing the advantage of his eminent services to the Institution as far as they can be rendered by him, hereby re-elect him to the office, and associate with him in the performance of its duties, Bro John Hodgkinson, one of the Vice Presidents.

This was, of course, carried unanimously. The members of the General Committee were then elected for that year.

Crucefix's health was rapidly deteriorating, and with continued haemoptysis and fatigue he would never be able to attend the much-vaunted stone-laying ceremony. He wrote to Dr Oliver just prior to his final journey to Bath, hoping that some relaxation and rest would delay the inevitable:

Grove, Gravesend
Sept 22nd 1849.
My ever dear Friend, I hopefully trust that I am out of immediate danger; but I have only a respite, the cough has returned, though not with all its late violence. Still the sputa bear too unmistakeable evidence that the most cautious restriction is absolutely needed.
Ever yours
Robert Thomas Crucefix

He travelled to Bath on 12th October 1849, and just prior to Christmas he again wrote to Oliver:

Bath, December 20th 1849.
My dear Friend, Although as yet I can neither dress nor undress myself, yet I have, after a month's close confinement, been out today and basked in the sun. The indulgence has greatly inspired me, and I almost dare to hope that our common Father may vouchsafe me still greater blessings. On the whole I am certainly better. Although the tenant of a sick chamber, my attention is naturally drawn to the season of the year, when the world is, as it were, almost morally directed to the enjoyment of Christmas, and the prospect of a happy new year.
Ever yours
Robert Thomas Crucefix

The Home in Croydon was in the Elizabethan/Tudor style, and by the end of 1849 the north wing was roofed and the foundations for the south wing had been completed. Sadly, during this period one of their greatest benefactors, Adelaide, the Queen Dowager, died. The society's flag on the building site was flown at half-mast.

In Bath, on 25th February 1850, Dr Robert Thomas Crucefix finally succumbed to his disease. He had a massive haemorrhage before slipping into unconsciousness and passing away. *The Gentleman's Magazine* recorded:

Somerset: March 4th 1850. At Bath, Dr Crucefix, well known in every part of the world where Freemasonry flourishes, by his benevolent exertions the Asylum for Aged and Decayed Freemasons was founded. The Institution known as the 'Widows Fund', established for the widows of Freemasonry, also owes its existence to his efforts, and of all other charitable institutions of the craft he was a liberal and zealous supporter.

His body was taken back to John Whitmore's house in Oxford Street before his burial in the family plot at St Mary's Church, Paddington Green. Later a bronze tablet was fixed to the wall above the central window at the Home, stating:

This Tablet perpetuates
The memory of
Robert Thomas Crucefix
The founder of this Asylum
Anno Mundi 5854.

CHAPTER 8
THE CONSECRATION AND NEW BEGINNING

It may be coincidental, but with the death of Dr Crucefix the attitude towards the Asylum appeared to modify. There was also a minor alteration in the title of Crucefix's brainchild, the *Freemasons' Quarterly Review*, which became known as the *Freemasons' Quarterly Magazine and Review (FQM&R)*. The editorial in the first edition commented on the start of 'a new relationship'.

The subscribers congregated at Radley's two days after the Doctor's death. Deep sorrow was expressed, for he had been the driving force since the charity's conception and there were serious concerns about its future without his guidance. They agreed that his obituary should be published in *The Times* so all could learn of their loss. However, the news about the positive progress of the construction of the Asylum brightened the proceedings, for the north wing was now complete and rumours abounded that the two charities were to merge. There were now no barriers separating the two committees responsible for the charities and, on 15th May 1850, regulations for the final amalgamation were presented and unanimously agreed. The joint committee requested the patronage and support of the Most Worshipful Grand Master the Earl of Zetland towards the new agreed venture.

The last Festival held solely for the Asylum took place on 19th June — from now on all fund-raising events would be combined. The Earl of Zetland had originally agreed to preside, but at the last moment was unavailable to attend. William Tucker, the Provincial Grand Master of Dorsetshire, agreed to take his place. Tucker's rise in the Craft had been even more meteoric than Crucefix's. He had been initiated into a Dorset Lodge in 1842, becoming its Master in 1843, and three years later he was appointed the Provincial Grand Master for Dorsetshire. But his prominence did not last long, for in 1853 he was suspended for wearing insignia of Christian Orders in Grand Lodge. The Festival had the same format as in preceding years, and after dinner the President gave the traditional toasts. The response was given by Bro Alexander Dobie, and everyone was delighted when the Chairman presented the toast to the memory of Dr R. T. Crucefix, which was drunk in silence.

It was evident that one individual was now doing his utmost to ensure that not only the merger but also the building of the Asylum would take place. This was Bro Alexander Dobie, the Grand Registrar and the Grand Master of Surrey, in whose Province stood the new Asylum. It was therefore suggested that he would be the perfect senior Freemason to officiate over the consecration of the Home, which was planned for 1st August 1850.

The day of the consecration was initially overcast, but by mid-morning the sun came out and soon carriages containing the elegantly dressed VIPs arrived. Just before noon four omnibuses appeared, carrying the 60 children of the Royal Masonic Girls' School; Mrs Cook, the Matron; Bro Crew, the school's secretary; and the members of the House Committee, closely followed by the representatives from the Boys' School. The main part of the ceremony was to take part in the Committee Room, recently furnished with a beautiful harmonium and a very handsome dog stove that had come from Leeds Castle and had been presented by Bro G. Barrett. Adorning the wall was the portrait of Robert Crucefix painted by Bro Mosely. A large marquee, provided by Messrs Lee of Leadenhall Street, was erected in the neighbouring grounds where lunch, supplied by Bro Benjamin Bean of the Greyhound Hotel, would be served for the 300 guests.

Provincial Grand Lodge was held in Croydon Town Hall and, on conclusion, the members adjourned to St James's Church where the Grand Chaplain, VW Bro the Rev J. E. Cox, presented a sermon based upon the tenets of Freemasonry and the attributes of the late Bro Crucefix. The packed congregation then collected a sum of £40. Bros Wilson, Faudel, Whitmore and Blake then marshalled those assembled to form a procession to march to the Asylum. They assembled as follows:

Two Tylers with drawn swords
Steward; Steward
The Girls of the Royal Freemasons' Charity for Female Children in couples

The Boys of the Royal Masonic Institution in couples
Juvenile Pipers and Band of the Royal Caledonian Asylum, in Highland Costume
Steward; Steward
Lodges and Brethren according to their numbers, the junior going first
Officers of Grand Stewards Lodge
Provincial Grand Pursuivant
Provincial Grand Organist
Past Provincial Grand Officers
Superintendent of Works
Assistant Director of Ceremonies
Bro Whitmore bearing the Cup containing wine; Bro Wilson bearing the Cornucopia containing corn
Bro Wright bearing the Vase containing the Oil
Provincial Grand Director of Ceremonies
Secretary of the Institution, Bro Farnfield, with the Book of Constitutions on a cushion
Treasurer of the Institution, Bro J. Hodgkinson
Past Grand Officers of England
Architect, Bro Daukes, with Plans
Members of the Building Committee
Vice Presidents of the Institution
Grand Officers of England
The Corinthian Light, borne by a PM

The Column of Junior Warden, borne by a PM
Provincial Grand Junior Warden, with a Plumb Rule
Steward; Steward
The Doric Light, borne by a PM
The Column of Senior Warden, borne by a PM
Provincial Grand Senior Warden, with a Level;
Provincial Grand Deacon
A Past Master bearing the Volume of the Sacred Law on a Cushion
Steward; The Grand Chaplain, the Rev J. E. Cox; Steward
The Deputy Provincial Grand Master, Bro J. Francis, with a Square
The Ionic Light, borne by a PM
Steward; Steward
Provincial Grand Sword Bearer
The Provincial Grand Master, Bro Alexander Dobie, Grand Registrar &c. &c
Steward; Provincial Grand Senior Deacon; Steward
Provincial Grand Tyler

The girls stood three deep on the terrace either side of the central door and the boys lined each side of the broad walk leading to the door. When the procession approached, they opened outwards to allow the Provincial Grand Master, followed by his Officers, to pass through and into the building.

An ode written by Bro Carpenter was read, followed by a reading from the Psalms by the Grand Chaplain, at the conclusion of which an anthem was sung. The architect presented the plans and elevations to the Provincial Grand Master, followed by prayers penned by Crucefix's great friend, the Rev George Oliver.

The Provincial Grand Master spoke of the works of all the

Masonic charities, and the ceremony was concluded with another anthem. The Provincial Grand Master spoke of the works of all the Masonic charities, and the ceremony was concluded with another anthem.

Lunch was served in the garden. The caterers had prepared for 300 individuals, but with sunshine an additional 200 turned up who had not paid, causing some commotion which was smoothly resolved. Grace was said by the Grand Chaplain. After lunch they were entertained by a song from Bro Ransford who had performed at many of the Annual Festivals. One of the older girls from the School, Eliza Birch, then delivered an address composed by the school's secretary, and Bros Crew and Dobie responded by describing the success of the Masonic charities. When they sat down, Miss Ransford delivered a delightful melody entitled *I love the merry sunshine*, a popular song of the period written by Stephen Glover.

Afterwards a list of the names of those ladies, such as Mrs Dobie, who had collected silver purses for donating five guineas towards the charity was read. Dobie called for everyone's attention and talked at some length of those two brothers responsible for the day: Bro Walton, who had been instrumental in the formation of the Annuity Fund, and, of course, Dr Crucefix. A toast was drunk in solemn silence. He continued with a speech on the principles of Freemasonry and how it was open to all from different persuasions. Finally he thanked the Ransfords, father and daughter, for their entertainment during the proceedings, and John Whitmore, the Secretary of the Building Committee, for planning and organising the day's events.

Whitmore responded:

> The part our most esteemed Chairman has played in this day's ceremony, I feel that no language of mine can sufficiently eulogize; I take leave, however, to make use of his own words. On a recent occasion, the Grand Master, having agreed to patronize the Charity, Bro Dobie told his Lordship that it was the brightest feather in the cap to be President of this Institution, and I now tell the esteemed Brother that it is the brightest feather in his cap to preside here today.

The celebrations then came to an end and all returned to their homes. That September, Bro Lee Stevens, who had stood by Dr Crucefix through thick and thin when the wrath of Grand Lodge had descended upon them both, penned an address which was subsequently published in the *FQM&R*. It illustrated the extent of the reconciliation between the

ABOVE **James Goodchild and his wife.** *Library and Museum of Freemasonry*

different factions, especially with Alexander Dobie.

> Dobie! Forgive, what in mistaken word
> And bygone days, I uttered: thinking then,
> Less of all else than of that best man,
> Who now, like thee, is better understood.
> His was my fealty; for, unselfishly,
> When sunshine friends — some whom my willing hand
> Had helped to raise, higher than I could stand —
> Shunned or maligned, He saved, He succoured me!
> To him, to Crucefix, I owed — still owe —
> Unbounded Gratitude! And fancied wrong
> To him, feelings awoke too deep, too strong
> To be controllable. Now that I know
> How misdirected, how unjust to thee,
> They were, Dobie! I pray thee, thus to pardon me!
> J. Lee Stevens
> Past Grand Steward

ABOVE **The Main Entrance to the Asylum.** *Harriet Sandvall*

The annuitants, in order of seniority, were invited to become residents, and the first eight were admitted into the Asylum towards the end of September 1850. It had been a surprisingly good year for the Earl of Zetland. His racehorse *Voltigeur* had won both the St Leger and the Derby. He composed a letter to be read by the Grand Secretary before the next meeting of Grand Lodge:

Aske, August 24th 1850.
By the arrangements made for the amalgamation of the Asylum with the Annuity Fund, it is stipulated that beyond the sum required for completing the building, a further amount is to be raised and funded as the source from which the necessary repairs of the building may from time to time be effected.

As the greater portion of the building is already completed, but some time may elapse before there will be sufficient money to erect the remaining wing, and then only would the subscriptions commence for a

repairing fund, it has occurred to me that repairs may be necessary before there would be any fund applicable to that object.

I would consequently suggest that Grand Lodge should make a grant of £500 (to be paid out of the Fund of General Purposes) towards formation of the Repairing Fund.
Zetland

This duly accomplished, RW Bro R. Galston reminded those present that every effort should now be made to raise the final sum needed to complete the building.

The MW Grand Master was to chair the first Festival under the new banner of the Royal Masonic Benevolent Institution (RMBI), but urgent business prevented him from attending, so Bro Cabbell, stepped in on the night. The Festival, held on Wednesday 12th February 1851, was very similar to those held previously; the speeches were polite or, as would be said these days, politically correct. Cabbell could not refrain from reflecting that the Institution owed its origin to the late Duke of Sussex, who had first suggested it eight or nine years ago. He continued:

Whatever differences of opinion there may have been, and however the Brethren may have taken up warmly different views, I am sure every Brother will give the illustrious Prince credit for an anxious desire of spreading the blessing of Charity over the length and breadth of the land. I must claim for him the honour of being the founder of the Institution. Although there have been differences of opinion, I know it was only rivalship in doing good — and that all will give each other credit for having the best intention, and will therefore unite in carrying out the objects of the Institution.

It is not recorded, and one can only imagine, what the supporters of the late Doctor thought; he was quietly forgotten. But it cannot be denied that the Annuities Fund had been the idea of the Duke of Sussex, and that its inclusion, along with the Asylum Fund, created the new charity, the Royal Masonic Benevolent Institution. The Festival raised the sum of £891 17s.

The era of confrontation appeared for the time being over, and ironically the death was announced of Bro George Radley, the owner of the hotel in Bridge Street, Blackfriars, where many of the early meetings had been held. He died on 16th June 1851.

The RMBI's first AGM, on 16th May 1851, was overseen

by the Grand Master. The accounts for the Royal Masonic Benevolent Fund for Aged Freemasons and their Widows and the Royal Masonic Annuity Fund were read and approved individually. That year, the 50 annuitants had received a total of £973, whilst the funds for the Asylum reached a total of £685 19s 10d, further increased by £500 bequeathed by the late Bro Colville Brown. It was agreed to appoint a warden responsible for order within the Asylum, whilst a gate-keeper would be appointed from one of the residents. A general maintenance man was hired for 5s a week, to pump water for domestic use, mow the lawns, and clean and maintain the walls. A local doctor, W Bro Thomas L. Henley, offered his services free as an honorary surgeon.

The method for electing annuitants and residents was complicated, so a committee was formed to clarify the problem. Its conclusion was that the total number of votes cast for unsuccessful candidates for the last two preceding elections should be carried forward as credit and be included with the votes in the next election. Any candidate over the age of 80 who still failed to achieve the required number of votes at three elections would be automatically added to the list of annuitants.

However, the completion of the Home was slowing down due to insufficient funds, and questions began to be asked. One such question appeared in the *FQM&R* in September 1851:

Why is the Asylum for Aged and Decayed Freemasons at Croydon allowed to remain in its present state? is a question which is frequently asked, not only amongst Masons, but in the general society of 'the popular world'. BECAUSE ABOUT £1200 ARE REQUIRED TO COMPLETE THE BUILDING, AND THERE HAS NOT YET BEEN FOUND SPIRIT ENOUGH IN THE ORDER, EVEN TO ATTEMPT TO RAISE THIS SUM!

The writer suggested a target of six months to raise the money and continued:

No Mason, who understands the terms of his O.B., could hesitate 'to put his shoulder to the wheel', if he would only set himself to see what HE could individually effect, towards completion of an edifice which affords a home and a shelter to many poor and decayed Brothers, whose lot would else be the Union Workhouse ... But what will the Grand Lodge of England say to the silence? some over-scrupulous Brother may be dispose to ask. We answer, THE GRAND LODGE OF ENGLAND IS

NEVER DEAF TO THE CALLS OF CHARITY AND BENEVOLENCE!

We believe, — in fact we know, — that Grand Lodge would be only too glad to congratulate the Craft upon the funds having been provided, which should make THE OLD MAN'S ASYLUM as noble and as enduring an institution as those of the Girls' and Boys' Schools.

This had the desired effect in some quarters, and one group met at the Windmill Hotel, Croydon, to present the proceeds of a benefit they had held earlier at the Grecian Saloon in City Road. They were apologetic that the sum was not greater, for it had been raining on the day, but there was still sufficient to give each resident 28s.

By May 1852 seven male annuitants and two widows were now in residence. One male resident had recently died, and another, who was severely disabled, left to stay with a friend who would care for him.

The most effective fund-raising events had always been the Annual Festivals, but overall donations were declining and they still had to support the 55 annuitants as well as the residents. The idea of holding a second ball was put to the Earl of Zetland but was rejected on the grounds that the first half of the year's calendar was full and if held in the second half it would probably be unprofitable. The conclusion was that the most convenient time for the ball was the second Wednesday in February in 1854, and Zetland agreed to preside along with the Right Hon Bro Lord Methuen, the President of the Board of Stewards, who would be responsible for the arrangements. The Festival was attended by 190 people and, as promised, the Grand Master did attend, accompanied by his deputy the Earl of Yarborough and Grand Officers as well as other distinguished Brethren. The customary cloth was removed to mark the commencement of festivities, and after the usual formal toasts to the Royal and Masonic dignitaries there was a silent toast to the memory of the late Duke of Sussex. The final toast, with much acclaim, was to the ladies in the gallery. The choral entertainment was performed by Mrs Lockey (late Miss Williams), the two Miss Wells, Mrs Temple and Bros Genge, Lawler, Shoubridge and Holmes; Bro Smythson accompanied them on the pianoforte. The evening raised £1,602 14s, yet even with this success, financial difficulties were not eased.

The generous legacy from the late Bro Colville Brown became the catalyst to stimulate the completion of the Asylum at Croydon. That, combined with the monies already in the fund, was sufficient to complete the project. Grand

LEFT **Dr George Oliver.** *Province of Lincoln*

RIGHT **John Lambton, Earl of Derby, in an engraving by H. Robinson.** *Author's Collection*

Lodge donated a further £350 towards expenses, and within a few months the building was complete, the Building Committee submitting its concluding report to Grand Lodge on 15th February 1855. There being no further purpose for this committee, it was finally dissolved.

Little was said at the time about the debt still outstanding, which would continue to be a concern for some time. The Male Fund had increased to £1,833 11s 8d and the Widows' Fund to £736 11s 7d, but the Committee and Freemasons in general were disappointed that they could only appoint two more annuitants. Many were worried about those desperately seeking relief and not being heard, and the spectre of the workhouse loomed greater than ever. The full effect of the Union Workhouse was now familiar to all. The infrastructure created by Sir Edwin Chadwick had been streamlined and perfected. Families were split and forbidden to communicate. Married couples over the age of 60 could request sharing a bedroom, although the various Workhouse Boards considered this unnecessary as, in their opinion, at that age most would prefer to live separately. Individuals entering the workhouse were split into specific categories such as age, sex, infirm or able-bodied; whatever their age, all were expected to work unless designated infirmed and were punished if they failed to comply.

Samuel Aldrich had been for some time a very active member of the RMBI and took a singular interest in the welfare of aged Freemasons, for he was not only a senior Freemason, Past Master of Lodge No 196, but was also the Master of the New End Workhouse in Hampstead. He knew precisely what conditions within Union Workhouses were like. His letter is recorded in the September edition of the *FQM&R*:

20th August 1855
Dear Sir and Brother,
I am anxious to invite the serious attention of the

members of the Craft to the painful results of the last elections of Male and Female Annuitants; I allude to the rejection of Thirty-three Brethren out of Thirty-five Candidates, and nine Widows out of thirteen; and to urge upon them the necessity of immediate and active co-operation in rendering the means of the Charity adequate to its wants.

I know many Brethren who would gladly exert themselves to promote the real object of the Institution — the relief of existing cases of distress — but their ardour is dampened by the 53rd Male Annuity Bye-Law — by the reflection that no such object could be gained — that nearly the whole of the results of their exertions, instead of being available for the pressing exigencies of the present, would be engulfed by the 'Permanent Fund'. It is much regretted that there should be any obstacle to active co-operation in support of the excellent Institution, whilst so many Brethren are crying for help. The Widows' Annuity Fund is limited to £4,000 (and that is a large sum), which is a practical recognition, by the Grand Lodge itself, and of the principle of the limitations, which appears to be as applicable to the one Charity as to the other. It is the general opinion of those conversant with such subjects that the Fund should not be allowed to accumulate beyond £10,000; and of many, that £8,000 would be amply sufficient for the purposes for which it is intended. I think, therefore, that it should be limited to one of these amounts, or increased only by bequest, so that all donations and subscriptions may be afterwards applied to meet the claims as they arise.

I have no doubt that the rejection of so many Candidates has deeply excited the sympathies of the Craft, and trust that it will lead to earnest endeavours on their part to prevent the recurrence of such painful results. Knowing by personal experience what may be done by individual exertions, I would strongly urge the more energetic amongst the Fraternity to do their utmost to stimulate their less active Brethren to subscribe to these Charities and to solicit donations and subscriptions from others. I am convinced that if the subject were to be properly agitated, and the principles of limitations adopted, such a sum would be annually raised as would render the Fund adequate to the relief of the necessities of all proper applicants, and thus entirely sweep away the systems of elections, which I cannot but regard as antagonistic to the principles of our Order. In aid of which and a humble example to Brethren generally, I pledge myself to continue to collect not less than Ten Pounds per annum, in favour of one, or both, of the Funds; and if the same course were adopted in 429 Lodges at only Five Pounds each, the large sum of £2,145 would be added, being a total of Three Thousand Five Hundred and Forty-five Pounds per annum.

I am, dear Sir and Brother, faithfully and fraternally yours,

Samuel Aldrich, Hampstead.

ABOVE **Thomas Dundas (1795-1873), 2nd Earl of Zetland, by Louis William Desanges.** *Library and Museum of Freemasonry*

This, and letters like it, added to the consternation of the Craft. The delay in selecting annuitants had to be resolved by one means or another and ideas were not short in coming. One such suggestion was published in the December edition of the *FQM&R*:

Sir and Brother,

The number of rejected candidates at the recent election of annuitants — thirty-three distressed Brethren, and nine widows — has created a general desire among the Craft to see some plan adopted by which this discreditable state of things be corrected, and every fit and proper object obtain relief as soon as the case can be examined. Bro Aldrich's letter of August 20 affords some suggestion, which, if carried out, would doubtless attain the end desire. But I am disposed to think that there already is a fund, and which continues to increase unnecessarily, that ought to be drawn upon instanter. The General Benevolent Fund, which we are taxed to provide, and hence one in which every Mason has an interest, has lately been increasing at about £1,000 per annum: it now amounts to, I believe, over £16,000. I ask, why should we continue to lay by this fund, for those who come after us? Why leave our own generation to pine for the want of relief? Here are means by which every case of distress can be aided, the fund is created for that purpose only, and no one, I think, would venture to say that the relief of these forty-two applicants is not a righteous and a holy purpose. I heard a Brother in the Lodge, No 206, only a few evenings since, when speaking of the Institution, say that the Committee being of opinion that a festival would be productive of benefit, had applied to the Grand Master to sanction it by his presence, but his lordship refused to comply with the request. Now, we all know that this Institution originated with the late Bro Crucefix, and hence has never enjoyed the favour of the Grand Master and his officials, but as it has now become an Institution recognised and ruled over by Grand Lodge to use the mildest term, it evinces singular bad taste to allow jaundiced views to interfere with the wishes of the Committee of one of our charities. I suggest then, to relieve the Committee from the difficulties of its position, that the Grand Lodge resolve:

That it is expedient that the Benevolent Fund be increased.

That so much of the fund as now exceeds £16,000 be voted in aid of the Royal Masonic Benevolent Institution, one-third to the males, two-thirds to the widows. That the surplus proceeds of the Benevolent Fund, at the next Quarterly Communication, after the accounts are made up, be annually voted in aid of such Masonic charitable institutions as have the most pressing claim on their fund.

Thus we should be doing justice to our own generation, and still leave a handsome fund for our descendants. Hoping the bread cast on the waters may be picked up ere many days. Thus we should be doing justice to our own generation, and still leave a handsome fund for our descendants. Hoping the bread cast on the waters may be picked up ere many days.

I am, fraternally yours,
H. W.
November 23

Aldrich raised his concerns in another letter, sent on 26th March 1856, and suggested that a simple solution could be found by each Lodge annually suspending one banquet and that the sum accrued should be presented to the RMBI. He again wrote to the editor of the *FQM&R*:

Dear Sir and Brother,
The fact that the funds of our Benevolent Institution for Aged Freemasons and their Widows, available for present purposes, at the disposal of the Committee, are wholly inadequate, is being felt by many members of the Craft, and there are some, I know, who are devising means to augment them, in the hope that all proper applicants for the annuity may be at once admitted. In order that their good intentions may not be frustrated

by the way in which Lodges vote assistance, I would remind them that all sums given as donations are invested in Government securities, are carried to the Permanent Fund of the Institution, so that the only present benefit derived therefrom is the amount of interest they produce in the three per cents. By the recently amended Bye-Laws, all yearly subscriptions are permanently applied to grant annuities; therefore I would strongly urge Provincial Grand Lodges, Private Lodges and individuals in England and Wales to give but one guinea annually to each; a fund would be raised that would be more than sufficient to provide for every claim. I will, with your permission, enter more fully into this subject in your next number.
Samuel Aldrich
Hampstead,
20 February 1857

In 1857, the Treasurer revealed that donations over the past three years had fallen dramatically, from £717 9s to £405 2s per annum, whilst the Widows' Fund had fallen from £213 10s to £152 4s. The number of applicants was increasing and, in spite of thirteen potential annuitants on the waiting list dying, the Committee still could only recommend an additional four men and four women. Amidst the gloom, Grand Chapter agreed to contribute £50 per annum towards the outstanding debts from the construction of the Asylum, and the Committee of Management was now in a position to announce that at least the Home was free from debt and in a good state of repair.

The Grand Master informed Grand Lodge in June 1856 that, thanks to essential building works, the funds for both Boys' and Girls' Schools had been exhausted, whilst the RMBI's capital was so low it would not be possible to have an election for annuitants that year. He hoped, under these circumstances, that the members would approve to both charities the sums of £1,000 each and a further £500 towards the Widows' Fund. This was seconded by Alexander Dobie and agreed by all those present. It began to look like the predictions of the Duke of Sussex were correct and that the Masonic Order could not sustain three charities.

Wednesday 17th June 1857 was the date set for the Triennial Festival, 150 people having registered to dine that evening at Freemasons' Hall. The Earl of Durham, SGW, should have presided, but neither he nor any of the leading Brethren in the Fraternity attended, which led to the comment in the *FQM&R*:

It is not for us to judge or attempt to account for their absence; we simply and regretfully record the circumstances.

The JGW, H. Fenwick, the MP for Sunderland, stood in and chaired the event. The candlelit gallery was filled with ladies in their beautiful ball gowns, who greeted the membership with applause as they entered for dinner. The cloth was removed and a grace was sung. The food, arranged by Messrs Elkington & Co, had provided a sumptuous meal accompanied by excellent wines. Dinner complete, the meeting then came under the direction of Bro Banks Junior, the toastmaster. Having taken the Loyal Toast and the various other formal tributes, various letters of apology were read. The first was from the Grand Master, apologising for his absence due to ill health, followed by the Earl of Durham, who had urgent business overseas. He did, however, contribute the sum of £20 towards the charitable funds. The Chairman rose to report on the financial position and the concerns in declining contributions:

Our beautiful building near Croydon is adapted for the habitation of thirty-four necessitous Masons, who can live there in homely comfort. The Home filled, I know, is what you would all like to witness; but at the present moment, partly from want of funds and partly from other causes, that beautiful building, with all its comforts, conveniences and appliances, has within its wall only fourteen or fifteen residents.

The final toast was to the ladies in the gallery, which was accompanied by loud cheers. The formal part of the evening thus concluded, the gentlemen retired to join their ladies in the gallery for the usual after-dinner entertainment. The evening raised £1,558 6s 6d, with an additional £30 donation from the Grand Stewards. They made a specific request that this additional sum should be used to purchase coal for the residents of the Asylum now that winter was approaching.

The Secretary, William Farnfield, could not hide his delight when he delivered his report to the AGM held in May 1858. The success of the Festival and the additional contributions from both Grand Lodge and Grand Chapter made it possible to increase the number of annuitants by two men and seven women. In addition, the Grand Master had reconsidered the frequency of the Festivals and had consented to hold a biennial event on 26th January 1859. A vote of thanks was also given to Dr Henley for his continued medical care to the residents.

There never was a more distinguished list of Stewards than those who organised the January festivities. It included the Provincial Grand Masters of Surrey and Norfolk — Alexander Dobie and Benjamin Bond Cabbell respectively. The Chairman for the event would be Bro Wyndham Portal, the Junior Grand Warden.

When Wyndham Portal presented the Loyal Toast he made specific reference to the fact that currently no members of the inner circle of the Royal Family were members of the Craft, but there were rumours circulating that this was about to change. He said no more, leaving the audience wondering who this could be. Portal toasted the RMBI and emotionally described a recent visit he had had to the Home:

Could I have induced you to go with me and see all that I saw, your heart would be melted at the sight of the old men, and old women thanking me — and, through me, you — for your kindness to them, and expressing their trust that your favours would be continued to them for the time to come.

He made a passionate comment on the vacant rooms, the paths that had not been gravelled and the library with no books. This had the desired effect, for when William Farnfield rose he announced that so far pledges amounting to £1,875 had been received and that Bro Kellock promised that his Lodge, St John's No 196, would make it up to £2,000. A ripple of excitement and enthusiasm spread throughout the room, but a sombre Bro Barrett exclaimed that no matter how generous the members had been, £2,000 was still not sufficient. What was required was not a biennial Festival but an annual one.

Despondency turned to hope when it was agreed that recently collected funds could now be invested in stock: £800 for the Male Fund and £500 for the Widows' Fund. Twenty-two out of the thirty-five candidates were added to the list of annuitants for consideration in May, and six widows out of the sixteen petitioned were to be admitted as residents. All rejoiced at the changing fortunes of the charity as donations exceeded expectations and there was now genuine hope that the corner had been turned, the Male Fund standing at £11,550 and the Widows' Fund at £3,430. The Asylum was now declared in a perfect state of repair, although it would be necessary to paint the outside wood and iron works and to whitewash and paint some of the interior; but these were deemed minor tasks.

To everybody's delight, the Grand Master sanctioned the idea of an annual ball, with the first to be celebrated on

Wednesday 25th January 1860, and as a consequence he suggested that a greater number of annuitants should be elected at the next ballot. Grand Chapter also announced that they would transfer £200 consolidated stock, with a 3% interest rate, to both funds.

Bros Joseph Smith and William Farnfield, both acting as Secretaries, agreed to support Col Burlton, Chairman of the Board of Stewards, in the organisation of the ball. The Lord Lieutenant for Warwickshire, Lord Leigh, who was also the PGM of that Province, agreed to chair the next event. It was announced during the evening that the Craft had at last gained a Royal member in the person of Prince Frederick of Prussia, who had recently married Victoria, the Princess Royal and the eldest daughter of Queen Victoria. He had been a soldier in the Prussian Army and had participated in a number of the wars of German Unification. Nevertheless he was liberally minded and hated war, and had done much to curb the belligerent ambitions of Otto von Bismarck. There was now an expectation that the Prince of Wales might follow in his brother-in-law's footsteps. Farnfield announced that the Festival had raised £2,096 18s 10d, and Lord de Tabley gave a résumé of the history of the RMBI, commenting on the Duke of Sussex's involvement in its foundation, and that since that day some 149 aged Freemasons had been beneficiaries.

There was now a general satisfaction that the cash flow and income from investments had stabilised the charity. Now the number of male annuitants had increased to 62 and females to 29, and by August 1890 there were only seven vacant apartments at the Home. However, controversy again surfaced that September when it became known that Farnfield had been ordered to take premature retirement on a reduced pension of £60 per annum. The reason given was his age, but the real motive was that the Grand Secretary, William Gray Clarke, had given him an ultimatum to choose between his role as the Assistant Grand Secretary or the Secretary to the RMBI. Gray Clarke considered he was spending too much time with the RMBI to the detriment of his primary job, but such was the pressure from the RMBI that this ultimatum was rapidly dropped and he was allowed to continue with both posts.

CHAPTER 9
STABILITY

The RMBI now appeared to be an integral part of the Masonic movement. The Home had finally been completed and the charity was financially sound thanks to the Festivals. Now Provincial Grand Masters were mobilised to support the movement, and one of the first was the PGM for Kent, William Archer Amherst, the future 3rd Earl Amherst, also known as Viscount Holmesdale. Born in Mayfair, he was the son of the 2nd Earl Amherst. After Eton he served in the Coldstream Guards during the Crimean War and fought at both Balaclava and Inkerman, where he was severely wounded. He was promoted to the rank of Captain during the siege of Sebastopol. With the end of the war he became the MP for West Kent, and subsequently the MP for Mid Kent. He was initiated into the Westminster and Keystone Lodge No 10 in 1856 and joined the Invicta Lodge No 709 in Ashford, Kent, in 1860, the same year he was installed as the PGM for Kent at Gravesend. Amherst was conscious that although the charity was controlled from London, a disproportionate number of beneficiaries lived in the Home Counties. Therefore, through his Provincial Secretary, he began to recruit supporters within his own Province. This would set an example to the rest of the Craft. A letter was sent to the *FQM&R* in December 1860:

Chatham, 14th December 1860
Dear Sir and Brother,
The R.W.Prov.G.M. Lord Holmesdale, having consented to preside at the Festival of the Royal Benevolent Institution for Aged Freemasons and their Widows on the 30th January next, 1861, and being desirous that the province should be represented on that occasion, I have sent my name as a Steward, and by your co-operation in obtaining donations. I find that this excellent Institution has great claims upon the Province of Kent from the fact that since the establishment for males in 1842, seven Brethren from the county have been elected Annuitants, five of whom were living as of the 1st of this present month, receiving in the aggregate £60 per annum. Total,

£176. I therefore think that the County of Kent is at present receiving a fair share of the bounty of the Craft, and on reference to the last list of subscribers printed you will find that very few Lodges in the Province are governors or subscribers to either branch of the Institution, neither does the Provincial Grand Lodge appear on the list.
Again begging the favour of your cordial co-operation, and a reply at your earliest convenience.
I am, dear Sir, yours, fraternally
Charles Isaac
P.G.Sec to Kent

The Festival proved a tremendous success, raising £2,982 1s. There was additional excitement with the announcement that HRH the Prince of Wales was almost certainly going to join the Craft. Farnfield was euphoric when he announced the outstanding success at the AGM and that, as a consequence, the number of annuitants could now be increased to 78 men and 45 women. Aldrich had the rules altered to allow those annuitants residing in the Home to be supplied with 2cwt of coal and 11lb of candles weekly in addition to his or her annuity.

There was one particular unsung hero worthy of mention, who had given his time and skills freely and frequently — Dr Thomas Henley. Month after month he attended to the annuitants' medical needs, supplying medicines and wines for tonics at his own expense. The Committee believed he should be rewarded with a testimonial, so on 22nd July at Freemasons' Hall he was presented with a silver salver.

The world was shocked to hear, on 14th December 1861, of the death of Prince Albert, the Queen's consort. His death has long been thought to have been caused by a virulent episode of typhoid fever, but recently it has been suggested that he may have been a victim of Crohn's Disease, a long-term condition relating to inflammation of the gut lining. The loss of Albert reduced Victoria to a state of mourning that would last the rest of her life, but at this particular

ABOVE **HRH Albert Edward, Prince of Wales, by Louis William Desanges.** *Library and Museum of Freemasonry*

ABOVE RIGHT **William Archer (1836-1910), 3rd Earl Amherst, by William Carter.** *Library and Museum of Freemasonry*

RIGHT **Crown Prince Frederick William of Prussia 1870.** *Author's Collection*

moment the loss of someone so integral to Great Britain and her Empire was a blow to the whole country. Nobody felt like celebrating and the expectations of Lord Holmesdale were dashed. The takings that year fell to £1,986 4s, and funds would not begin to recover until the 1863 festival overseen by RW John Havers, which raised £2,203.

The Boys' and Girls' were treated to a holiday in Brighton on Friday 4th August, and as the railway to Brighton ran beside the Asylum, it was decided a fraternal gesture should be shown to the children. Early on the morning of the allotted day a large flag, borrowed from Bro Bean, the landlord of the local Greyhound Hotel, was flown from the upper windows of the Warden's House. The elderly residents lined the track to cheer the youngsters as they passed, the men in full regalia and the ladies with their best Sunday dresses. This was repeated on the return journey to London.

The year 1865 would be the second time that Earl de Grey, Lord Ripon, had chaired a Festival, and he took the opportunity to highlight the dichotomy existing within Masonic society: there was a desperate need to find funds for charities, yet there still lurked an inbuilt fear that there would always be some who would abuse the situation.

Wealth has risen in this country to a pitch the world has never before seen, but at the same time in no past history has there been greater or more painful distress than there is now in this country. There never was a time when, in a condition of civilisation, it was more necessary that charity should be dealt with wisely, considerately, and judiciously, for without discrimination charity may be made the object of mischief rather than good.

The death of Sophia Jane, wife of the Grand Master, came in the late spring of 1865. The daughter of Sir Hedworth Williamson, she had married the Earl of Zetland on 6th September 1823, but they had no offspring. She departed this life on the evening of Sunday 21st May at their London home at 19 Arlington Street. She was 61 years old.

The financial situation slowly recovered, so that by the time of the Festival held on 30th January 1867, Lord de Tabley, PGM Cheshire, was able to say that every year, with the exception of 1862, the charity had raised more money than the preceding year. The day before the Festival he had visited the Home and had met the 28 residents. He commented that at this moment there were only six apartments vacant and said that he wished that every Brother would go there and see the quiet and comfort their poorer Brethren enjoyed in their old age, who had been shipwrecked in their passage through life.

He continued with a description of the characters he had met and those who had impressed him, such as a blind man who had once been a well-known artist, as well as an elderly widow of a Brother whom he had known and had fallen on hard times. That year they raised £2,692, enough to support 88 male and 56 female annuitants.

The artist he mentioned was almost certainly John Harris, a well-known painter of miniatures and an architectural draughtsman. Harris was born in 1791 and initiated into Freemasonry in 1818. He had exhibited at the Royal

ABOVE **Earl de Grey and Ripon 1863.** *Author's Collection*

Academy, where he came to the notice of the Duke of Sussex, who much admired his paintings. It is thought that the Duke may have commissioned him to produce a set of Tracing Boards for the Three Degrees to be used by Lodges after the creation of Grand Lodge in 1820. In 1845, he submitted his work in a competition and they were officially adopted by the Lodge of Emulation. Over the next few years he slowly lost his sight and was eventually admitted to the Home at Croydon as a pensioner, along with his wife May in 1857. He remained there until his death in 1873.

James Norris was as old as most of the residents, but he was still appointed as the Home's Warden in 1868. Born in 1790, he had been initiated into Sincerity Lodge No 174 in 1812 and, apart from a short break, remained a member until he became an annuitant. He continued as Warden until his death in 1884, having been a Freemason for 72 years.

Rev George Oliver, aged 85 years, died on 3rd March 1867. He had been a staunch supporter of Dr Robert Crucefix

ABOVE **Earl of Zetland.** *Library and Museum of Freemasonry*

ABOVE RIGHT **The Havers address to the RMBI.** *Library and Museum of Freemasonry*

AN ADDRESS

DELIVERED AT

THE FESTIVAL

OF THE

Royal Benevolent Institution,

FOR

AGED FREEMASONS AND THEIR WIDOWS,

JANUARY 28th, 1863,

BY

THE R. W. BRO. JOHN HAVERS,

JUNIOR GRAND WARDEN.

REPRINTED FROM THE "FREEMASON'S MAGAZINE,"
And to be obtained (Price Sixpence) from
BRO. RICHD. SPENCER, MASONIC DEPOT, 26, GREAT QUEEN STREET,
AND (BY PERMISSION) OF
BRO. W. FARNFIELD, SECRETARY TO THE INSTITUTION,
FREEMASONS' HALL.

The Proceeds of Sale will be devoted to The "WIDOW'S FUND."

throughout the early struggles and as a consequence he too endured persecution. One of his last acts was to pay his subscription to the Provincial Benevolent Fund. His funeral was held at St Swithin's Church, Lincoln, where he was laid to rest in the churchyard by his wife, Mary Ann.

In 1868, the long-expected news came that HRH Albert Edward, Prince of Wales, had been initiated into Freemasonry, not in England as expected but in Stockholm and by the King of Sweden. The Prince's initiation encouraged some of his brothers, in particular Arthur, Duke of Connaught, and Leopold, Duke of Albany, to become Freemasons.

The Earl of Zetland resigned as Grand Master in 1870 and on his retirement was made a Knight of the Garter. He died the following year at Aske Hall and was succeeded by George Robinson, Earl de Grey and 1st Marquess of Ripon.

William Farnfield gave up his post as the Secretary of the charity in 1872. He had been the Assistant Grand Secretary from 1854 until his retirement from that post in 1866, receiving a pension of £250. He had also been the Secretary of the Male Annuity Fund since its inception in 1842, and previously to that the Secretary of the Asylum Fund in the early 1830s. Farnfield had been initiated into the Lodge of Union No 256 in 1825 and remained a subscribing member until his death on 27th February 1876, aged 79. He was laid to rest in Tooting Cemetery. In his early life he helped form the Lodge of Emulation, where he was described as taking a warm and an active interest in the affairs of the Lodge. Farnfield was succeeded by James Terry, who would over the next few years become a leading light in the charity.

When the Prince of Wales was appointed as the Past Grand Master in the United Grand Lodge of England, the members of the charity thought it opportune to invite him to chair their main fund-raising event. The date set for their 31st Festival was Monday 23rd February 1873. Some 400 people paid 23s each to attend the event at the Freemasons' Tavern. It was arguably the most prestigious Masonic event since the formation of UGLE and would be the first time since his life-threatening illness, typhoid, two years previously that the Prince of Wales had attended anything in public. The band of the Coldstream Guards played as he entered for dinner, accompanied by the Grand Master, Lord Ripon, and a retinue of Provincial Grand Masters. The first toast, after the meal, was to the health of the Queen and the increased happiness of the Craft, which was followed by the National Anthem. Lord Ripon then proposed the toast to the Prince of Wales, who responded by saying that while he had been admitted to the mysteries of Freemasonry through a foreign lodge, at heart he was really an English Freemason and he had been struck by the kindness of the Brethren since his return to England. He concluded with the toast to the Grand Master. Lord Ripon replied:

> I can assure you sir that I esteem it a great honour to be present on this occasion, on which you have been pleased to give your personal support and sanction to one of our Great Masonic Charities.

The Prince of Wales' speech was a milestone in the history of the charity, for it traced the journey from the charity's foundation in the early 1830s, through the political and financial difficulties of the intervening years, until accepted and supported by the leaders of the Empire as well as the rulers of the Craft:

> Most Worshipful Grand Master and Brethren, the toast which I have now the honour of proposing to you is, I may say, the so-called toast of the evening. I have to beg you to drink 'Success to the Royal Masonic Benevolent Institution for Aged Freemasons and their Widows.' [Applause] I was certain that this toast would be most cordially responded to, and from the assemblage that I see before me, in particular, are deeply interested in this great charitable and excellent Institution. It shows me, Brethren, that you agree in those great objects, and those great events of our Craft of which our Worshipful Grand Master reminded you, those of charity; and I feel sure,

> Brethren, that although many have preceded me this evening, and many have explained to you far better than I shall be able to do, the objects and principles of this charity, you will be as liberal as it is in your power to be. As you are doubtless aware, Brethren, my late grand-uncle, the Duke of Sussex, who was formerly your Grand Master, and who I have always understood took the deepest interest in all that concerned our Craft, was one of the first to suggest the Institution for Aged Male Freemasons, and the suggestion taken up by Grand Lodge, under his Presidency, and the sum of £4,000 a year was voted. Since that time — seven years afterwards our most worthy and excellent, and may I say revered late Grand Master, the Earl of Zetland, who nobody regrets more than I do not to see here this evening supporting us in this occasion, extended this Institution to the Widows of Freemasons. Although those funds were separate, we may consider them as so far united that not only do our male aged Brethren receive support, but their widows also. The few statistics that I have to recall to your attention, I will now just mention. In 22 years as many as 147 widows were relieved, at the cost of over £19,000 by annuities of £25 each. As many as 352 indigent Freemasons were assisted at the cost of over £40,000 by annuities of £26. It is proposed that after the next month male annuitants should receive £36 and female annuitants £28 a year, therefore an increase of £10 and £3. I feel sure that we should all do our utmost to give our cordial co-operation to effect this. I believe I am not incorrect in stating that we have entire trust in those who have the management of the Institution, and as it is under the auspices and Presidentship of our Worshipful Grand Master, I feel sure that he will be with us and give his utmost attention to the interests of the Institution. It is well and economically managed. From what I understand about certain annual income, it is unfortunately small. The male annuitants receive only £1,300 a year, while the expenses are over £4,000 a year. The female annuitants receive under £800 a year, and the expenditure is £1,200 a year. For some years past the annual expenses have been £4,000 or £5,000 per annum. This sum, this deficit I may say, has to be made up by donations and subscriptions. Let me therefore impress upon you once more most heartily to do your utmost to render this deficit as small as you possibly can, I feel sure that you will do so, and I feel sure that no long speech of mine will be necessary to make you do it. It is said that brevity is the soul of wit, and on this occasion I beg to

ABOVE **John Havers.** *Library and Museum of Freemasonry*

ABOVE RIGHT **Installation of HRH Albert Edward, Prince of Wales, as Grand Master.** *Author's Collection*

RIGHT **James Terry.** *Library and Museum of Freemasonry*

adopt the proverb. I once more thank you, Brethren, for the cordial manner you have supported me, and if by taking the Chair this evening I may have in any small way augmented the funds of the Institution, I shall return home feeling that I have done pleasant duty. [Great Applause] I call upon you now to drink in bumper, 'Success to the RMBI for Aged Freemasons and the Widows of Freemasons'.

The last toast was, as usual, to the ladies. The party then adjourned to the Temple to attend a grand concert under the directorship of Bro Seymour Smith.

A crisis was averted the following year caused by the resignation of the Grand Master because of his conversion to Roman Catholicism. The Prince of Wales was invited by Lord Carnarvon, the DGM; John Havers, the JGW; and

Aenias J. McIntyre, the GR, to undertake the duties of Grand Master, which he accepted, and on 28th April 1875 he was installed at the Royal Albert Hall. This was, at the time, the greatest assembly of Freemasons ever held in Great Britain.

The 1875 Festival, presided over by the Earl of Shrewsbury and Talbot, the PGM of Staffordshire, followed the same pattern as former dinners. The menu has survived, and would have been typical of the day. It consisted of the following:

Soups
Clear Mock Turtle. Game Jardinière
Fish
Turbots in Lobster Sauce. Crimped Cod in Oyster Sauce Fried Smelt. Stewed Eels
Entrees
Bouchées à la Pompadour. Fricandeaux with Peas Salamis of Plovers with Olives
Removes
Roast Capons. Mushroom Sauce. Hams. Tongues Haunches and Saddles of Mutton. Boiled Fowls with Cauliflower
Second Course
Pheasants. Wild Fowl. Chips. Sea kale
Sweets
Fruit Jellies. Russian Charlottes. Pine Apple Trifles Compotes of Oranges. Goronflots. Tartlets. Iced Pudding Desserts

ABOVE **John Albert Farnfield.** *Library and Museum of Freemasonry*

It was customary for the Secretary, James Terry, to attend the two annual events held at the Home. One was held in the summer, whilst the other was in the New Year. These were always enjoyed by both residents and friends, and for the summer event of 1881 Bro Seymour Smith had prepared a little musical-comedy entitled *Seaside Jottings: The Adventures of Theophilus White in search of Quiet*. William Seymour Smith, a Professor of Music at the Royal College of Music, taught singing and was himself a composer of cantatas. An accomplished organist, he was much in demand at Masonic functions. That year's event took place in the Great Hall and Terry took this as an opportunity to announce that this would be the last concert held in this venue — the RMBI now had sufficient funds to expand and redevelop the site. A vote of thanks was given by the Warden, James Norris, followed by a rendition of *The Vacant Chair*, a typical Victorian romantic melodramatic song by the American songwriter Henry Washburn. It was sung on this occasion by a resident, Kezia Bonorandi, and her two friends:

We shall meet but we shall miss him,
There will be one vacant chair;
We shall linger to caress him,
While we breathe our evening prayer.
When a year ago we gathered,
Joy was in his mild blue eye;
But a golden chord is severed,
And our hopes in ruin lie.

Chorus
We shall meet but we shall miss him,
There will be one vacant chair;
We shall linger to caress him,
While we breathe our evening prayer.

At our fireside, sad and lonely
Often will the bosom swell,
At remembrance of the story

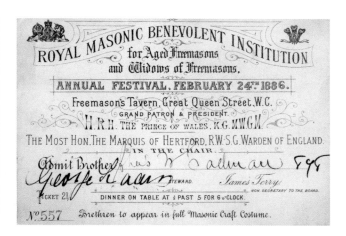

How our noble Willie fell;
How he strove to bear our banner
Through the thickest of the fight,
And uphold our country's honour
With the strength of manhood's might.

True, they tell us wreaths of glory
Evermore will deck his brow;
But this soothes the anguish only
Sweeping o'er our heartstrings now.
Sleep today, Oh early fallen!
In thy green and narrow bed;
Dirges from the pine and cypress
Mingle with the tears we shed.

The alterations to the building began shortly afterwards and were completed by Christmas. The main hall was made larger with the addition of an adjoining retiring room and outside toilets, and a staircase was built to give access to the additional rooms on the ground floor. *The Freemasons' Chronicle* commented:

The appearance, on entering the main door, will at once strike the visitor, who has been accustomed to the form in which the Institution had previously existed, and must impress him with the wisdom which has been displayed in the enlargement.

Most of the work was staggered, so as not to upset the residents, and was carried out by Mr Gaskin, who also

replaced the flag pole blown over in a storm in November of that year.

The Committee assembled in the newly refurbished hall on the morning of 4th January 1882 and chatted informally to the old folk; all agreed that it was a large improvement. The total cost was £937 11s 7d, and all thought it money well spent. A special banquet was arranged for 2pm in the Great Hall held under the chairmanship of Dr Strong, the honorary surgeon, accompanied by James Terry, Raynham Stewart and Thomas Cubitt. The highlight was the unveiling of an inscribed tablet over the entrance to the Great Hall:

This Hall was enlarged
A.D.1881
Under the supervision of the
HOUSE COMMITTEE
W Bro Raynham Stewart P.G.D.
John A Farnfield. V.P.
Charles J Percival. V.P.
Thomas Cubitt F.G.P. V.P.
Samuel Rawson P.Dist G.M.China
Robert Griggs James Terry
Architect Secretary

The John A. Farnfield mentioned was the son of William Farnfield. He would be appointed to the brevet rank of Past Assistant Grand Director of Ceremonies for the extraordinary meeting held at the Royal Albert Hall to celebrate Queen Victoria's Jubilee in 1887.

There were the usual toasts, including one especially to Bro Norris, the Warden, and his daughter (the Matron) for preparing such a magnificent feast. The entertainment consisted of the Criterion Hand Bell Ringers, and the Glee Singers, under the direction of Bro Tipper, followed by a

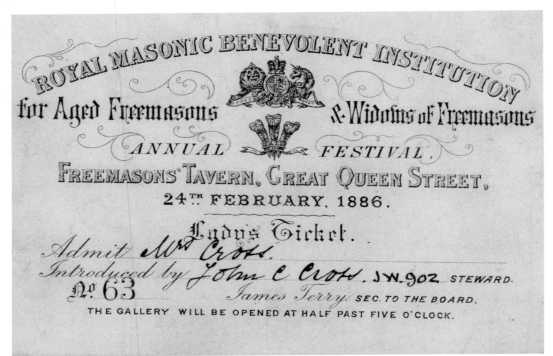

recital given by Miss Constable on the pianoforte. Bro C. J. Percival presented a series of humorous readings in broken Dutch, and the actor Bro Frederick Binckes gave his splendid rendition of Shakespeare's 'Apology' from *Othello*. Finally James Terry announced that he had just received a telegram from the old folk of East Lancashire saying that they were at this very moment drinking a toast to their 'Fellow-Annuitants at the Croydon Institution'.

The design of the Home attracted many over the next few years, including liverymen from the City's Livery Companies as well as representatives from the City of London's architect's office with a view to the design of their own alms-houses.

At these biennial events each resident received a small gift; invariably a pound of tea and, for the ladies a packet of 10 cigarettes, whilst the men would get tobacco and often a bottle of whisky. They would at times also receive objects that would be of daily use like a milk jug or a snuffbox.

Just before the Christmas celebrations of 1882, a magnificent oil painting of James Terry was unveiled in the Great Hall to add to the portrait of Crucefix. Terry was now becoming an important figure in Freemasonry. The eldest son of James and Sarah Terry, he was born in St John's Road, Clerkenwell, on 21st May 1831. He trained as a law stationer and worked in the Inns of Court, and married Amelia Mary Boulter in 1854. His Masonic career began with his initiation

into the United Strength Lodge in February 1860, and within three years he was elected as its Worshipful Master. He was instrumental in founding the Urban Lodge in 1867 and was its Secretary for seven years. He was the Provincial Director of Ceremonies for Hertfordshire and was appointed Provincial Grand Standard Bearer in 1869. His association with the Asylum began when he accepted the appointment as the Collector of the RMBI in June 1864, and when William Farnfield eventually retired, Terry was appointed as its new Secretary.

The Home was now 20 years old. It was designed to house 32 elderly people and was supervised on a daily basis by a Warden who received a small stipend of £20 per year. Wardens were also elderly annuitants, usually of good character. Throughout its existence there were a number of Wardens, all housed in their central apartment within the building. The one important criterion for all was the need to have a partner who would act as Matron. The first Warden in 1851 was Mark Oliver Iron, who moved into the Asylum at the age of 68 years. He had been an upholsterer, originally from Ipswich, but now had fallen upon hard times. He was accompanied by his daughter who acted as Matron. Little is known of his early life, although he appeared at the Old Bailey as a witness in 1828, a victim of theft in a somewhat embarrassing circumstance. In his own words:

I am an upholsterer, and live at Ipswich, in Suffolk. On the 1st of February I was in Newgate-street, going to the Four Swans, in Bishopsgate-street; I had taken more wine than agreed with me — I was not particularly drunk; I was intoxicated, I know — I had been drinking at an Inn in the Haymarket, where I had dined; I do not know what time I came away. I came on to Fleet-market, and got in company with a female, close by the market; she asked me to treat her with a glass of wine; I went into the wine-vaults, and gave her a glass — finding I had no change, I took out my pocketbook; I then had seven 5l. notes, of Mills', of Hadley Bank, safe; I had taken the numbers down on the Tuesday before — they were Nos. 70, 636, 327, 816, 1351, 1443, and 4128; the landlord said he would not trouble me to change, but told me to take care and put my pocketbook into my pocket; I did so, and went on to Newgate-street; a person stopped me in Newgate-street, and pulled me about — my pocketbook and its contents were taken — I missed it before I got out of Newgate-street — this was on a Friday. About half-past nine o'clock next morning, the 1st of February, I saw one of the notes — I lost it on Thursday night, the 31st of January, after twelve o'clock, I mean — I saw it at the coach-office of the Four Swans; I had stated when I got to the inn that I had been robbed, and in the morning I went to Messrs. Hankey's, where they were payable, and stopped the payment of them, just as they began business; at half-past nine o'clock that morning I found the prisoner in custody in the coach-office, with the note No. 327; he said he had taken it off a person for a watch that morning — I did not hear him say where. The Hadley coach puts up at the Four Swans. I have not found any other note.

The miscreant, Hyam Phillips, was convicted for felonious receiving and transported for 14 years.

The Wardens were expected to complete a diary recording daily events. These provide a fascinating record of the lives of the residents, and include their misdemeanours, parties and Festivals. Residents were expected to apply for leave of absence, which was invariably granted. In some instances they would be absent for some weeks, but it was an offence if they were absent without permission and beyond the agreed period. The application for visitors was especially important as they would have to stay in the residents' lodgings. Inevitably the occasional romance occurred, as illustrated on 14th November 1876 when the Committee sat specifically to discuss two residents wishing to marry; this,

after much deliberation, was agreed.

Not everything in the Home went smoothly; punishments and reprimands could be swift and decisive. A retired builder was evicted for expressing his unwanted affections towards another resident who was a 50-year-old retired nurse. On another occasion a resident was walking in the gardens when he noticed a strongbox lying under some shrubs which had been forced open but was still full of papers and also contained a gold wedding ring. He recognised it as belonging to another resident, who confirmed that it was his box and that a sum of £1 4s was missing. He was convinced that he had placed it in one of a set of drawers the previous evening. The Warden noticed that a window had been opened, although the resident had assured her that he had shut it the previous evening. The police were contacted and the next day a detective arrived and made a detailed examination of the rooms and surrounding gardens. He confirmed that, in his opinion, this was not the work of a common criminal as he would have taken everything. The culprit, who almost certainly was a fellow resident or member of staff, was never found.

Most of the residents lived happy and contented lives in their old age, but occasionally this was not so. In 1889, a cleaner wishing to light the fire of a resident, knocked on the door but had no reply. Suspecting that the gentleman was asleep she attempted to open the door but found that difficult. She went to the Matron and between them they forced open the door, only to find the resident hanging by a short rope from a hook on the back of the door. The coroner gave a verdict of temporary insanity. Life in the Home could have its moments of excitement too, such as a herd of cows straying onto the grounds and badly damaging the perimeter fencing. Over the next 30 years, cows became a major nuisance.

Iron recorded, on 3rd May 1858, the extraordinary dedication of Dr Henley who had attended on Bro Povey, who was very sick. He treated him and charged nothing, saying he would be happy to be called at any time, as would his partner Bro Strong, should there be an emergency. These doctors were much loved and respected by the residents, as was shown when a large party assembled in the January of 1877 to present to Dr Strong his testimonial reward, which was a gold watch bearing the following inscription:

Presented by the Residents of the Royal Masonic Benevolent Institution at Croydon for Henry John Strong Esquire M.D. in grateful appreciation of many acts of loving kindness evinced by him, as Honorary

Surgeon for Thirteen Years during which time he faithfully and assiduously ministered to their comfort and alleviated their sufferings in every way.

Dr Henry John Strong, a man of great kindness with a keen sense of duty, was also presented with a microscope cabinet with a suitable inscription, whilst his wife received a golden locket. He loved microscopes and had joined the Croydon Microscopical Society. He even presented papers on bone structure, later published by the Royal Society of Microscopy, and was part of the British Medical Society deputation that called on officials in Whitehall about the implementation of the Public Health and Adulteration of Foods Act in 1872. This Act made it compulsory for every council to appoint a medical officer of health and was fundamental in forming a whole range of legislation relating to food, sanitation and the control of infectious diseases, which ultimately led to a healthier environment. Over the years there were three doctors dedicated to the Home: T. L. Henley (1851-1862); H. J. Strong (1862-1892); and Lt-Col J. A. Wayte MC (1892-1951).

Iron died in 1861 and was succeeded by John Commins, a printer born in Dorset in 1793; his wife Harriett acted as Matron. He had been initiated into All Souls' Lodge in Weymouth in 1817 and was at one time the Junior Grand Deacon for the Province of Dorset. Commins became an annuitant in 1855. He recorded in the diary that in the July of 1861, 12 girls from the Royal Masonic Institute for Girls visited the Home specifically to prepare and serve tea for the pensioners. Commins remained at the Home until his wife died on 24th July 1867 when, unable to find a relative to act as Matron, he was compelled to resign his position and moved to his son's home in Norwich. Dr Strong presented him on leaving with a pair of gold spectacles from the residents as a token of his uprightness.

James Norris succeeded to the post in 1868. Born in Shoreditch on 21st January 1790, he had been a tailor, at one time employing seven individuals. He became a Freemason in the Lodge of Sincerity in 1812, subsequently resigning to join the Yarborough Lodge, only to rejoin his Mother Lodge in 1851 — the Master at the time was a Bro Terry. He was elected an annuitant in 1862 and lived in the Home with his eldest daughter, who acted as Matron. In 1881, they were joined by his other daughter, Mary Hodges Norris, who eventually became the Assistant Matron.

Since the opening of the Home there had been repeated complaints about the lack of books in the library. This was resolved when, in 1870, W. D. Hughes donated a number of important publications, including a large number of contemporary novels. Later, others would add to this, updating the collection until every shelf was full.

Christmastide was often a period of great kindness. In 1870, three dozen bottles of sherry were sent to the residents by Freemasons. This was followed by a monster cask of ale which was recorded as 'beautiful it was'.

Nationally important events were also celebrated. The Board gave each resident 15s 6d to celebrate the birth of the Prince of Wales' son, the Duke of Clarence, in June 1864, and each resident received 10s to honour the Queen's Golden Jubilee in 1887, £5 for the Diamond Jubilee, and 10s 6d for King Edward VII's Coronation in 1902.

Since its opening, an individual had been employed to mow the lawn and generally keep the grounds tidy, but eventually it was necessary to employ a full-time gardener to tend the beautifully laid out gardens with shady trees and colourful flowerbeds. By the end of 1884 the gardens had a magnificent heated greenhouse with sufficient coke to keep it warm throughout the winter months.

In 1884, James Norris died. His daughters were extremely popular with the residents as well as the Board, and so the eldest daughter was appointed to fill her father's position and continued to act as Matron, assisted by her sister. Jane was extremely efficient, and it was recorded that:

On her shoulders rests a considerable amount of responsibility, and when, as has more than once happened, a resident has proved himself unsociable or litigious, her task has been neither an easy nor an enviable one. But the manner in which she has fulfilled her part has given the utmost satisfaction to the Committee, as was shown by the presentation to her early last year of a valuable diamond and ruby ring, in token of the high esteem and respect in which they held her, and of the grateful sense of loving care with which she had tended the residents at Croydon.

Jane eventually died in early 1912 at the Home, aged 95 years.

On Thursday 24th April 1902, the Treasurer, John Albert Farnfield, died whilst staying in Hastings. Farnfield had been the Solicitor to the charity for many years (his practice was at 90 Lower Thames Street). A bachelor, he lived at 363 Brixton Road with his mother and younger siblings. His funeral was conducted by his great friend, the rector of St Matthew's Church, Brixton, and was attended by the House Committee of the RMBI, headed by James Terry. Farnfield had bequeathed £500 towards elderly unsuccessful

candidates. John Farnfield was the son of the first Secretary, William Farnfield, and his death severed the last direct link with the founders of the charity.

ABOVE **The Reception of HRH the Prince of Wales as Past Grand Master, 1st December 1869 by Sigismund Rosenthal.** *Library and Museum of Freemasonry*

CHAPTER 10

THE PROBLEM WITH SUCCESS

In the latter part of the 19th century, life was still hard in the industrial cities of Great Britain, but there were some noticeable advances. Housing was beginning to improve, and most had access to clean drinking water. Municipal boroughs began to open public laundries and baths. Disease and infant mortality were still high but were declining. This was not a sudden revolution but a slow, unstoppable evolution.

The deaths of paupers in workhouses led to an Inquiry in 1864, and soon infirmaries, initially attached to workhouses, were becoming the hospitals in industrial areas. Eva Lückes, at the London Hospital in Whitechapel, developed training schools for nurses, and Dr Barnardo, also from the same hospital, began his crusade for poor and abandoned children. In April 1862, the American philanthropist George Peabody introduced decent and affordable accommodation for the 'artisans and laboring poor of London'. Chadwick's report on the sanitary conditions of the labouring population recommended sanitary engineering as a solution, which gave an opportunity for Bazalgette to improve the sanitation of London. The revolution in transport permitted easier access to fresh food, but more important was the introduction of the Elementary Education Act of 1870, which enabled all children between five and 12 years of age to have access to a basic education.

These simultaneous events provided better living conditions and it was now becoming evident that the population was beginning to live longer; the number of applications for relief from elderly Freemasons and their widows was increasing. A Special General Meeting was convened in May 1890 to formulate a change in the rules. These were as follows:

Male Fund

Every candidate must have been a subscribing member to a Lodge as well as a registered Master Mason for a period of fifteen years. Under the old rules he was required to be a registered Master Mason for fifteen years and a subscribing member of a Lodge for only ten years of that period.

The income disqualifying a brother from becoming a candidate was reduced from £40 to £32 per annum. On the death of a male annuitant, his widow, provided she had been married to him for seven years, became eligible to receive half her late husband's annuity for a period of five years. Under the old rules it was necessary that the widow should have been married to him for five years, and the term for which she was entitled to receive her half-annuity was three years.

Widows' Fund

The minimum age for election was raised from 55 to 60 years.

The husband of a widow applicant must have been a subscribing member of a Lodge as well as a registered Master Mason for at least fifteen years, instead of a registered Master Mason for fifteen years and a subscribing member for only ten years. She must also have been married to him at least seven, instead of five, years; and if a widow of an annuitant, for at least five, instead of three, years previous to the presentation of his position.

Longevity was but one of the problems perceived by the Committee of Management — over the previous two decades there had been a substantial increase in the membership of Freemasonry. The organisation was becoming popular with the upper and middle classes, due partly to the support by the Royal Family but also to the social life.

In 1902, Bro James Stephens became Treasurer of the charity and James Terry decided to retire as Secretary, although he continued to visit the Home until his death on 17th April 1909. He was succeeded by Bro P. Colville Smith, the son of Sir Philip Protheroe Smith of Truro, on a salary of £500 per annum. Colville Smith had been educated at St John's College, Oxford, and was initiated into Apollo Lodge in 1886. He eventually qualified as a barrister-at-law.

In 1907, *The Freemason* reported:

ABOVE **A few of the residents.** *Library and Museum of Freemasonry*

RIGHT **Right Honourable Arthur Oliver Villiers Russell (1869–1935), 2nd Baron Ampthill, GCSI, GCIE painted by Arthur Stockdale Cope.** *Library and Museum of Freemasonry*

Concerning the aims of objects of the Masonic Benevolent Institution it is necessary to say but little, for every member of the Order is frequently afforded facilities for becoming acquainted with them. Suffice it to say that those aged Freemasons and widows who are fortunate enough to be elected as annuitants are protected from want for the remainder of their days. The male annuitant receive £40 per annum, and the widows £32. It must be remembered that the majority of these pensioners are resident with, or near, relatives and friends, and the annuity is received in such a manner that their neighbours need not be acquainted with the source of their income. This, surely, is one of the most kindly modes of dispensing charity, for the feelings of the recipient are considered and studied in every detail ... The number of old people now in receipt of annuities is the largest ever known in the history of the Institution, being no less than 620.

Bro C. E. Keyser, a trustee of the RMBI, suggested in January 1907 that a perpetual presentation should be able to be purchased for either sex for the sum of £1,627 10s 0d. This was agreed, and he subsequently purchased, from his own pocket, perpetual presentations for both the Provinces of Berkshire and Hertfordshire. Keyser was an accomplished and wealthy antiquarian, having been educated at Eton and

Trinity College, Cambridge, and was initiated in the Isaac Newton Lodge. He made a considerable fortune on the Stock Exchange, and this, when combined with his inheritance, enabled him to purchase the estate of Aldermaston Court in 1893. He was a generous benefactor, both in Freemasonry and in the public sector, where he funded a convalescent hospital during the South African War. He was appointed Provincial Grand Master for Hertfordshire in 1924.

It was proposed by Bro Alfred Robbins at the AGM that annuitants' families, if they too were penniless, should be awarded £5 towards funeral costs. This was agreed and immediately implemented. Robbins was an influential Freemason, becoming known as the 'Prime Minister of English Freemasonry'. He was born in 1856 in Launceston,

Cornwall, and became the London correspondent for the *Birmingham Daily Post* in 1888. Robbins joined Freemasonry in Gallery Lodge No 1928; this was the Lodge for members of the Press Gallery of the House of Commons. In 1907, he and the Grand Master, the Duke of Connaught, were instrumental in setting up London Rank. He later served as President of the Board of General Purposes from 1913 until his death in 1931.

Nationally the spectre of the workhouse was still of general concern to the population, but a series of international events were about to create new and exciting developments. Back in May 1889, the German Chancellor, Otto von Bismarck, had presented the Old Age Pension and Disability Act before the Reichstag in Berlin. This had reduced the age of retirement to 70 — later, in 1916, it was reduced to 65 —for all German industrial and lower paid white-collar workers. In Great Britain, Charles Booth, a rich shipping magnate, had used a series of multi-coloured maps to demonstrate the distribution of the poor throughout London, and in 1897, Joseph Chamberlain had introduced the Workmen's Compensation Act, giving employees the right to receive damages if accidentally injured at work, and mentioning for the first time a scheme for an old age pension. This would be one of the first Acts in the United Kingdom that would eliminate one of the principal reasons for admission into the workhouse — namely, being poor. Previously, the Liberal Government had appointed a Royal Commission, presided over by Lord Aberdare, to report on the aged, poor and destitute. This was further investigated by another committee, chaired by Lord Rothschild, charged to investigate the possibility of introducing an old age pension. In 1899, Lloyd George recommended that the needy and deserving over 65 years of age should be awarded 5s per week.

The Royal Commission of 1905 recommended that workhouses were no longer appropriate for the poor, homeless and destitute. Instead, more appropriate accommodation with properly trained staff should be found. The Union Workhouses were only of use as a deterrent for 'incorrigibles such as drunkards, idlers and tramps'.

However, it was not until 1907 that the small sum of £1.2 million was set aside to form a non-contributory pension scheme, which was to start on 1st January 1909. The benefit level was set low in order to encourage workers to make their own provision for retirement; the recipient had also to have earned less than £21 10s per annum and have passed a good character assessment. It excluded all those in lunatic asylums or prisons, those convicted of drunkenness, and any person who was guilty of 'habitual failure to work'.

In 1909, David Lloyd George introduced a budget to pay for old age pensions and other reforms, in what became known as the People's Budget. He declared:

> *This is a war Budget. It is for raising money to wage implacable warfare against poverty and squalidness. I cannot help hoping and believing that before this*

BELOW **Asylum for Aged, Worthy and Decayed Freemasons.**
Library and Museum of Freemasonry

ASYLUM FOR WORTHY AGED AND DECAYED FREEMASONS, CROYDON,
PURSUANT TO THE UNANIMOUS RECOMMENDATION OF THE UNITED GRAND LODGE OF ENGLAND, 6 DEC. 1887

generation has passed away, we shall have advanced a great step towards that good time, when poverty, and the wretchedness and human degradation which always follows in its camp, will be as remote to the people of this country as the wolves which once infested its forests.

The Budget was initially rejected by the House of Lords, causing a constitutional crisis that involved the King, but after much debate and another general election it was eventually passed in December 1910. Lloyd George's National Insurance Act of 1911 provided for a compulsory insurance for lower paid workers and set a fixed fee per person for medical cover. Workers who earned under £160 per year had to pay 4d per week, whilst employers paid 3d and the government 2d towards the scheme. Workers could now receive up to 10s per week if sick. These actions largely removed the need for the elderly to retire into Union Workhouses when too old to work, and also delayed the necessity of the workhouse for the working family, but it was still a long way before the closure of such establishments.

In 1914, Lloyd George received this letter:

May I appeal to you on behalf of the aged to succeed and supplement the Old Age Pensions Act by providing out of National Funds Old Age Homes for the destitute over 70 years of Age? The figures enclosed show the great savings which would be effected by substituting Old Age Homes for the Workhouse. Your promised housing scheme offered a fine opportunity of providing for aged as well as robust labourers at one stroke. Earnestly commending the needs of the Homeless Aged to your heart and conscience.

It would, however, take the Local Government Act of 1929 to begin to remove the powers of the workhouses, which were finally abolished in 1930, although the institutions continued under the new name of Public Assistance Institutions controlled by local councils. As late as 1939, nearly 100,000 individuals, including over 5,000 children, were accommodated in former workhouses. The last vestiges of the Poor Law were not eliminated until the National Assistance Act of 1948 under Clement Attlee's post-war Labour Government.

In the meantime, life at the RMBI Home continued with few practical changes. The Home's medical Officer, Bro Strong, PAGD, resigned in 1893 but would continue to act in a consultative role until his death. He was replaced by his younger partner, J. Wayte, a Freemason, who took over the medical practice at 108 North End, Croydon, in December 1893. Born into an old Warwickshire farming family, in Meriden, on 28th March 1862, he married Constance Harriett Ward whilst studying at Oxford and they had three academic children. They were themselves quite enlightened for the day, allowing their daughter, Dorothy Margaret Anne (1890-1956), to study at Oxford. Her elder brother, John Woollaton Wayte (1892-1954), was a medical student. The youngest son, Samuel Wilfred Wayte (1895-1917), studied at Kings College, Canterbury, and his name appears on the school's war memorial. Samuel, like his father, was awarded a Military Cross, but sadly was killed whilst serving with the Royal Field Artillery on 17th October 1917.

In 1910, Edward VII died. He had always been an active Freemason and had done much to popularise the Fraternity. On 4th May he contracted severe bronchitis and the following day his condition deteriorated whilst he was giving his final audience to official visitors. He collapsed on 6th May and, after a series of heart attacks, died at 11.45pm with the Archbishop of Canterbury at his side. Cheerful to the end, he said his goodbyes to the assembled friends and family. He lay in state in Westminster Hall, and his funeral was attended by all the European crowned heads of state. Herbert Asquith eloquently stated:

> I went up on deck and the first sight that met my eyes in the twilight before dawn was Halley's Comet blazing in the sky ... I felt bewildered and stunned ... we had lost, without warning or preparation, the Sovereign whose ripe experience, trained sagacity, equitable judgement and unvarying consideration counted for so much. For two years I had been his Chief Minister ... his unbroken confidence lightened the load which I should otherwise have found almost intolerable.

James Stephens was pleased to note at that year's AGM that the Home had been redecorated and was in a good state of repair and, in memory of the late King, all unsuccessful candidates were elected as annuitants to the RMBI, bringing the total to 847. King George V succeeded his father. He had never been involved in Freemasonry and, although his sons would join, he refused. To celebrate his Coronation, £5 was presented to each resident and every annuitant received 10s 6d.

On 31st January 1912, Jane Norris died at the Home; she was 95 years old and had been Warden since the death of her father in 1885. She was succeeded as Warden by J. H. Beale.

A most memorable outing took place on 4th February 1913, when Eustace Jay, the Manager of the Empire Palace, invited the residents to a special performance at his theatre. Originally known as the National Palace of Varieties when first built in 1895, it was redesigned in 1906 by the well-known theatre designer G. R. Sprague and renamed The Empire. Built on three levels, it had seating for 1,868 people and was equipped with eight dressing rooms for the various leading music-hall figures of the day such as Vesta Tilley, who had appeared there on Monday 15th April 1912. Bro Albert Ford had organised the event, which was crowded as the residents intermingled with the celebrities in the foyer. The proprietor of the Rising Sun Public House, Robert Dove,

BELOW **James Terry in a painting by an unknown artist.** *Royal Masonic Benevolent Institute/Cecil Barton*

LEFT **Miss Jane Ann Norris, the Matron, and Mrs Mary Hodges (nee Norris).** *Library and Museum of Freemasonry*

RIGHT **Open Day at the Croydon Home.** *Royal Masonic Benevolent Society*

The British Army was not huge like those of France, Germany and Russia; Britain's strength lay with the Royal Navy, although the government was conscious that the Army must dramatically increase in size. The Minister of War and eminent Freemason Lord Kitchener of Khartoum set about recruiting such an army. In the meantime, the British Expeditionary Force had already fought its first action at the small Belgian town of Mons and now the major part of the Army had arrived at Ypres and was entrenched across the Menin Road, a few miles outside the town. It was here that the first of the bloody battles of Ypres would take place. At home there was still an element that believed that the whole thing would be over by Christmas, but already the steady trickle of casualties was passing through Charing Cross Station just a few hundred yards from Freemasons' Hall in Great Queen Street.

The first wartime President for the RMBI Festival was the Provincial Grand Master of Northumberland, Col Charles Warren Napier Clavering. He had been recently recalled to the colours at the outbreak of the war and currently commanded the depot of the Somerset Light Infantry. His first regiment, as a young subaltern in 1878, had been the 13th Light Infantry and he saw action in the Burmese War of 1885-87. He was eventually appointed as Lieutenant-Colonel of the 1st Battalion Prince Albert's Somerset Light Infantry. Always an active Freemason, he was a member of many military Lodges, including the Khyber Lodge, Lord Frederick Roberts of Kandahar's Mother Lodge.

The Festival was held in March 1915, by which time the population was beginning to appreciate the sheer horror of this war. The Christmas peace, when troops of both sides met in no man's land, was the last vestige of sanity, and as the Festival was enjoyed in London, two major battles — at Neuve Chapelle and Artois — were beginning which would account for 11,000 British casualties. Col Napier Clavering

presented the gentlemen with cigars, and Miss Dove presented boxes of confectionery to the ladies. On behalf of all the residents, Bro Webb thanked all those who had organised the event.

Those halcyon days of the Edwardian era were not to last. On 28th June 1914, the heir to the Austro-Hungarian throne, Archduke Franz Ferdinand, and his wife were assassinated in Serbia and within a month the major powers in Europe were preparing for war. In Sir Edward Grey's memoirs, he recalls the date of 3rd August:

> We were standing at a window of my room in the Foreign Office. It was getting dusk, and the lamps were being lit in the space below on which we were looking. My friend recalls that I remarked on this with the words: 'The lamps are going out all over Europe; we shall not see them lit again in our lifetime.'

The next day Great Britain and her Empire declared war on Germany.

The three charities hoped life would continue as near normal as possible but were concerned about the practicalities of holding Festivals. After some deliberations, they all agreed that even during a time of hostilities it would be advantageous.

commented on the current difficulties in his speech at the Festival:

> It is a very difficult matter, on the occasion of a Festival like this, not to allude to the great crisis through which we are passing, but I endeavour to say as little about it as possible, and then only in allusion to the Festival of the evening. I have had from the Secretary some particulars about the Institution which shows how absolutely necessary a Festival of this kind is. There was some idea about postponing the Festival this year, but it was decided, and I think wisely, to hold it.
>
> We are determined that no war shall interfere with the love and affection we feel for our old folk who have fallen by the wayside.

This wartime Festival proved a success and raised in excess of £35,000, of which £7,892 was raised in the Province of Northumberland.

The Festival over, a meeting of the Committee of Management was held to discuss a more appropriate situation for the charity's offices, and it negotiated a temporary move to the basement of Freemasons' Hall until more suitable accommodation could be found, and there it would remain until 1931. The charity was not slow to modernise, and in October 1915 it purchased an expensive Elliot Addressograph machine that had to be imported from the USA.

His Grace the Duke of Richmond and Gordon, the Provincial Grand Master of Sussex, presided over the Festival in 1916, a year when the war would intensify to levels of even greater slaughter than those of the Crimean and the Napoleonic Wars combined. His speech was reported as follows:

> Many had been the rumours for some days prior to the Festival that, notwithstanding the war and the almost universal slump in business of every description, there was going to be a great collection for the 'Poor Old People' but few seemed prepared for the announcement that the Festival had yielded over £34,000, the fourth highest sum collected at any Festival in the history of the Institution.

It is with some jingoistic irony that the toast to the other Masonic charities was given by the Deputy Provincial Grand Master of Sussex, Major R. Laurence Thornton, who commented that whenever the Sussex Regiment was in the front line, the German troops opposite were afraid. This was based on the fact that, as of that moment, the regiment had the smallest number of prisoners of war in German camps than any other British regiment.

On 27th May 1916, Bro Charles Keyser, PGW, presented a portrait of the Treasurer, James Stephens, painted by Hugh G. Rivière. It would hang in the Great Hall of the Institution at Croydon along with those of Crucefix and Terry.

James Stephens, more familiarly known as Jimmy, had a most industrious and distinguished career within the Masonic community, becoming patron of both the Royal Masonic Institutions for Girls and Boys and in 1909 the President of the Board of Benevolence. Born into a working class family in Judd Street, St Pancras, on 23rd January 1850, he was the second son of a carpenter, Robert Stephens, and his wife Mary Ann, who had recently arrived in London from their native Cornwall. Robert Stephens worked hard and prospered and his family grew in size. They moved, as their lot improved, to the more salubrious district of Paddington, which enabled Robert to expand his specialised business of ladder and barrow making. When James was a teenager he and his younger brother were apprenticed in his father's business. Robert Stephens died in 1881, by which time he had accrued several properties, including four houses in the Harrow Road, and a substantial and profitable business. James married Ellen Leontine Ada Dew at St Mary's Church, Paddington, in 1875 and set up his ladder making business at 225 Pentonville Road. In 1878, he was initiated into Hyde Park Lodge No 1425 and thereafter joined many other Lodges in London and Buckinghamshire. He became a Grand Officer in 1897, and in 1923 was promoted to Grand Junior Warden. At the outbreak of the war he lived in Maida Vale with his wife and sister-in-law, Louisa Carter, and a couple of servants. He eventually died there on 3rd March 1929, aged 80. His funeral was attended by the Lord Mayor of London and many other dignitaries.

Life within the charity continued much as normal, with only the occasional event to disturb what otherwise was a peaceful haven. In August 1915, two individuals petitioned for permission to marry, which, after much discussion, was refused as it was considered inappropriate. On 14th October, Mrs Truelove, an annuitant of some 30 years, celebrated her 100th birthday, and a horse and carriage were hired for the day to take her on a journey around London. She was also presented with £5 for any additional comforts, and a photographer was present to record the occasion. Martha Ann Truelove had been born on 7th August 1816 in Woolwich, the daughter of Richard Harrison, a private in the

SOME OF THE BRETHREN who are residing at the Institution
at East Croydon

THE SITTING ROOM OF A RESIDENT

ABOVE LEFT **Residents playing bowls.**
Royal Masonic Benevolent Institute

ABOVE **A room in the Croydon
Home.** *Royal Masonic Benevolent
Institute*

LEFT **RMBI Jubilee 1892.** *Royal
Masonic Benevolent Institute*

Royal Marines, and his wife Ann. She was baptised on 25th August at St Mary Magdalene Church, Woolwich. She had been a domestic servant before she married James Truelove, a waterman. They were both annuitants; when he died in 1889, she continued living on her own. In 1921, the General Court awarded her another £50 on reaching the age of 105. She eventually died in 1924, aged 108.

The celebrations of the bicentenary of the formation of Grand Lodge were held at the Royal Albert Hall on 23rd June 1917. This was arguably the most important event in the Masonic calendar for that year. There were to be no festivities due to the war, but a number of representatives were present from various Grand Lodges throughout the English-speaking world. The Grand Master, the Duke of Connaught, presided and James Stephens was called on to speak:

> Brethren — There are present with us today distinguished Masons from Grand Lodges in the Dominions beyond Seas and in the United States of America, and to each and all of these I give from myself in your name a most cordial welcome. Had the times and season proved propitious, the number of such Brethren would have been largely increased; but we regard those assembled with us today as representatives of the might of the Masonic host, which now embraces the English-speaking world. To British Brethren beyond Seas we accord our wholehearted fraternal greeting, asking them to tell, on their return home, how very deeply all in the Motherland appreciate the devotion that has been shown to her so abundantly in the period of unexampled stress. To our American Brethren we say how sincerely we recognise that spirit of love and truth and loyalty to freedom which have led their nation to join with our own and with our Allies in the present great struggle. From the beginning we have felt that the cause we defend is that of Masonic Brotherhood in its noblest aspects, and in that victory of our course will ensure the spread throughout all lands of the three Grand Principles on which our Order is founded, and the triumph of which was never more necessary — and, we trust, never more assured — than this hour.

The heartfelt warmth felt at the time by Freemasons towards the charities — particularly the Home in Croydon — can be best illustrated by a speech delivered by Sir Alfred Robbins on 15th September 1917 to the Bon Accord Lodge No 3750 at its meeting held at the Great Eastern Hotel near Liverpool Street Station, during which he stated:

> We have also that other great Institution, known generally and affectionately as 'The Old People's'. In the Home at Croydon there is room for only some ninety inmates, but the accommodation is found sufficient for the number of those who have no home or friends to whom they can go, and who wish to settle in a little place like that. I find on a regular visit, year after year, that the people there are comfortable and happy, and, what is even more to the point, independent. Each has his or her own suite of rooms; and they are not merely content but happy, because they are treated by everyone who visits them as a brother or sister. Yet this is the least part of the Benevolent Institution, which altogether has some 1,200 aged Brethren and widows under its care.

During 1917 the Secretary of the RMBI, Bro Colville Smith, was promoted to Grand Secretary. The most important item at the next AGM in the October was the election of a new Secretary, resulting in the appointment of Bro William Resbury Few. William was the son of Charles Few, a solicitor, and his wife Jane, and was born in Wandsworth, London, on 15th July 1860. The youngest of four children, he was baptised in the local church of All Saints. His mother had died when he was only eight years old and he was brought up by his eldest sister, Emily. He was educated at Wellington School in Somerset and initiated into the Royal Somerset House and Inverness Lodge No 4 in 1889. He qualified as a solicitor and joined his father's practice at 11 Surrey Street. When his father died in 1887 he left him a substantial inheritance, and he married Gertrude Mabel Wright on 15th March 1893. They had a daughter, Audrey Githa Few, in 1902.

Every cloud has a silver lining, and in a small way that was the position that the RMBI found itself in. Inflation caused by the war left many organisations casting around for opportunities to curtail benefits and cut down on spending, but the RMBI, to the contrary, actually had sufficient funds to increase benefits on the grounds of the higher cost in living.

Throughout the war the Royal Navy blockaded Germany and in retaliation the Germans responded with submarine attacks on convoys in the Atlantic. This action, along with panic buying, restricted food supplies and other consumables so that, by the end of 1917, Britain found it necessary to introduce rationing; this remained in place until 1920. Rationing affected the dining for the Festival at the

LEFT **The Great Hall at the Asylum.** *Royal Masonic Benevolent Institute*

RIGHT **Two residents outside the main entrance.** *Royal Masonic Benevolent Institute*

Connaught Rooms in 1918, presided over by the Chairman of Lloyds Bank and the PGM for Gloucestershire, Sir Richard Vassar-Smith. *The Freemason* reported:

> If 'festivity' is synonymous with that which is known generally as 'high feeding' then it was not a Festival, for the Menu was strictly in accordance with the new regulations.

The meal, delightfully presented, and eaten with the usual enjoyment, consisted of vegetable hors-d'oeuvres, soup, fish, eggs and spaghetti, plain pudding and coffee (no sugar). The article continued in a rather sombre tone, reflecting the attitude of the evening:

> There were Brethren there — men in high position in the world of commerce and finance — whose hearts were bowed down with sorrow for the loss of sons on the battlefields of Europe. There was, perhaps, not one Brother in the assembly free from anxiety as to the fate of a beloved son, relative, or close friend in determining right and might. All, however, put aside personal inclinations and sorrows to show their sympathy with the wounded survivors in the battle for life.

The Armistice came at 11am on 11th November 1918 and, to celebrate, each annuitant received a £1 Victory Bonus. However, this was not the official victory — that would only come after the Treaty of Versailles was signed on 28th June 1919, but that Christmas the nation rejoiced. *The Freemason* commented:

> The thoughts of many will turn this year towards 'The Old Folks Home' with more calmness of mind and pleasurable anticipation of meeting than has been possible during any one of the four preceding Christmastides ... Let us not forget that the aftermath of war will bring with it much misery; we have not yet arrived at the piping times of peace, nor has the long, long trail of suffering yet come to an end.

The first post-war RMBI Festival was chaired by the Marquess of Zetland, who stated:

> Indeed, in this year, when I hope we shall celebrate the conclusion of Peace after more than 4 years of devastating war, it would give every one of us, and particularly myself as your Chairman to-night, intense satisfaction if the announcement were such that the peace year Festival will stand out prominently among the Festivals of the Royal Masonic Benevolent Institution. I may also state, for the information of those who are not already aware of the fact, that, to mark further this year of Peace, the Most Worshipful Grand Master has graciously pleased to give his consent to the jewels for this year's Festivals of all three charities being worn as permanent jewels.

Charles Keyser announced in May of 1919 that each annuitant would receive a £5 Peace Bonus, and a month later the world was at peace.

CHAPTER 11
BETWEEN THE WARS

The First World War had left the country destitute, with unemployment levels rarely if ever experienced before. This inevitably had an effect on the charities as they strove to raise money from a Masonic population already strapped for cash.

The New Year celebrations at the Home in 1920 were held on the second Wednesday of the year. The Lodge of Tranquillity No 185 had for the last 27 years generously provided the residents with their treats. However, this year an additional concert was arranged with the added attraction of a film show, to the delight of the residents.

The Province of Kent, under Col Fiennes Cornwallis, ran the 1920 Festival. The Cornwallis family played an influential part in Freemasonry at this time. Fiennes Cornwallis was born in 1864 at Chacombe Priory in Oxfordshire, the son of Maj Fiennes Cornwallis and Harriet Elizabeth (née Mott). The family name was originally Fiennes Wykeham-Martin but was altered to Cornwallis by royal licence in 1859. Fiennes Cornwallis was educated at Eton and married Mabel Leigh, daughter of Oswald Peter Leigh, in 1886. He became Conservative MP for Maidstone in 1888 and was subsequently appointed a Lieutenant-Colonel, later the Honorary Colonel of the West Kent Imperial Yeomanry. They had seven children, the eldest of whom, Lt Fiennes Wykeham Mann Cornwallis, was sadly killed by the IRA in May 1921 during the Irish War of Independence. Col Fiennes Cornwallis was raised to the peerage in 1927, becoming the 1st Lord Cornwallis of Linton.

During the festivities Bro Keyser was pleased to report that since 1916 all worthy candidates now received the advantages of the Institution. He gave a brief history of the charity, emphasising that the primary function of these Festivals had always been to raise money for the annuitants and residents. He further stated that up to 1903, only the gross figure collected nationally had ever been recorded, but that from then on the amount raised within the President's own Province would also be documented. Festival targets were introduced to help Provinces plan their fund-raising

events and achieve their final goal. Such a fund-raising event occurred in 1923, when the Province of Cheshire organised a day trip to Llandudno for 500 members and their families. An eventful day was enjoyed, with some preferring the seaside whilst others cruised to view the Menai Bridge. The band of the *Indefatigable* under the baton of Bandmaster John Williams entertained them on their return journey. This event, along with others, contributed to their target of £50,000. Two years later they exceeded their target by reaching £62,213 3s; the national sum raised was £106,607 13s 5d.

Since the deaths of the Norris sisters, there had been two further Wardens — J. H. Beale (1912-1924) and A. E. Turton (1924-1927) — and it was during their tenure that the Home was upgraded with modern facilities such as electric rings and kettles. Later, the sanitation system was modernised, floors were relaid with new linoleum and cupboards were fitted into each room.

Certain families have played exemplary roles within the charity since its foundation. In the 19th century it was the Farnfields; then came the Terrys. James Terry was succeeded as Secretary by his son James Edmund Terry, who was born in Clerkenwell on 6th October 1861. He was the eldest child, followed by his two younger sisters, Kate Sarah Terry and Jessie Eliza Terry. Initially employed as a bank clerk, he soon became a successful stockbroker, marrying Gertrude Mary Smith, the daughter of Henry Smith, a City bank manager, in 1891. The family prospered and moved to Weybridge where they had a daughter, Muriel Gertrude Terry, who sadly died when only six years of age. Their son, James Arthur Terry, born in 1904, would later be involved in the expansion of the RMBI. In 1909, James Edmund Terry joined the Committee of Management, which he would eventually chair, a position he held until his death in 1937.

The value of an annuity was determined every three years, but at a time of high inflation as a consequence of the war, the original sum was insufficient by the time of the third year. Widows received at this time £40 to £48, whilst the men got

ABOVE **Sir Phillip Coleville Smith**. *Library and Museum of Freemasonry*

BELOW **Christmas at the Croydon Home**. *Library and Museum of Freemasonry*

ABOVE RIGHT **James E. Terry**. *Library and Museum of Freemasonry*

£48 to £52. Conversely, the amount raised by the Festivals had substantially increased. James Stephens decided that the most effective way forward was to assess payments annually as well as immediately increasing the annuity to £56 for widows and £64 for the men. It was proposed at the Special General Meeting held in July 1922 and duly passed. However, the suggestion that daughters and sisters of Freemasons should also be admitted to the scheme was rejected.

The First World War had been funded by borrowing huge sums; consequently there was now a large national debt. Unemployment began to rise dramatically, reaching 2.5 million by 1922, which forced the government to allocate £10 million to fund public works. The Goschen Committee was set up to look into the need for relief loans for the Poor Law Authorities (workhouses). In December 1922, *The Freemason* reported an increase in the numbers requesting help:

> For many years past there has been an increasing number of applicants, and the fact that elections were only held annually was a matter for deep sympathy. However, Bro James Stephens, with his usual thoroughness in all matters of charity, urged that an increasing number should be relieved, relying upon the Brethren to confirm that policy by their subscriptions. By his sturdy advocacy the policy was successful, and this year the whole of the candidates have been accepted without ballot, and over 1,400 Brethren and Widows are now receiving annuities.

The organisation now began to struggle, forcing it to update the rules and regulations, especially relating to widows, whose numbers had increased dramatically as a consequence of the war. James Stephens proposed at the Committee Meeting of 14th February 1923 that:

> No widow shall be eligible to be admitted a candidate under the age of sixty years, nor unless her late husband has been for ten years a subscribing member of a Lodge, except in the case of his petition having been accepted by the Committee before expiration of that period, or his having been a subscribing member of an English Lodge for not less than five years and having continued a subscribing member to the time of his decease. A widow must have been married to her late husband for at least five years, and if the widow of an annuitant, the marriage must have taken place at least five years previously to the presentation of her husband's petition.

ABOVE **Charles Edward Keyser**. *Library and Museum of Freemasonry*

> If qualified in other respects, a widow shall be eligible to be accepted a candidate at an earlier age than sixty years if suffering from blindness, paralysis, or other affliction certified by two medical men which, in the opinion of the Committee, permanently incapacitates her from earning a livelihood.

Charles Keyser, now Grand Senior Warden, convened a meeting of the Committee at Freemasons' Hall on 8th May 1923. James Stephens was requested to chair a group, selected equally from members of both the House and Finance Committees, to resolve the ambiguous nature of the rules. This task would take seven years to complete.

In early 1926, William Resbury Few's health began to fail and had now deteriorated to such an extent that it was essential to appoint a deputy, possibly a potential successor. This, sadly, became a reality when, on 18th November, he

LEFT **HM King George VI (1895–1952) from a painting by Herbert James Gunn**. *Library and Museum of Freemasonry*

ABOVE **Mrs M. A. Truelove 1916**. *Library and Museum of Freemasonry*

finally succumbed to his illness. Sir Alfred Robbins read the following eulogy at his funeral:

Bro Few fulfilled every expectation I had formed of his work as Secretary of the RMBI. I used to meet him regularly on the first Wednesday of every succeeding New Year, when I was privileged to take the Chair at the yearly festivity given to the inmates of our Old People's Home at Croydon by the generous Brethren of the Lodge of Tranquillity and the Playgoers Lodge. It was not merely the question of securing the materials for such a feast when the funds were kindly given by these special friends of the Institution, the two Lodges named. During the closing periods of the War and immediately afterwards, the almost insurmountable difficulty was to procure the materials, and all in accordance with traditional custom and usage. It was a task in which Bro Few seemed to revel, and his delight in ensuring that his old friends should not suffer any appreciable diminution in the provision made for them, and to which they had been so long accustomed, was inspiring to witness. I shall always bear with me, when remembering Bro Few, the recollection of a Freemason for whom I had not only admiration, but affection, and he has left a gap in my Masonic acquaintance very difficult, if not impossible, to fill.

There were two very important decisions made in February 1927. The first permitted the wife of a petitioner to sign her husband's application if he was incapable of so doing. Likewise she was now allowed to receive his annuity directly if her husband was being maintained free of charge at their home. The second was that petitioners could not apply for an annuity if they were already receiving a government award because their son had been killed during the war.

The day before the Annual Festival was an opportunity for that year's President to visit the Home, attend a meeting of the Committee of Management and meet the residents. In 1927, the President was an old friend, namely RW Bro Charles Keyser, the Provincial Grand Master for Hertfordshire. On this occasion he met the newly appointed Matron, Miss M. Houlton. The ball was a great success, but the Festival raised only £21,000 from the Province of Hertfordshire and £68,349 12s 10d nationally. This sum was disappointing, but with the industrial turmoil as a consequence of the recent General Strike, not really a surprise. In order to raise his own Province's amount, Charles Keyser generously presented a gift of £10,000 from his own pocket. The cost of running the Home had now reached £7,000 and, although the residents were limited to the number of apartments available, the number of annuitants was steadily increasing: they had exceeded 1,800 by December 1927.

Major Cecil Clare Adams, a decorated war veteran, was appointed as Few's successor on 4th December 1926. He eventually retired in 1961, and became the RMBI's longest-serving Secretary. Adams was the son of the architect Harry Percy Adams and was born in Woburn Place, St Pancras, on 4th March 1891. Educated at Radnor Park School, Folkestone, and then Winchester College, he joining the Royal Engineers and was awarded the Military Cross as well as being Mentioned in Despatches. He was seconded to the Military College at Kingston, Ontario, and whilst there married Louisa Augusta Kirkpatrick on 28th May 1917. He and his wife returned home in 1920. Adams had been initiated into the Pentangle Lodge No 1174 in 1912 in Rochester, Kent, becoming its Master in 1916. By the age of 36, he was already a Deputy Grand Standard Bearer.

The summer festivities at the Home had for a number of years been known as the Stewards Day, and 700 visitors came on 14th July 1928, including James Stephens and Cecil Adams and his wife. The entertainment was provided by the English Imperial Military Band conducted by Captain Harry Godfrey. Those attending enjoyed the day, wandering around the beautifully kept gardens, now at their very best.

The year 1929 was a painful one for the RMBI, for on 3rd March, the Treasurer of the charity, James Stephens, PGW, died at his home in Maida Vale. He was buried at Kensal Green Cemetery. That year also saw the death of one of the

charity's greatest benefactors, Charles Keyser, who passed away on 29th May.

Lord Ravensworth, the PGM for Durham, presided over the 87th Festival, which was a rousing financial success. During the evening Lord Ampthill presented Lord Ravensworth with a golden salver to commemorate not only his 60th birthday but also his tenth year as a Provincial Grand Master. His wife, Lady Isolda Blanche Ravensworth, received a set of tortoiseshell toilet brushes and mirrors bearing her monogram I. B. R. surmounted by a coronet.

The new Treasurer was to be Henry George Charles Lascelles, 6th Earl of Harewood, KG, GCVO, DSO, TD. A member of the Royal Family, having married the King's only daughter, Princess Mary, he was a Captain in the Grenadiers during the First World War and was twice wounded, and later served in the Yorkshire Hussars Yeomanry. His appointment as Treasurer meant that from now on this

LEFT **Right Honourable Fiennes Stanley Wykeham (1864–1935), 1st Baron Cornwallis, from a painting by May Bridges Lee**. *Library and Museum of Freemasonry*

RIGHT **RMBI Festival meal**. *Library and Museum of Freemasonry*

BELOW **Sir Alfred Robbins**. *Library and Museum of Freemasonry*

position would be more of a figurehead than an active, hands-on officer. The Rt Hon Lord Cornwallis, Deputy GM and Provincial Grand Master for Kent, was also appointed to the Board of Trustees. The new decade started well, *The Freemason* declaring:

> What a wonderful Institution is the RMBI with each resident enjoying two rooms with the shared use of a kitchen with a nice garden. They are given coals and light all provided free of charge.

The Home was looking smart, having been recently improved. The terraces had been newly paved and tarred, and the recently discovered dry rot had now been removed. On New Year's Day the 'old folk', as they were now known, were entertained by the Playgoers Lodge No 2705, who had assembled a range of artists to perform the works of Edward German, Sir Arthur Sullivan and songs of 'olden days'. George Thomas and Kitlee thrilled those present with his ventriloquism and magic tricks.

Lord Ampthill had agreed to preside over the 88th Festival. Born Arthur Oliver Villiers Russell on 19th February 1869 in Rome, he was the eldest son of the 1st Baron Ampthill and Lady Emily Theresa. His mother had been one of Queen Victoria's Ladies of the Bedchamber. He attended Eton and

New College, Oxford, where he had a distinguished rowing career. A better sportsman than an academic, he gained only a third class degree in modern history in 1888. He married Lady Margaret Lygon in 1894, and she, like her mother-in-law, also became a Lady of the Bedchamber, this time for Queen Mary, and was awarded Dame Grand Cross of the British Empire in 1918.

As a diplomat Arthur Russell became Joseph Chamberlain's Private Secretary and proved so efficient that, in 1897, he succeeded Sir Arthur Havelock as Governor of Madras. He became Viceroy of India in 1904, succeeding Lord Curzon, albeit for a short period, until a permanent successor could be found. On his return home he was appointed Deputy Lieutenant of Bedfordshire in 1909. He had joined Apollo Lodge in 1890 whilst at Oxford, and became the PGM for Bedfordshire in 1908. He commanded a battalion of the Leicester Regiment during the war and was twice Mentioned in Despatches.

Lord Ampthill knew at the time that his Festival would be less popular than the following year's event, for word had leaked out that the next Festival was to be chaired by HRH the Duke of York. Sadly the amount raised dropped even more dramatically than expected, from £43,855 the previous year to £23,276. This was due to a number of factors: the previous year the Stock Market in New York had crashed, and in Great Britain unemployment had doubled.

In 1911, an idea for a Masonic Hospital had been suggested, and by 1916 enough money had been raised to buy the former Chelsea Women's Hospital on the Fulham Road. It was initially used for wounded soldiers and became known as the Freemasons' Hospital and Nursing Home, but by 1929 there was a need to build a larger hospital. The Royal Masonic Hospital would be completed at Ravenscourt Park in 1933. Running parallel with this project was the Masonic Million Memorial Fund for the rebuilding of Freemasons' Hall, which was now nearing its completion. These combined projects inevitably stretched the demands of the membership at a time of a national economic recession.

As early as October 1929 a Committee, consisting of the Grand Secretary, Sir P. Colville Smith, selected members of the House and Finance Committees and representatives of the Duke of York's own Province of Middlesex, met to arrange the 1931 Festival. Tickets would be in great demand, and the usual accommodation would not be large enough to cater for such numbers. A number of venues were suggested, but the final choice was the Addison Hall at Olympia. Olympia was originally opened as an exhibition centre in 1886, but it had now been enlarged to 50,000 square metres

ABOVE **Sir Phillip Colville Smith, CVO, Grand Secretary (1917-1937) from a painting by Henry Macbeth-Raeburn.** *Library and Museum of Freemasonry*

primarily to accommodate the British Industries Fair. (The Craft had previously used the venue for a fund-raising dinner for the Masonic War Memorial in 1925, and on that occasion 8,000 people had paid 17 guineas each to attend.) Messrs Lyons & Co, the official caterers, prepared three miles of tables for the Festival to seat the 3,100 guests who were expected for the event on 12th March 1931; 1,360 waitresses and 700 cooks were employed. The total cost was £8,910.

There was much excitement as the day approached. Everything had to be perfect for the Royal Family, and already the total number of Stewards had reached 6,674, a number far exceeding that of any previous Festival. The Province of Middlesex had raised £45,000, approximately £10 per member, and the Craft as a whole had exceeded £116,000. There was only one cloud on the horizon. On 14th March 1931, the death was announced of Sir Alfred Robbins, aged 75 years, at his home, 32 Fitz-George Avenue, West Kensington. He had been an influential supporter and had done much to guide the Craft in the early part of the 20th century. King George V had created him a knight in the birthday honours list of 1911.

The Duke and Duchess of York had agreed, as was customary, to visit the Home on Tuesday 10th March 1931, two days before the Festival. The weather had been cold over the previous weeks, and London had been covered by a thick

A short address on the history of the Institution will be given in the Hall at 4.30 p.m.

THE CONCERT HALL.

There are now about 2,500 Annuitants receiving help, of whom 32 are Residing in the Homes at Croydon. The cost of these Annuities is about £135,000 per annum.

The next Festival will be held on Wednesday, 23rd February, 1938, when the Chairman will be R.W.Bro. The Rev. Canon J. C Morris, *M.A.*, Vice-Patron, Past Grand Chaplain, Provincial Grand Master for Surrey.

Ladies and Brethren who are prepared to serve as Stewards on that occasion, are asked to give their names as early as possible to the Secretary.

ABOVE **Stewards' Dinner 7th July 1937 Programme.** *Royal Masonic Benevolent Institute*

RIGHT **James Terry.** *Library and Museum of Freemasonry*

PROGRAMME OF MUSIC

to be performed by a portion of

THE BAND OF THE CORPS OF ROYAL ENGINEERS.

(By permission of Major-General L. V. Bond, and the Officers of the Corps.)

1.	MARCH ...	...	"The Triumph of Right"	...	...	*Lovell*
2.	OVERTURE	...	"The Arcadians"	...	...	*Wood*
3.	FANTASIA	...	...	"Faust"	...	...	*Gounod*
4.	WALTZ ...	...	"Gold and Silver"	...	...	*Lehar*
5.	SUITE ...	...	"Ballet Egyptien"	...	...	*Luigini*
6.	ENTR'ACTE	...	"In a Pagoda"	...	...	*Bratton*
7.	SCENES FROM ...	...	"Swing Time"	...	...	*Kern*
8.	(a) INTERMEZZO	"Standchen"	...	...	...	*Heykens*
	(b) MORCEAU	"The entry of the little Fauns"	...	...	*Pierne*
9.	SELECTION	...	"The Gondoliers"	...	...	*Sullivan*
10.	ENTR'ACTE	...	"Fragrance"	...	...	*Ancliffe*
11.	SUITE ...	...	...	"La Feria"	...	...	*Lacomb*
12.	DESCRIPTIVE PIECE	"The Dicky Birds Hop"	...	...	*Gourlay*
13.	SELECTION	...	"A Musical Comedy Switch"	...	...	*Hall*
14.	INTERMEZZO ...		"Rose Mousse"	...	...	*Bosc*
15.	FINALE	...	"A Musical Jig Saw"	...	...	*Aston*

"God Save the King."

Director of Music : Lieut. D. W. JONES, L.R.A.M., A.R.C.M., p.s.m.

BRO. JAMES TERRY, P.G.S.B., SECRETARY OF THE INSTITUTION.

blanket of snow only a few days before the festivities. On the day of the Festival it was crisp but the sun shone in a bright blue sky. The doors were opened at 5.30pm, and the band of the Royal Regiment of Artillery conducted by Captain E. C. Stretton MVO entertained the guests until 7pm, when, to great applause, the Duke and Duchess were escorted to their table, which was decorated with carnations and foliage. Unlike previous festivals, both the gentlemen and their ladies dined together, the Duchess sitting on the Duke's right whilst Lady Ampthill sat on his left. The principal guests sitting on the top table were those who had done much to make the day a success and included Lord and Lady Cornwallis and the Earl of Harewood. Dinner was served after grace by 650 waitresses so efficiently and with such aplomb that no knife or fork was dropped or glass spilled, it being commented at the time that Messrs Lyons & Co showed themselves once again to be 'Organisers of Victory'.

Dinner completed, Lord Ampthill rose to propose the toast to the Chairman, praising the Duchess as follows:

Public opinion is reflected in the Press and there is never a week during which we do not find in our newspapers fresh evidence of the warm place HRH the Duchess of York has won in the hearts of the British people by whom she is believed to be as good as she is beautiful — in short, an ideal Princess.

This was received with rapturous applause and was followed by a boisterous chorus of 'For they are Jolly Good Fellows'. The Duke responded by toasting success to the RMBI. Lord Harewood rose at 10pm and, showing no ill effects from a recent hunting accident, delivered a short speech in which he mentioned the recent death of Sir Alfred Robbins. He graciously thanked His Royal Highness for taking the chair. The royal couple then took time to stroll around the room before making their final exit at 11pm.

Amidst all this joy the daily routine of the charity continued. It was now accepted that spinster daughters should become eligible to apply for an annuity. Cornwallis became a trustee, filling the post vacated by the death of Charles Keyser. Everything at the Home appeared a bed of roses, but financially the country was in dire straits. It owed an enormous debt to America, which had to be paid regularly, and reparation money extracted from Germany after the Treaty of Versailles had stopped. In order to avoid a financial collapse, a budget was essential to balance the economy and restore British credibility throughout the world. The King persuaded Prime Minister Ramsay MacDonald to form a coalition government on 24th August 1931, hoping that uniting the best talent from all the political parties would help solve the problem. The general election in October 1931 gave a landslide victory for the coalition, enabling the formation of the second National Government. Neville Chamberlain was appointed Chancellor of the Exchequer and began to formulate a budget to restore stability. War Loans were converted into national bonds, which reduced the interest payable on the national debt. This alone had the potential to save £25 million per annum.

Members of the Finance and House Committees met on 16th June 1931 to consider what to do with the Institution's 5% War Loan. James E. Terry stated that the City was in a quandary over the matter, and after some discussion it was decided that he should solicit the opinions of Holland & Balfour, the well-known stockbrokers. The 5% War Loan had been issued by the British Government in 1917 as a means of funding the war. The repayment date was planned for 1947, but certain sums could be withdrawn after 1st June 1929. The run on the pound in 1931 caused it to slip from $5 to $3.25, necessitating the Bank of England stepping in and injecting large amounts of liquidity into the system. This caused interest rates to fall from 5% to 2% and by June there was the inevitable rush to sell off War Loans. The RMBI held £262,967 in War Loans — a substantial amount — and agreed that to sell them at this moment would lose an estimated £1,600 per annum in interest, but to hold the stock might involve the Institution in a larger loss in the future if the government decided to pay off or convert the loan. The Sub-Committee did consider other forms of investment, but in the present financial climate these were of little value. There was but one course, and that was to wait.

In June 1932, Neville Chamberlain announced a conversion offer for all the 5% bonds into a new issue that held an interest rate of 3½%. This was a clear loss, but with a bank rate as low as 2%, there was little option. In fact it was hailed as a patriotic duty to convert; therefore the Sub-Committee recommended selling them all.

Far from the rarefied atmosphere of national and City finances, life at the Home in Croydon continued much as normal. The average age of the residents was calculated to be 75 years for the men and 77 years for the widows, with the oldest inhabitant being 88 years. A special celebration was held at the Board Meeting in the summer of 1933, when Dr John Wayte, the physician to the Home, received the rank of Honorary Patron of the RMBI in token of his many years' service to the old folk.

The Royal Masonic Hospital was nearing its completion. It had cost £335,000 to build and equip, and was officially declared open by King George V and his consort Queen Mary on 10th May 1933. Although another great milestone in the history of Freemasonry in England, it was yet another factor complicating the funding of the other Masonic charities. The predictions made by the Duke of Sussex so many years before — that the RMBI would be a financial burden on the other charities — were again coming true. On 10th November 1933, *The Freemason* published a letter from Major Adams:

Dear Sir & Brother,
I have been requested to bring to your notice the fact that this Institution is now, for the first time in its history, obliged to dispose of a portion of its investments to meet its current expenditure.
The proceeds from the last Festival have not been

sufficient to pay the annuities for this year, and the action is therefore being taken in order to provide funds for the payments which became due on 1st December.

As the needs of our 'Old People's' Institution have never been as big as they are at the present time, we shall be grateful if you will give this all possible publicity. We hope that the situation will be fully realised by the Craft, and an adequate response given at our Festival next February.
Yours sincerely and fraternally
Cecil Adams, Secretary.

As if an echo from the past, a correspondent wrote that the funding crisis of the charities could be solved if each member were to contribute £1 per annum. It must therefore have been some relief when the Festival of 1934 raised the third ever highest total, with the sum of £108,259 19s 5d.

Not long after the cessation of hostilities, Grand Lodge set up the Masonic Million Memorial Fund to rebuild Freemasons' Hall to commemorate the 3,000 Freemasons who had perished during the conflict. Plans were well advanced before it occurred to the charity that there was no mention of space for them within the new building. The Pro Grand Master, Lord Ampthill, attended a meeting on 9th January 1934 to resolve this problem. He suggested that a letter should be sent to the Grand Secretary stating their wish to remain with Grand Lodge, and that he, in turn, would present it to the Planning Committee. After much discussion and petitioning to Grand Lodge, the Institution was finally offered some accommodation in the new building. Initially the charity accepted this offer, but nobody in the room showed much enthusiasm, considering it far too inadequate. James E. Terry then suggested that there was an opportunity to take out a seven-year lease on the premises of 20 Great Queen Street on the other side of the street from Freemasons' Hall. Lord Ampthill, who was on both committees, immediately seconded this as a preferred option, and the vote was carried unanimously. However, this property was only leased, and there was concern by some who thought that the RMBI should invest in its own property rather than spending money on rent. W Bro F. W. Davy answered that, having taken legal advice, he was of the opinion that the Institution's charitable money could not be used to purchase property — only lease or rent it. A general discussion ensued over this vexing question, and when it came to the vote, the proposition was lost by five votes to two, so the newly leased offices at 20 Great Queen Street would remain the headquarters of the RMBI for the foreseeable future.

Lord Ampthill died of pneumonia on 7th July 1935. *The Times*, making reference to his rowing career, recorded:

> *Oarsmen they lived, and silver goblets mark*
> *The well-timed prowess of their trusty blades:*
> *In death their rhythm kept, they now embark*
> *To row their long last course among the Shades.*

His Masonic career had extended over 40 years, and his energy, enthusiasm and support would be greatly missed by the Masonic fraternity.

In January 1936, the death was announced of King George V who, unlike his father and sons, had never been Freemason. He was succeeded by his Masonic son, now Edward VIII, and as one of his first actions he graciously granted his patronage to the Institution. His reign was shortened by the abdication crisis, and the position of King passed to his younger brother, the Duke of York, who now became George VI.

Over the next few years, funds from the various Festivals trickled in but there would always be concern that Provinces with few Lodges would inevitable raise smaller amounts, and the RMBI needed £104,000 annually. The number of annuitants had now exceeded 2,500 and, at £68 for married men, £64 for single men and £56 for widows per annum, there still was not enough money.

The Chairman, Thomas Henry Woollen, passed away on 26th August. Woollen was a colourful character with many interests in life. Born in Sheffield, he was the younger son of Matthew Woollen, a manufacturer of bone knife handles. Initially Thomas followed in his father's footsteps but he studied hard and eventually qualified as a mechanical engineer. A keen cyclist, he became active in wheel design and was awarded a silver dessert service for his services by the National Cyclists' Union in 1903. While living in Sheffield he married Elizabeth Lowde, and in the early 1900s the family moved to London and lived in Hendon. He became actively involved in the development of the motorcar and the Royal Automobile Club, and was an official timekeeper at Irish, German and French Gordon Bennett races, up to 1905. He officiated at the 1903 race in Ireland when British racing green was introduced.

For a short period James E. Terry acted as Chairman, but sadly he too died a year later, on 20th September 1937, and was succeeded by J. Wilkins, with John E. C. Stubbs as his deputy. During Terry's short Chairmanship he did manage

ABOVE **James Stephens from a painting by an unknown artist**. *Library and Museum of Freemasonry*

to persuade the Committee to grant the staff two weeks' annual leave, an act of kindness ahead of its time.

The Home at Croydon was designed for poor and aged Freemasons and their dependants, but one criterion was essential: they had to be fit. This was beginning to be a more frequent problem and it was becoming increasingly necessary for an elderly person to be placed in a nursing home, particularly if they suffered from dementia. The Home at this time housed 32 elderly people — seven married Brethren, two unmarried and 23 widows; of these, eight widows and two Brethren were over 80 years old, the oldest being two ladies of 87. The average age was 75 years. The Matron since 1932 had been Mrs A. L. Diggins, and she was to hold this position until 1958.

The residents' costs were met by the House Committee, which could only permit funding up to the individual's annuity. This generally was insufficient, but under the rules of the Institution they could receive no more. The Samaritan Fund could not be used as it was not set up to support such demands, yet clearly there was a need to find additional monies. The Joint Committee decided it could adapt Rule 86 to allow greater versatility and permit the RMBI to provide additional monies to fund nursing care. These were hard times and money was becoming increasingly difficult to raise, especially under the looming threat of another major European conflict.

Finance was becoming even more acute. Prior to 1916, there had always been contested elections that controlled the number of annuitants. There were then only 1,347 individuals receiving a total of £44,611. Since elections were terminated, the numbers of annuitants had increased to 2,600, costing £150,000 per annum. The Festival income was no longer sufficient and the financial situation had finally become unsustainable. It would be fair to say that not everyone was sympathetic towards the RMBI, and echoes of the 1840s began to appear in the Masonic Press. The

Secretary of the Province of North and East Yorkshire wrote to *The Freemason* expressing his opinion:

Dear Sir & Brother,

I would like to make one or two comments on the circular that has been issued by the Royal Masonic Benevolent Institution, appealing for funds for the 1939 Festival.

I think it high time that the Board of Management took into their serious consideration the advisability of disposal of the Croydon Homes.

For the sake of a few number of Annuitants (thirty two) the funds of our Institution are being mulcated to the tune of about £1,500 per annum. Simply on the grounds of 'sentiment'. Why should this small number be singled out to be the recipients of a cost of £50 per head per year more than the 2,570 Brethren and Widows?

So far as my experience of fifty years in the Craft goes, I have never heard of a single Annuitant from this Province being elected, nor do I think we have ever had one at the Croydon Homes, which have had their day, and in my opinion should be disposed of, and the capital added to our funds. The amount placed in the last balance sheet £7,000 must be an exceedingly conservative one, as an asset of the Croydon Homes; but whatever the value of the Homes, the time has come when the Board should make up their mind to dispose with them.

The cost of £10,000 mentioned in the circular should be divided under each head — say £8,000 for office expenses and £1,500 for the upkeep of the Homes, or whatever the correct figures are; as phrased it is too ambitious. It was only the other night at a banquet a Brother in his speech said that the cost of the Homes amounted to £10,000 per annum, and there is little wonder, as the paragraph is worded, at his statement.

The last cannot continue to fritter away £1,500 a year for sentimental reasons. With the state of the Funds as they are at present one thing is certain — either the number of applicants must be cut down or the grants reduced (and I should deplore to see this to our present Annuitants), or the age limit increased. The funds of the Institution are not in a position to stand an annual expenditure of £160,000.

With the calls of the other two Institutions and the Hospital, the Board of Management cannot expect Festivals to average £130,000 a year. It is too much to expect the Craft to do.

Yours faithfully and fraternally

F. W. Laughton PGD

Provincial Grand Secretary North and East Yorkshire.

The House and Finance Committees were, of course, conscious of the arguments. They therefore took the unusual step of inviting representatives from all the Provinces to solicit their opinions, and as a consequence they came to a conclusion that could potentially save £30,000 by raising the age limit for candidates from 60 years to 65 years.

The next Festival was held by one of the country's largest Provinces, Essex, and although just over £110,000 was raised, it was still insufficient to cover the required sum. Good news came when it was announced in 1939 that the Grand Master, HRH the Duke of Kent, would not only accept the Presidency of the RMBI but had also agreed to become the President of its next Festival.

That autumn, Germany invaded Poland and, on Sunday 3rd September, Great Britain found itself, for the second time in the 20th century, involved in a global war.

ABOVE **Duchess of York at home 1931.** *Royal Masonic Benevolent Institute*

CHAPTER 12
WAR AND PEACE

The British had delivered their ultimatum to the German Government at 9am on 3rd September 1939, to which they received no response within the designated time. Great Britain and her Empire were again at war with Germany.

Since May 1924 a sub-committee of the Imperial Defence Committee had been set up to study the effects of aerial bombardment on Great Britain. The conclusions were grossly misleading, as the total size of the German bomber force was exaggerated and its effects on cities such as London were based largely on events during the Spanish Civil War. Experts assumed that for every ton of bombs dropped there would be 50 casualties, and it was assumed that the enemy had the capacity and potential to drop 100,000 tons within 14 days of the declaration of war; however, this figure was never achieved.

Air-raid precautions were immediately introduced as soon as war was declared. Gas masks were issued and blackout imposed. Plans for the evacuation of children from London were immediately set into motion and all places of entertainment were closed. Schools were to remain empty until November.

Within a week Grand Lodge asked members not to attend the Quarterly Communications to prevent large numbers congregating in one space. Instead, a small number of Grand Officers assembled for an informal meeting to cover any urgent business. The Assistant Grand Master addressed the meeting:

> Brethren, We are meeting this evening in circumstances which I think are unprecedented in the history of the Craft, and it has been necessary to take the grave step of issuing a circular to the members of Grand Lodge concerning this meeting ... Many of us remember what Masonry meant in the last war, not only to our Brethren but to those from the Empire who were in this country. It is a little early to consider the problems which vary so much all over the country, but in the meantime we know

> that Masons in their individual capacity will give that support to their King and Country in accordance with their Masonic Duty.

It was also suggested that private Lodges followed suit.

The absence of hostilities became known as the phoney war, and soon life returned to virtual normality. The RMBI originally decided to cancel the Annual Festival for 1940, but as nothing seemed to be happening it was agreed to hold the event. Subsequently, Festivals were held throughout the war, although in a somewhat limited format. In 1940, Masonic and morning dress were worn, but the usual concert after the formal proceedings was cancelled.

The Home, situated in the southern suburbs of Croydon, was on the direct flightpath for the centre of London and near to three important fighter stations — Biggin Hill, Kenley and Croydon Airport —and was potentially liable to be damaged. On the evening of 15th August, bombers from *Erprobungs Gruppe 210*, based in the Pas-de-Calais, attacked Croydon Airport, producing columns of black smoke that drifted across the town. A number of these bombers and their fighter escorts were shot down on their return flight. This was the first of a series of attacks, but others would soon follow. Fortunately the Home, although adjacent to a railway line, escaped damage.

The Secretary, Major Adams, was immediately recalled to the colours and posted to the War Office with the rank of Colonel, and there he remained until 1944. In his absence the Chief Clerk, Bro W. Dance, was appointed as Assistant Secretary and was responsible for much of the administration. He did a great deal to make the wartime Festivals the success they were.

Just prior to the outbreak of war, King George VI installed his younger brother, the Duke of Kent, as the Grand Master. The Duke of Kent had been initiated into the Navy Lodge No 3612 in 1928 and was appointed Senior Grand Warden at the Masonic War Memorial meeting held at the Royal Albert Hall in 1933. He had agreed to chair the Festival the year he

was made Grand Master, but circumstances of state prevented this from happening. This was fortuitous, for now he could preside over the Centennial Festival.

It was agreed in 1941 that, due to the current difficulties, certificates should be issued rather than Festival jewels. These would be replaced at the end of hostilities with an appropriate metal medal.

The Centennial Festival for the RMBI was held on 25th February 1942, and, despite the circumstances, it proved to be a splendid evening even though restricted to men. The Brethren met at the Grand Hall of the Connaught Rooms in Great Queen Street. The MW Grand Master, HRH the Duke of Kent, occupied the chair assisted by RW Bro Lt-Col Sir Francis J. Davies, the Deputy GM, and the Assistant Grand Master, Brig-Gen W. H. V. Darrell. The Duke of Kent addressed those present:

RW Deputy Grand Master and Brethren,
I am very grateful to you, Deputy Grand Master, for the kindly terms in which you have proposed my health, and to you, my Brethren, for the warm welcome you have given me.

ABOVE LEFT **Lord Cornwallis.** *Cecil Barton and The Kent Museum of Freemasonry*

ABOVE **HRH George Duke of Kent in a painting by S. Elwes.** *Library and Museum of Freemasonry*

BELOW **HRH Princess Mary, the Princess Royal, Dowager Duchess of Harewood arriving at Harewood Court.** *Royal Masonic Benevolent Institute*

The Craft has recently suffered a great loss by the death of our late Grand Master. The Duke of Connaught had a deep affection for Freemasonry and followed its activities very closely. He was much interested in this Festival and would have been eager to hear the results. We have lost a great leader, but his example will ever remain with us.

When I accepted the Chairmanship of this Festival some years ago, I was looking forward to this occasion as one of my first engagements after my return from Australia, where I was then expecting to take up the position of Governor-General.

There is no need for me to tell you why those plans were changed, as the reason for the alteration has affected all our lives.

I am pleased, however, that nothing has occurred to prevent me from fulfilling my promise and I am happy to be among you.

We are today celebrating the One Hundredth Anniversary of this wonderful Institution.

I have not attempted to ascertain how much has been expended during those hundred years on the purpose for which the Institution was founded, but when I remind you that during the first year, five annuities of £10 a year were granted, whereas today more than 2,600 Brethren and Widows are receiving assistance at an annual cost of £140,000 you will appreciate what has grown from the sowing of those first seeds.

It is understandable that we as Freemasons are proud of our great institutions, which are admired the world over, but let it not be thought that Freemasonry is primarily an organisation for charitable purposes.

Grand Lodge had been in existence for half a century before the first of those Institutions was founded, and as the Craft expanded it would have failed in part of its principles if it had not taken under its care those of its own who needed a helping hand.

And so we have had handed on to us the duty of carrying forward the work which our forebears so naturally and wisely commenced.

And we are particularly concerned today with those to whom life has not been too kind.

Everyone has respect for the aged, and when declining years are accompanied by misfortune our sympathies are aroused.

It is difficult for those in more affluent circumstances to realise exactly what our annuities mean to those who receive them.

While the amount of our grant cannot, particularly in these days, provide any degree of luxury, it does make just that difference between penury and a feeling of independence.

Yesterday, my wife and I spent a very happy afternoon at Croydon and we enjoyed the opportunity of having a few words with every one of the residents.

I could not help thinking how inappropriate the original name of the Institution at Croydon would have been today. It started life as 'The Asylum for Worthy and Decayed Freemasons', but fortunately it was changed to 'The Home for the Royal Masonic Benevolent Institution'. Those whom we met there were undoubtedly 'worthy' but I can assure you they were by no means 'decayed'.

A more cheerful and happy band of people it would be difficult to find, and I am certain every visitor must realise how justified the Institution is in asking for its support, though the Homes are only a small part of its work.

The last four years have shown a net deficit of £40,000 on the accounts of the Institution — that is a large sum to make up.

You have heard the results of this Festival. As President of this Institution, a position which I am proud to hold, and as your Chairman today, I wish to thank you all, everyone who has contributed, for the truly remarkable response which has been given to the appeal.

Anyone who is concerned with the maintenance of a voluntary Institution in these days must have many anxious moments, as money is needed in every direction and must be found, and there is little to spare for objects which in normal times we like to support.

But that anxiety is removed for this year and our Committee can go forward with lighter hearts.

It has, of course, meant labour and while we appreciate to the full the work of the Charity Stewards and Almoners of the Lodges, the Charity Associations and the numerous Brethren who have worked unceasingly for today's success, I know you would wish me to add a word of thanks to Colonel Adams's staff under the leadership of Bro Dance, who, in his Principal's absence on War Service, has borne a heavy load.

As you have heard, this Festival has been supported by Brethren in all parts of the world, including countries which are, at this moment, suffering under the heel of the invader. May their restoration be speedily accomplished.

ABOVE **HRH Princess Mary, the Princess Royal, accompanied by Sir James Stubbs at the opening of Harewood Court.** *Royal Masonic Benevolent Institute*

ABOVE **J. M. S. Coates, PGM Northumberland, laying the foundation stone at Scarborough Court.** *Royal Masonic Benevolent Institute*

Brethren, as your Chairman, and as your Grand Master, I want to thank you most cordially for your support. I shall long remember this happy occasion.

Before I resume my seat, I wish to propose, just formally, but very sincerely, the Sister Institutions.

It is our usual custom to do this and we do not want to break it as it is the one occasion when, in wishing them successful Festivals, we recognise the complete harmony which exists between us in carrying out our respective parts of the common duty.

The meeting concluded with the list of donations, which made a grand total of £96,501. There was a great cheer when the sum received from a Lodge of refugees from the Channel Islands was announced. To celebrate the Centenary each annuitant received a gift of £10.

Later that year, on 25th August 1942, Prince George, Duke of Kent, was killed. He had taken off in an RAF Short Sunderland flying boat from Scotland heading towards Iceland when the aircraft crashed into a hillside killing all but one crew member. The Duke was first buried in St George's Chapel, Windsor, but later his body was exhumed and reburied at the royal burial ground at Frogmore. The Rt Hon Earl of Harewood was asked to be the acting Grand Master and as a consequence he resigned his post as Treasurer of the RMBI. On 12th December, the Earl was confirmed as the Grand Master and was later invested at the Royal Albert Hall

in the presence of the King on 1st June 1943.

The Province of Sussex put in a tremendous effort for the 1943 Festival. The luncheon, chaired by their PGM, Major Lawrence Thornton, was attended by 400 from that county, and to commemorate the occasion each received a cardboard Steward's badge. The Province raised over £42,000 as part of a national total of nearly £97,000.

The new Treasurer, Lord Cornwallis, was elected at the 1943 AGM and his deputy was John E. C. Stubbs, a patron of the charity and a PGD. Wykeham Stanley Cornwallis, the 2nd Lord Cornwallis, was born in 1892 at Linton in Kent, the second son of Fiennes Cornwallis, who had presided over the 1920 RMBI Festival. He had a privileged upbringing, being educated at Eton and at the Royal Military Academy at Sandhurst, and was commissioned into the Royal Scots Guards with the rank of Captain. During the First World War he was wounded, Mentioned in Despatches and awarded the Military Cross.

RW Bro Reginald P. St John Charles, PGM South Wales, supervised the next Festival. The phoney war had long since passed and the country was now enduring frequent nightly attacks. Large parts of London, especially around the City, docklands and the major railway hubs, had been seriously damaged by continual nightly bombings, but worse was to come when, on 22nd June 1944, a flying bomb crashed into Drury Lane a few hundred yards from Freemasons' Hall, blowing out some 1,045 panes of glass in 252 windows, and on 25th January 1945 some 22 incendiary bombs fell on the roof and in the courtyard of Freemasons' Hall. Thankfully, all were extinguished.

In December 1943, it was agreed that the safest measure was to have the next Festival in the City Hall in Cardiff. On 25th February 1944, at 2.30pm, a large body assembled wearing their plastic jewel in the Great Hall of Cardiff's fine

City Hall to hear announced the second highest total ever achieved — over £136,000. Spontaneous applause and loud cheers broke out, followed by several renditions of *For He's a Jolly Good Fellow* and then the rousing chorus of *Land of My Fathers* echoed around the Great Hall. The ladies were admitted and listened to a concert given by Bro William Mortimer and his orchestra. The Assistant Secretary, Bro Dance, was teased for his unsuccessful attempts to pronounce the various Welsh names. The concert and speeches over, the PGM and his guests retired to the Masonic Hall in Guildford Street to partake of the best high tea that rationing would allow.

John Wilkins, the Chairman in 1944, pointed out that the rooms leased at 20 Great Queen Street were quite inadequate. W Bro Lance Hall, a solicitor who had been specifically invited because of his expertise, was of the opinion that the charity had the power to purchase a site and build offices thereon. John Stubbs pointed out that there were sites in Great Queen Street that could be purchased, and all agreed that this should be investigated. Throughout that year Grand Lodge endeavoured unsuccessfully to purchase land, but eventually, some two years later, the Institution leased four floors of 19-21 Great Queen Street from Grand Lodge. A few years later, the whole building was purchased.

In 1944, an attempt was made to modernise the name of the charity. Initially called the Home for Worthy and Decayed Freemasons, it had become known as the Royal Masonic Benevolent Institution when the former united with the Royal Masonic Benevolent Annuity Fund in 1850. Now the name was felt to be outdated and the Royal Masonic Fellowship was suggested, but this also was thought unsuitable. Finally, with no agreement, the name remained unchanged.

Just weeks before the end of the war in 1945, the 103rd Festival returned to the Connaught Rooms. It was held under the auspices of the Province of Suffolk, and raised over £97,000.

The war in Europe ended officially on 8th May, and Victory over Japan (VJ Day) came on 15th August 1945. Both events were celebrated by the nation and each annuitant was given £5 to commemorate the victory. Colonel Adams returned in the December of 1944, and his hard-working Assistant, W. H. Dance, PAGSt B, who had done so much to keep the Institution running during the war years, retired in March 1946.

Churchill had declared, back in 1940:

Hitler knows that he will have to break us in this Island

or lose the war. If we can stand up to him, all Europe may be free and the life of the world may move forward into broad, sunlit uplands.

Hitler had failed, but the devastation caused was enormous. The cost of the war would take many years to pay back, but at this moment the country enjoyed its sunlit uplands and celebrated with the largest birth rate in its history; a generation of 'baby boomers' was born, which again one day would have repercussions for Masonic charities.

A large part of the country's wealth had been consumed in winning the war and vast areas of its cities had been laid to waste. The structural damage to the houses that survived, combined with the troops returning home for demobilisation, created a housing crisis — 170,000 houses had been destroyed in London alone, and an additional 700,000 were damaged. There was one dominating question: How to house the population?

At a meeting held in Freemasons' Hall in 1946, T. Lidstone-Found suggested that the charity could open Homes on a paying basis, specifically for Freemasons and their widows, who, due to current housing difficulties, might be in need of accommodation. He reasoned that such a scheme would be open to any Freemason who could afford to pay between 30s (£1.50) and £3 per week, and gave a number of examples of Homes run on these lines. It was well known that the Province of Lancashire was contemplating such a system, and he proposed the cost per head need not exceed 35s (£1.75). More importantly, these Homes could be situated all over the country. The RMBI questioned the legality, for although it found the scheme attractive it was dealing with monies that had been given for a specific purpose and Charity Law was quite specific that it could not be used for alternative projects. The Finance Committee was tasked with a feasibility study and to report back if it was achievable; only then would it be presented to the Grand Master for approval. By the spring of 1946 the Committee came back:

Your Sub Committee have taken Counsel's opinion and report that under the existing Rules and Regulations it is not possible to allocate the present monies subscribed to the Institution to provide Hostels accommodating Brethren and Widows able to contribute the full cost of their upkeep.

There is, however, scope for extending and altering the existing Homes. There will be a number of Annuitants whom the scheme sought to benefit, who will be eligible in view of the increased financial limit which is proposed by the Finance Committee shortly.

If this report is accepted, the Sub Committee are prepared to go into the matter and make further report at a later date.

A further statement was presented by John Stubbs, the Chairman of this Sub-Committee, that:

At the earliest possible moment the RMBI building at Croydon be demolished and a new building erected on the same site to accommodate 100 residents and staff.

The scheme envisages the establishment of one or two bedrooms, dining-sitting room, bathroom, kitchen etc. There will also be a sick-bay with a qualified nurse. Rent and rates will be free and electric light and central heating will be provided. The Finance Committee and House Committee be appointed to carry out the scheme.

The Home in Croydon was nearly 100 years old. It had been designed as Victorian alms-houses, which in this post-war era was deemed old-fashioned and generally outmoded. The logical solution was to demolish it and build a modern structure. However, another member of the Committee, L. W. Lewis, argued that they should not be limited to a rebuild in Croydon if an alternative site was thought more appropriate. The cost of the project was estimated at around £200,000 with an annual outlay of £10,000.

The Marquess of Zetland, PGM for Yorkshire (North and East Ridings), held the first peacetime Festival and raised a record sum of £142,000, his own Province contributing just over £40,000. This spectacular sum improved the balance sheet, which in turn would support the RMBI's housing development plans.

Specifications for the new Home were enthusiastically drawn up. A site of at least five acres was thought an ideal size. It should not be hilly, must be reasonably clear of fog and be no more than a quarter of a mile from shops and a cinema. Ideally it should be within 20 miles of central London. It was accepted that the Home should be suitable for a range of old folk, some of whom might require constant attention.

Three potential sites were quickly found, all located in the Brighton area. The President of the Board of General Purposes, Sir Ernest Cooper, was invited to join the committee members when they went to inspect them, and they adjourned to the nearby home of one of the members, W. F. Blay, at 6 Eaton Gardens, to make their decision. All were agreed that the ideal site was Melrose Hall, Wilbury

Road, Hove, currently priced at £18,000.

A Building Committee was formed early in 1947 and a local architectural company, Messrs Denman & Sons of Queens Road, Brighton, was instructed to draw up plans, Messrs Gardiner & Theobald being commissioned to act as quantity surveyors. The architect, J. L. Denman, a well-known Freemason, soon presented a set of plans for consideration by the Building Committee, who were so impressed with the designs that they were immediately accepted. The new building would be called Harewood Court, in honour of the Grand Master.

The Bishop of Crediton, the PGM for Devonshire, presided over the 1947 Festival, which raised over £187,000. Colonel Adams thought this an appropriate time to announce that the charity was in the process of purchasing a plot of land sufficient to build a new Home in Hove, which was enthusiastically received. However, the announcement proved a little premature, for later that year it became evident that Melrose House was not suitable. It would take another two years before an appropriate site, at 11 The Drive, Hove, could be purchased, ironically adjoining the previous plot. Planning permission was sought and finally approved in 1953.

In the midst of these negotiations, the 64-year-old Grand Master, the Earl of Harewood, died on 24th May 1947. His successor would be His Grace the Duke of Devonshire, who was invested at the Royal Albert Hall the following year.

Having taken the momentous decision to move to Hove, they began to explore avenues into the field of convalescent and rest homes. However, these schemes were firmly licensed by the newly formed National Health Service and at this time it was felt that it would be inappropriate to proceed into potentially difficult territory.

The editorial of the Christmas edition of *The Freemasons' Chronicle* was invariably penned by a Masonic Anglican Priest, who gave the customary yuletide message along with a brief résumé of the Masonic charities. In the 1949 edition was an artist's impression of Harewood Court, with a brief explanation:

It may be recalled that with the view to providing accommodation for annuitants unable to live in homes of their own, the fine block of 104 modern flats, shown in the illustration, is to be built at Hove, Sussex, close to the sea, as soon as building operations can be licensed, but no appeal for its erection is made additionally to the Craft on this account. In increasing measures, on the hand, is its generous support urged for the maintenance of the annuities to the aged beneficiaries numbering some 2,000 on the register. With rising costs, the expenditure for the current year is estimated at approximately £12,000, towards which £40,000 can be derived from investments, leaving a balance of £80,000 to be found through the generosity of Lodges and Brethren, if accounts are to be balanced. The 108th Annual Festival is to be held in London on Thursday 23rd February, and take the form of a luncheon. The fact that the Chairman on this occasion is to be RW Lord Cornwallis, KBE, MC, Provincial Grand Master for Kent, a most deservedly popular figure in Freemasonry, offers additional appeal for support by reason of his being the Treasurer and a Trustee of the Institution.

In the summer of 1950, John Edward Charles Stubbs died in Hove. He had been, for three years, the Chairman of the Committee planning the new Home and had played an active role within the RMBI since 1919, joining the Finance Committee in 1924. John Stubbs had been born in Bermondsey in London in 1874, the son of a seaman, and grew up around in the docks, eventually becoming a master stevedore. He gained his admission by redemption to the Freedom of the City of London by way of the Worshipful Company of Fruiterers. He was succeeded as Chairman by W. F. Blay, and James A. Terry became his deputy.

The year 1950 also brought the sad and sudden news of the death of the Duke of Devonshire. Edward William Spencer Cavendish was born in 1895 and inherited his father's title in 1938, becoming the 10th Duke. He had fought in the Dardanelles Campaign of 1915 and then spent the remainder of the war in Military Intelligence in France, ultimately witnessing the signing of the Treaty of Versailles in 1919. During the Second World War he was appointed as the Parliamentary Under Secretary of State for India and Burma from 1940 until 1942, and then for the Colonies from 1942 to 1945. His death was recorded as a heart attack whilst staying at Eastbourne, but in recent years suspicion has been drawn to his physician, Dr John Bodkin Adams. Dr Adams was later convicted of fraud, but many believe he was a notorious serial killer, estimated to have murdered up to 160 individuals who died under his care.

In 1952, James A. Terry was appointed Chairman of the Board of Management, and his deputy was Lt-Col W. O. Davies. James Terry's first announcement was to confirm the granting of the licence enabling them to proceed with the planning of the foundations and the ground floor flats. Just before the Coronation of Queen Elizabeth II in June 1953,

the Charity Commission approved the sale of the Home at Croydon.

Now the way was clear to begin building the new Home. Nine well-known builders were invited to tender for the job, which was awarded to a firm of well-respected builders founded by William Willett. Willett himself had died of influenza in 1915, but was noted for the leading role he had played in supporting the introduction of British Summer Time. Building started immediately, and by Christmas all the steelwork for the eastern section had been erected. The architectural plans for the central and west wings were approved by February 1954. In the original design the central wing was thought strong enough to support the communal dining room on the first floor, but the architect, having assessed the difficulties, now considered it more appropriate to move it to the ground floor in the proximity of the sitting rooms. A further recommendation placed the Electricity Board's transformer substation in the basement. By July the bell and fire-alarm systems were approved, and two laundries containing three washing machines were fitted in the east and west wings. The Coronation had highlighted the importance of television, and Central Rediffusion was engaged to install an aerial on the roof with connections to the main sitting room and to each apartment.

The first part of the building had now been completed and, in July 1955, 26 residents, accompanied by the Matron, Mrs A. L. Diggins, moved from the Home in Croydon to Harewood Court. Each flat, with the exception of those on the ground floor, had a glass-enclosed balcony. The kitchens were fitted with an up-to-date cooking range and a refrigerator, now considered an essential item in this new Elizabethan age. There was a comfortable sitting room and next to the mantelpiece was a Radio Diffusion Bakelite switch allowing access to the BBC Light, Home and Third piped radio programmes. The bedroom was furnished with a built-in dressing table and fitted cupboards, whilst the bathroom was equipped with grip handles to assist the elderly. James Terry commented at the Festival of 1956 that these new flats would serve as a shop window for the works carried out by the charity. He also emphasised that the Home was only part of its function; the Institution still supported 1,900 annuitants, which needed £200,000 per annum. He assured those present that 18s in every pound was devoted to the benefits granted by the Institution to its annuitants.

The RMBI now began advertising the vacant flats and assessing the many applications requesting accommodation. An unexpected gift of bedding, sheets and linen arrived from the Royal Masonic Hospital and much of the furnishings were provided by Mark Grand Lodge to commemorate its centenary. The Grand Master, the Earl of Scarborough, was delighted to open the Central Hall, now named The Scarborough Hall in his honour, in February 1956.

With the second phase of the building nearing completion, it was now appropriate to plan the gardens. The grass turf was laid in early 1956 and as a consequence Colonel Adams was instructed to purchase an Abco motor mower. W Bro Turton offered to purchase a teak seat for the garden, and James Terry and Cecil Adams each consented to purchase a tree. The fountain was given by the architect, J. Denman, and John Hart supplied the hedges and rose gardens. Everything looked in order for the customary visit of that year's Festival Chairman, W. Proctor-Smith, the Provincial Grand Master of Cheshire. During this visit he was delighted to present to the old folk a television for the newly named Adams Room.

The following day Proctor-Smith commented:

No reply could be complete without the grateful reference to the Staff at the Homes, and first to the Matron, and her two Assistants. She is regarded in turn by the residents as an angel and a magician, and she well deserves their affection for she does great work. There is the Doctor, too, who devotes much time, care and patience to the old folks and their ailments. Also the Office Staff of the Institution need to be remembered for the ever helpful part they play, not least the Secretary, W Bro Colonel Cecil Adams, for his constant interest. It is learnt that both himself and Mrs Adams are shortly to enter the Royal Masonic Hospital, for surgical attention, and the best wishes of all accompany them for the success of their treatment, happily not of very serious character.

The now vacated old Home at Croydon, built and opened with so much love, pomp and pride, now closed with barely a mention in the Masonic world. Bought by Croydon Corporation, who renamed it Davidson Lodge, it continues to this day as alms-houses for the local population.

CHAPTER 13

NOBODY COMES TO THE HOMES TO DIE BUT TO LIVE

In 1959, the charity was confronted with a pleasant dilemma. An anonymous benefactor wished to donate £50,000, provided there was some tangible reference to his late wife, Edith, and his current wife, Elsie. However, it had previously been agreed that no matter how generous the donation, a benefactor could not dictate the name of any part of a Home. This gift inevitably reopened the question of Homes for fee-paying Freemasons. James A. Terry reminded them that according to the lawyers when the subject was last raised this remained outside the current rules. Nevertheless they asked John Stubbs, the Grand Secretary, if the gift could be redirected through Grand Lodge, thereby circumnavigating the problem, but Stubbs thought this unlikely.

In the meantime, Stevens confirmed that the property next door to Harewood Court was vacant and could be purchased to erect a small nursing home; rooms could be then named 'Edith' and 'Elsie'. After considerable discussion it was proposed:

That the offer of an Anonymous Donor to give a sum to total approximately £50,000 for an additional Home for Annuitants be accepted with grateful thanks; such Home to be at Bexhill if possible, and to be known as the Edith and Elsie Home; and to be used for the reception, without payment, of Annuitants who are in need, temporarily or permanently, of more medical and nursing attention than can be provided either at their own homes or in Harewood Court. If for any reason it proves impracticable to find or to build or to equip such a Home, the Brethren present recommend that either two wings, or other parts of Harewood Court, be named as Edith and Elsie. It is also recommended that the Donor be granted the right to nominate a properly qualified Annuitant.

This seemed to satisfy all parties.

In the June, Colonel Cecil Adams, the longest-serving Secretary, announced his retirement. It was agreed that his replacement should be an installed Master Mason aged over 50 years, and once appointed he would shadow Adams until the latter finally retired. He was to receive a salary of £1,750 per annum. They interviewed nine candidates before offering the post to J. D. E. Barnard, but he could not commence work for some time and had to decline the post. Sqn-Ldr D. A. Lloyd was then offered the position and he accepted. Colonel Adams duly retired in March 1961, but sadly he died in Putney Hospital just two years after retiring, on 20th April 1963.

David Alun Lloyd had been a navigator in the RAF Volunteer Reserve and, whilst attached to No 139 Squadron equipped with Mosquito aircraft in 1944, was awarded the Distinguished Flying Cross to add to his Distinguished Flying Medal. The citation reads:

Flying Officer David Alun Lloyd, DFM (128538), Royal Air Force Volunteer Reserve No 139 Squadron. As pilot and navigator respectively these officers have completed a large number of sorties, including attacks on such well-defended targets as Berlin, Hamburg and centres of the Ruhr area. They have invariably displayed great skill, courage, and resolution, qualities that were well in evidence during a recent sortie against the German capital. Whilst over the North Sea a severe storm was encountered but Flight Lieutenant Holloway flew through it and on to the enemy coast. Whilst over the target the aircraft was hit by shrapnel and one engine was rendered useless. Nevertheless Flight Lieutenant Holloway flew the damaged aircraft to a home-based airfield. On the return flight, Flying Officer Lloyd, although deprived of the use of some of his instruments, navigated the aircraft with his usual skill and initiative. This is the second occasion within recent weeks in which they completed their mission with one engine out of action. Their achievements have been worthy of much praise.

LEFT **Right Honourable Henry George Charles Lascelles (1882–1947), 6th Earl of Harewood, from a painting by William Nicholson**. *Library and Museum of Freemasonry*

ABOVE **Harewood Court, Hove 1970.** *Royal Masonic Benevolent Institute*

possibility that the charity could change its rules to admit fee-paying Freemasons. Both the lawyers and the Charity Commission could find no objection to the scheme, provided the rules were correctly modified. This now opened the way for future development. Fortuitously a long-standing Freemason generously donated £100,000 for a new Home in Northumberland, but this created two urgent problems that would have to be resolved. The first was to reorganise the administrative staff, to cope with the increased workload that would be generated as a consequence of the plans for expansion; the other was to form a General Purposes Committee, to supervise the individual building projects as

The entertainment in the new Home at Hove was now supported by new Lodges in the area as well as old friends like the Lodge of Tranquillity and the Playgoers Lodge. The Brighton Masonic Club organised a number of visits to the theatre, and in July 1960 arranged for a coach trip to visit the South Downs, the residents enjoying a high tea at the village of Patcham.

In 1961, Norman Lancelot Hall CBE, a solicitor, fully aware of the wish to build Homes in other parts of the country, questioned the validity of the advice previously given by lawyers back in 1946. The Secretary as a consequence began consulting various legal firms on the

RIGHT **Harewood Court, Hove 1970.** *Royal Masonic Benevolent Institute*

125

LEFT **Squadron Leader David Alun Lloyd, Secretary of the RMBI.** *Royal Masonic Benevolent Institute*

ABOVE **HM the Queen Mother at the opening of Devonshire Court, Leicestershire.** *Royal Masonic Benevolent Institute*

they developed. The Secretary was asked to co-operate with the PGM of Northumberland in selecting a suitable site in the vicinity and then seek the assistance of the Royal Institute of British Architects on likely local architects to design the Homes both in Newcastle and potentially in the Midlands. James A. Terry, as a final gesture at this important meeting, presented the RMBI with a silver cigar box to commemorate his 25-year membership of the House Committee.

The Secretary soon located two sites, one near Newcastle and the other close to Leicester. In the New Year, the Chairman, V. A. Elgood, together with some of his Committee, visited Newcastle to meet Bro William Leech, the Planning Officer for Northumberland County Council, accompanied by G. D. Shields, the Provincial Grand Secretary. They were driven to Cramlington, a suburb on the outskirts of the city, and there William Leech offered to donate a 4½-acre site adjacent to a dual carriageway, which was gratefully accepted, and strongly recommended that his planning consultant, Mr Elphick, be appointed as the project's architect. David Lloyd was then instructed to communicate their intentions to the local PGMs and request that they nominate suitable Brethren to form a local Building Committee. Mr Elphick went to London on 29th May 1963 with his plans, and, with minor modifications, they were accepted. Interestingly the central heating had been designed to use oil but could easily be converted to natural gas as a consequence of the newly discovered gas and oil fields in the North Sea. Another novel design enabled the residents to communicate with staff by a two-way call system. Almost as an afterthought they included a Chapel of Rest, as it was inevitable with the age of the residents that it would be an essential requirement.

W Bro Haird was appointed to be the architect for the Home in Leicester.

The Secretary now turned his attention towards a 2½-acre site at Holme Chase, near Chislehurst in Kent, which was purchased for £35,000. The architect chosen was Bro J. Greenwood and his first task was to organise the demolition of the current buildings on the site. His brief was to include in the final drawings a plan for an additional 10 flats or bungalows for the more independent residents.

In no time at all, the organisation had three building projects up and running. The Secretary's next task was to plan the various celebratory milestones — the turning of the first sod, the foundation stone, and the final opening. At the

ABOVE **Devonshire Court, Leicestershire.** *Royal Masonic Benevolent Institute*

Home in Leicester the first sod would be cut by 15th June 1964, followed by the stone-laying ceremony during September and the completion around December 1965; hopefully attended by a member of the Royal Family. It was agreed that in the absence of a Royal, the Grand Master would conduct the ceremony.

However, the Cramlington project was now experiencing difficulties. The Secretary had repeatedly written to the architect but seemed to have made little progress in persuading him to conform to their ideas, and the project was now beginning to fall behind schedule. This was not helped by the sudden escalation in the cost of local labour due to redevelopment of large parts of Newcastle. The charity agreed to pay an additional £3,000 to alleviate this labour crisis. Devonshire Court, as the Home in Leicester would be called, was now likely to be completed first, and the foundation stone was laid by the Grand Master on 20th May 1965.

RW Assistant Grand Master Maj-Gen Allan Adair laid the foundation stone at Cramlington on 1st October. It was a cold, damp autumn day after weeks of incessant rain, so a marquee had been erected to shield the guests and the site was floodlit. After inspecting the building site Maj-Gen Adair requested that the foundation stone be raised. Then adjusting the stone and striking it four times with the Maul, he stated:

> *With temperance, fortitude, prudence, and justice let our work be founded.*

Taking the Plumb Rule, he proved the stone to be vertical at

90°, then with the Level he proved the stone horizontal, and finally striking the stone three more times with the Maul he declared:

> *By virtue of the power in me vested and in the name of the Great Architect of the Universe, I declare this stone well and truly laid. With the implements of our Craft, may there be raised a superstructure, perfect in all its parts and honourable to the builder.*

The ceremony concluded with the singing of the hymn *O God, Our Help in Ages Past* followed by prayers. A banquet was later held at High Gosforth Park, in Newcastle upon Tyne. The Home would be known as Scarborough Court.

Princess Marina, the widow of the late Grand Master, was invited to open the Home in Chislehurst, and she requested that it should be named Prince George Duke of Kent Court, after her husband. The stone-laying ceremony was performed by Lord Cornwallis on 19th April, after which David Lloyd presented him with the building plans, and Lord Cornwallis commented that both he and the late Duke of Kent had been close friends. A cavity had been made in the wall beneath the foundation stone to deposit a canister containing coins, stamps and papers of the time. This ceremony also ended with the customary rendition of *O God, Our Help in Ages Past* before the group adjourned for lunch at Crown Woods School in Eltham. Lord Cornwallis was presented with a rose bowl as a memento of the day.

Devonshire Court was officially opened on 2nd November 1966 by Her Majesty the Queen Mother. She was greeted by Colonel R. A. St G. Martin OBE, the Lord Lieutenant of Leicestershire. The Grand Master, the Rt Hon Earl of Scarborough, in his welcoming speech reminded Her Majesty of her visit to the Home in Croydon back in 1931. He informed her that this was the first completed Home, with three others under construction, and that these projects were now so popular that he would not be surprised if others were to follow. In her response, Her Majesty stated:

> *I remember very well my visit to your Home in Croydon many years ago, and how much I was impressed by the spirit of cheerfulness amongst residents and staff. The King, when Duke of York, was keenly interested in Freemasonry and often spoke of the wonderful charitable work which the Institution did for many people all over the world. In Devonshire Court we have evidence of the enterprise of the Institution and of the wise humanity of a scheme which combines privacy, so*

precious to the elderly, with arrangements for communal feeding and recreation. These will provide a feeling of security and dispel loneliness which darkens the lives of so many old people in the busy modern world. Thanks to the miracles of modern medicine, the expectation of a long and useful life increases steadily. In itself this is a great blessing, but it also creates problems, problems which the old should not be asked to face alone, and which a home like this can help to solve. I pray that all those who live in these pleasant surroundings will find here a real home and true peace in the evening of their lives.

Finally, James A. Terry thanked Her Majesty and presented her with a desk bell inscribed 'R.M.B.I., Devonshire Court, 2nd November 1966'.

Within a few months, HRH Princess Alexandra of Kent had opened Scarborough Court, and her brother, the Duke of Kent, opened the Prince George Duke of Kent Home on 24th July 1968. The Earl of Scarborough greeted his successor, the new Grand Master, as he descended from the helicopter. Princess Marina should have opened the Home but had suddenly been taken ill, and the Duke had stepped in at the last moment.

The predictions of the Earl of Scarborough were now coming to fruition. The Home at York, Connaught Court, was nearly finished, and Harewood Court's additional wing was also near to completion. Two further Homes were in the pipeline: one at Sindlesham, a small village in Berkshire, and the other in Porthcawl. The Berkshire stone-laying ceremony was performed by Lord Harris in September 1970, James A. Terry reminding those present of the events that had led to this Home:

It is an important occasion, as it marks, and I use that word advisedly, the close and practicable co-operation of two great branches of Freemasonry. The building of the Home at Sindlesham has been made possible by the happy coincidence of an offer from the Grand Lodge of Mark Master Masons to contribute the sum of £500,000 towards the cost of building the Home and the desire of the Province of Berkshire, through its Masonic Hall Company, to place part of their beautiful site at Sindlesham at the disposal of the Institution.

BELOW **Devonshire Court, Leicestershire.** *Royal Masonic Benevolent Institute*

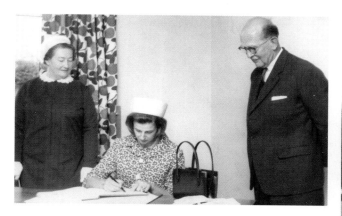

To mark the splendid gift, the Right Worshipful Brother the Rt Hon The Lord Harris, MC, VL, OSM, PJGW, Trustee of the Institution and Most Worshipful Grand Master of the Lodge of Mark Master Masons, has been asked to carry out the stone-laying ceremony. In addition, to commemorate for all time this close connection between Craft and Mark, the Home will be called 'Lord Harris Court'.

ABOVE LEFT **Princess Alexandra opening Scarborough Court, Cramlington, Northumberland.** *Royal Masonic Benevolent Institute*

ABOVE **The arrival of HRH the Duke of Kent to open the Prince George Duke of Kent Court, Chislehurst.** *Royal Masonic Benevolent Institute*

Prayers were recited by the Rev Canon Richard Tydeman, Past Grand Chaplain. The tools employed on this occasion were those previously used by Lord Cornwallis at the Prince George Duke of Kent Home. A collection taken during lunch raised the sum of £314 for the Matron's Amenity Fund.

It was a beautiful day on 21st September when James Terry invited Lord Cadogan to lay the foundation stone at Porthcawl and announced that he had just received permission from Her Majesty the Queen to name this Home Albert Edward Prince of Wales Court, and to commemorate this honour, the very tools used by Prince Albert Edward (later Edward VII) on his visit to India in 1876 were used to lay the stone. They were made of ivory with precious stones and gold wire inlay. The architect, Bro Dale Owen, presented Lord Cadogan with a silver rose bowl, and a collection was held in aid of the Matron's Amenity Fund during luncheon and raised £370, exceeding that collected at Sindlesham. This Home would take three years to complete, Lord and Lady Cadogan returning to open it officially on 24th September 1973, when James Terry presented Lady Cadogan with a patchwork cloth made by a 92-year-old annuitant. The day ended with the singing of the Welsh National Anthem, and as the official party left there was a chorus of *We'll Keep a Welcome in the Hillsides*.

The year 1977 marked the Queen's Silver Jubilee and in the January, H. J. C. Stevens, the Chairman of the Finance

and General Purposes Committee, disclosed the financial state of the Hannay Masonic Residential Trust, an organisation associated with the Province of West Lancashire. The Provincial Executive let it be known that they could no longer afford to support this Trust; neither was it feasible to create a special fund because all their efforts were now focused on the 1981 Festival on behalf of the RMBI. The RMBI, which had a large stake in Ecclesholme in Salford, was invited by the Province to be accountable for its completion, combined with the additional tasks of managing the Trust's two other Homes: The Tithebarn at Great Crosby, and Fairlawn in Lytham St Annes. The following resolution was passed:

> *It is agreed in principle that the RMBI will take over financial responsibility for the running of the Hannay Homes from the beginning of the next financial year, i.e. 1st April 1977, and as a consequence of this it will be necessary for the RMBI to exercise control over the finances and running of the Homes.*

The Tithebarn was a large, refurbished family home set in ornamental gardens. Fairlawn at Lytham St Annes would eventually be sold, whilst Ecclesholme would be opened by

HRH the Duke of Kent on 24th November 1977.

It was announced at the 130th Festival that a single donation of £100,000 had been given specifically to contribute towards a new Home at Llandudno, and to celebrate her Jubilee the Queen had approved that it should be named Queen Elizabeth Court. Noel Grout, the Assistant Secretary, organised the opening in 1979, which was performed by the Assistant Grand Master, RW the Hon Edward Baillieu, accompanied by the Mayors of Llandudno and Aberconwy. The weather in the days leading up to the opening had been appalling in Llandudno; consequently a large marquee had been erected in the grounds, but when the day finally came the conditions changed and instead of the gloom it was a beautiful sunny day. The event began with the singing of the Welsh National Anthem, and lunch had been prepared by the students of Llandrillo Technical College at Rhos-on- Sea. A total of 400 individuals had been invited for tea, although over a thousand people ultimately turned up. James Terry represented the RMBI, accompanied by Mrs J. Blandford, the Matron of Queen Elizabeth Court, accompanied by the Matrons from the charity's other Homes. Coincidentally, as the Assistant Grand Master left the marquee to tour the grounds a flight of the Red Arrows passed overhead. Despite his protestations to the contrary, many assumed that Noel Grout had organised this with the Royal Air Force. The Home is surrounded by magnificent gardens, and in 1989 won a Silver Trophy for the quality of its flowerbeds and lawns.

David Alun Lloyd officially retired as the charity's Secretary on 31st December 1978, although his last few months were spent on holiday in South Africa. On his retirement, H. C. Cottrell, the new Chairman of the General Purposes Committee, stated:

ABOVE **Prince George Duke of Kent Court, Chislehurst.** *Royal Masonic Benevolent Institute*

> *Brethren this is the end of an era; for 18 years Alun Lloyd has been the Principal Officer of the RMBI. When he arrived we had one Home at Hove and the main business of the Institution was paying annuities. It was very quickly apparent that on the one hand this did not meet all the needs; on the other hand the Craft was willing to provide support in meeting further needs. So a long-running partnership of Bros Stevens and Lloyd was established with a document which was drafted to enable us to start the Homes. The memorial in the crypt of St Paul's referring to Christopher Wren states, 'If you want to see his memorial, look around you'. If you seriously want to see Alun Lloyd's memorial, go to one of our Homes.*

Squadron-Leader David Alun Lloyd died in South Glamorgan on May 1988, aged 70.

Sadly, on 5th October 1977, James A. Terry announced the sudden death of Bro Henry John Charles Stevens, who had been Chairman of the Finance and General Purposes Committee since 1958. A Londoner, born in 1898 and known to most as Steve, he had been singled out by Colonel Adams for his financial acumen and invited to join the Finance and General Purposes Committee. He had for many years worked in Fleet Street as a chartered accountant. As its churchwarden, he had a special attachment to St Bride's Church, and on his death he bequeathed a sum of money to fund an organ scholarship. In his obituary in *The Daily Telegraph* he was described as a man of complete integrity

ABOVE **Prince George Duke of Kent Court, Chislehurst.** *Royal Masonic Benevolent Institute*

ABOVE **The Duchess of Kent at the opening of Connaught Court.** *Yorkshire Post*

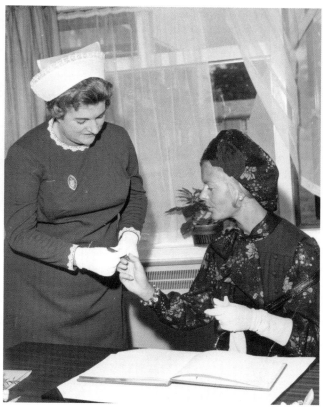

and single-mindedness. He, along with the Secretary David Alun Lloyd, had been responsible for instigating and implementing the new expansionist policies of the charity.

Over the next twenty years the demand for retirement Homes increased. Rooms in historic houses were regularly advertised in the more prestigious newspapers, and more and more mansions were coming onto the market. One such house was in Warham Road, Croydon; built between 1869 and 1870, it was originally surrounded by 18 acres, but most had been sold to a nearby school. In 1949, it was sold to a consortium from the Food & Tobacco Trade and the Licensed Victuallers Benevolent Associations for use as residential accommodation for its members, and a west wing had been added to provide additional rooms. The RMBI purchased the property in January 1977 and immediately applied for planning permission to redevelop the site. The residents occupying the Home were allowed to remain, the last passing away in April 1988. The building was then completely refurbished and designed to accommodate 60 residents and was officially opened on 23rd July 1980 by the Earl of Cadogan. It was renamed James Terry Court after the three generations who bore that name and had faithfully served the RMBI for an unbroken 116 years.

The last James Terry retired in 1980. He had been born in Weybridge in 1904, was educated at Eton and had been initiated into Apollo Lodge whilst at Oxford. This had to be performed by dispensation as he was still only 19 years of age. He was first introduced to the RMBI back in 1923 when his father, James E. Terry, had taken him to the annual New

Year's feast, sponsored by the Lodge of Tranquillity. He later recorded that his job had been to serve the Brussels sprouts. James Terry married Elizabeth May Prittie Perry in 1927. She was the daughter of an Irish stockbroker and had been born in Soochow, China, in 1903. They had four children — two boys and two girls. Having joined the House Committee in East Croydon in 1937, he became its Chairman in 1951 on the death of his father. He was appointed Past Junior Grand Warden in 1965, and afterwards received the Grand Master's Order of Service to Masonry in 1980. Following his wife's death in 1986, he eventually moved to the RMBI Home at Sindlesham where he died two and half years later, on 21st March 1996, aged 92 years. There were over a hundred relatives and friends, including two Grand Secretaries, Sir James Stubbs, and Commander Michael Higham, at his funeral. His ashes were placed in the gardens at Lord Harris Court amongst his favourite heathers.

When the Old West Suffolk Hospital at Bury St Edmunds, Suffolk, became redundant the RMBI purchased the property and engaged a local builder from Thetford, R. G. Carter, to redesign and extend the building. When completed, the stone-laying ceremony was arranged for 9th

March 1978 and performed by Lord Cornwallis, who allowed his name to be used for the new Home. The Province of Cambridgeshire donated a substantial sum for a library, to be named the Nourse Library in memory of a previous PGM. Mrs H. D. Horswill was appointed its first Matron, and the Home was opened by Lord Cadogan at 3.15pm on 18th June 1981.

Since the formation of the United Grand Lodge in 1813, the General Funds of both the Antients and Moderns had been controlled by a Board of Benevolence and Charity. In April 1974, an extensive report on the then five Masonic charities was published by Lord Justice Bagnall. It recommended that the Board of Benevolence, whose origins could be traced back to 1720, should be formed into a new charity to be known as the Grand Charity. It would now become the Central Masonic Charity, responsible for making Masonic and non-Masonic donations on behalf of the entire Craft. It was launched in 1981, thanks largely to the efforts of John Stebbings, its first President, and Sir James Stubbs, the Grand Secretary.

One of the most historic buildings ever purchased by the RMBI is situated at Branksome Dene near Bournemouth. Built in the 1840s, it has spectacular views of the Isle of Wight and a winding path leads down a leafy chine onto a sandy beach. It had once been the summer home of Lord and Lady Wimborne. Lord Wimborne, Ivor Bertie Guest, was such a snob and social climber that he was lampooned in *Vanity Fair* as 'the paying Guest'. Lady Wimborne's nephew was Winston Churchill and it was here, as a young man, that he

spent his summer holidays. Other notable inhabitants were Sir Ernest Cassel, who bequeathed it to his granddaughter Lady Edwina Mountbatten. George Arthur Dunn, the noted hatmaker, also lived here in the 1920s. Prior to the outbreak of the Second World War, it became a hotel noted for its vegetarian meals and, with the coming of peace, was purchased by the Grand Order of Israel and Shield of David Friendly Society for elderly blind Jews. The Home was later purchased by the RMBI and renamed Zetland Court, the Province of Dorset paying for the restoration of the house and gardens to their former Victorian splendour. Residents began to be admitted in 1982, but the formal opening did not occur until 21st April 1983 and was performed by the Duke of Kent. On that day the PGM for Hampshire and Isle of Wight gave the Grand Master a cheque for £250,000 to fund the Richard Bond Nursing Wing.

Inflation had become so high in the 1970s that Alan Fletcher Ferris, Chairman of the Committee of Management, had stated that it was no longer economical to purchase and convert existing buildings into Homes. Therefore the intended structure planned for Exeter would be brand new. In 1979, the PGM for Devonshire, RW Bro W. A. Kneel, launched an appeal to raise £2 million to house 60 residents in the south-west. His successor John Huxtable continued the project and it was finally opened on Dunsford Hill, overlooking Exeter, in 1987. Clarke Construction of Exeter had submitted the successful tender, and the Home was constructed using Devon red bricks and a slate roof. Noel Grout, the Chief Executive (as the Secretary was now

LEFT **Connaught Court, York.** *Royal Masonic Benevolent Institute*

ABOVE RIGHT **Connaught Court, York.** *Royal Masonic Benevolent Institute*

RIGHT **Roland Wade standing by the statue of the Duke of Sussex.** *Royal Masonic Benevolent Institute*

known), stated that from then on the philosophy of the Institution was that nobody comes to the Homes to die but to live. The Matron, Mrs G. Lynch, was truly a daughter of Masonry, having trained at the Masonic Hospital in London and been a previous Matron of Cornwallis Court. The Earl of Cadogan was invited to perform the opening ceremony on 1st October 1987, but numbers had to be restricted because of space; even so, every Lodge Master and his wife from the Provinces of Cornwall and Devonshire were invited. A storeroom was later modified as a Chapel and consecrated by the Bishop of Crediton in 1991. This work was funded by the Province of Devonshire and the furniture funded by the Province of Cornwall.

The life of a Home Manager has never been easy, tranquil or even mundane. The death of a resident is always distressing and sometimes traumatic. These Homes are the residents' homes, and the staff often act as part of their family and can be confronted by extraordinary and difficult circumstances. One such incident occurred at Cornwallis Court when the Deputy Matron was called to a resident who had suffered a minor heart attack at a local public house. On another occasion, a resident who had poor eyesight had mistaken a bottle of radiator fluid for his bottle of cough medicine. In October 1987, much of the south-east of England was devastated by a hurricane, the Chairman remarking on the extraordinary efforts made by Home Managers and their staff in such a difficult situation. Some Homes were without electricity for several days and many trees had been uprooted. The greenhouse at Prince George Court in Chislehurst was destroyed, and the roof and flag pole were severely damaged at Cornwallis Court.

It is not unknown for a royal personage to request an impromptu visit, and the Private Secretary to the Duke of Kent wrote in April 1987, stating that the Duke would like to visit one of the Homes and meet the residents. In particularly he wished to visit the first Home he had himself opened at Chislehurst. The staff and residents were, of course, delighted to receive him, and he later wrote to congratulate the Matron, saying how impressed he was and how clean the place appeared. It has often been the custom to celebrate a Home's birthday, so in July 2008, the staff of Prince George Court personally invited the Grand Master to celebrate their 40th birthday. Somehow the local Provincial Office and the Central Office in Great Queen Street were not informed, resulting in sudden panic when the news was discovered. However, the day went well and the event was attended by the Provincial Grand Masters for East and West Kent, Jonathan Winpenny and Michael Bailey, along with the newly appointed Chief Executive, David Innes, and Dr John Reuther, one of the trustees. The Duke was welcomed by the Matron and then introduced to the residents and staff before joining the residents for lunch.

When Lord Harris died in the November of 1984, Alan Fletcher Ferris, the Chairman of the Committee of Management, was invited to fill his vacated place on the Board of Trustees. Ferris had been initiated into Ceres Lodge No 3501 in 1948, and eventually became the Provincial Grand Master of West Lancashire in May 1981. He succeeded James A. Terry as Chairman on the latter's retirement. Ferris died in October 1993, and at his funeral there were, by request, just two wreaths: one from his family and one of red roses from the Duke of Kent.

In 1985, a decision was made to scrap the Festivals as they were now considered outmoded. Lord Burnham, PGM for Buckinghamshire, was to preside over the last. When Dr Robert Thomas Crucefix had chaired the event in 1836, he raised the sum of £700; this year's total was £1,529,144. The year also saw the appointment of RW Bro Brig E. W. C. Flavell, DSO, MC, TD, DL, PGM for Berkshire, as the new Treasurer following the death of Lord Cornwallis, who had died in 1982. Edwin Flavell enlisted when only 17 years old,

ABOVE **James A. Terry.** *Royal Masonic Benevolent Institute*

in 1914, but by his 20th birthday he was commissioned and now held the rank of Major. He was awarded the Military Cross with two bars. In the Second World War he commanded the 1st Parachute Brigade in the North African Campaign, where he gained a DSO. His final command was the 6th Airlanding Brigade during the Normandy offensive of 1944.

However, it soon became apparent that the decision to terminate Annual Festivals was premature. The charities successfully petitioned for their restoration, and they were reintroduced in 1989. That year witnessed the reorganisation of the various management committees. There had always been two principal committees overseeing the charity: the Finance Committee and the Building & Management Committee. These were salaried staff, whilst those appointed were voluntary. Historically, the Treasurer was appointed, but in recent years the Treasurer had been a member of the

ABOVE **The Rev Canon Richard Tydeman.** *Royal Masonic Benevolent Institute*

BELOW **Lord Harris Court, Sindlesham.** *Royal Masonic Benevolent Institute*

Royal Family or of noble ancestry; now this position was addressed as President. The Secretary, who traditionally was employed, became known as the Chief Executive Officer (CEO). The various Boards had merged over the years, until in late 1980 they were reduced to two. The Committee of Management now became the Council and represented the Craft, whilst the combined Finance and House Committees became known as the General Purposes Committee and would continue to perform the basic decision-making forum. This Committee would meet four times a year and was formed from the Executive (consisting of the Chief Executive, Finance Director, Care Director and Head of Human Resources) the President and elected members from

the Council. A subsidiary Supervisory Board was later formed to meet more frequently and comprised the Executive along with the Chairman of the main General Purposes Committee, his Treasurer and one other elected representative. In 1989, the President was H. C. Cottrell, the CEO was Noel Grout and Chairman of the Finance and General Purposes Committee was Roland Wade.

The demand for residential accommodation, especially in the South-East, was increasing, and the quest for suitable sites was ongoing. In December 1990, H. C. Cottrell reported that two potential sites had been identified that might alleviate some of the problems: one was Nascot Grange in Watford; the other was in Banstead, Surrey. In September 1991, the President announced that Noel Grout would be stepping down as the Chief Executive and that his position would be filled by Miss Jane Reynolds. Noel Grout would remain to supervise the charity's 1992 Festival under the Province of East Kent. The day Jane Reynolds arrived, she was invited to address the Board and give a brief résumé of her background in the voluntary care sector. Her previous appointment was as General Manager of a large Health Service hospital and she, by coincidence, had been responsible for closing the NHS facilities at Nascot Grange.

Mr Timothy French, who had been the architect for Cadogan Court, was selected to design the Watford development to house 40 residents, and it would be renamed Prince Michael of Kent Court. It was constructed by Lacey Simmons, the company used for the converting and rebuilding of James Terry Court. The Mark Province of Hertfordshire kindly commissioned a portrait of Prince Michael of Kent to hang in the Home and also paid to equip the newly constructed library.

The quest for a new Home in Surrey had identified a site at Banstead, but it was really too small and was rejected. Instead an Edwardian building in 28 acres near Hindhead was chosen. Two names for the Home were put forward: Alvernia and Shannon Court. Shannon Court was chosen, and it was opened in 1995 by the Countess of Shannon, wife of the then Provincial Grand Master of Surrey, the Earl of Shannon. Maggie Holloway was appointed its first Manager.

Harewood Court, the replacement for the first Home in Croydon, was now nearly 50 years old and beginning to need expensive renovation. In early 1993, the President circulated a paper entitled *Harewood Court — The Way Forward*. The Institution's main policy had always been to provide residential and nursing care and not sheltered accommodation. However, the flats were not registered for residential homes; consequently the Institution was currently breaking the law. This could be resolved if a 40-bed unit could be found in the vicinity, which would provide a more appropriate atmosphere in which to care for those needy residents at Harewood Court, and a sum of £4.5 million was put aside for the project. It inevitably caused concerns about the long- term future of Harewood Court, especially with the residents. The President visited the Home to assure them that not only was their home safe but it would always be the policy of the RMBI to look after their interests. The building, however, did need substantial reconfiguration, to the communal spaces as well as to the individual flats. In the meantime a local property, situated on the seafront at Hove, was purchased. This had been designed by the renowned cinema architect Robert Cromie for Ian Stuart Millar, an eccentric industrialist. It was completed in 1937, but Millar lived there for only nine years, after which it became a nursing school. The house is of architectural importance, being an excellent example of the Art Deco style, built of specially commissioned Italian purplish grey bricks and enclosed within a surrounding wall. In April 1994, once the building had been refurbished, the residents, mostly from Harewood Court, moved in. The new Home would be known as Barford Court.

A particularly violent thunderstorm struck parts of Great Britain in January 1993, the worst affected area being along the North Wales coast. Llandudno suffered a disastrous and devastating flood, necessitating the evacuation of 500 people as cascading water swept cars and caravans away. The water level rose dramatically by two-and-a-half feet, polluting the town with sewage and effluent. The ground floor of Queen Elizabeth Court was completely submerged, making it uninhabitable. Some residents were evacuated to Ecclesholme, whilst others took refuge with their families. The Home did not reopen until the end of July.

By 1995 the waiting list for accommodation had risen to 789. There was a particular demand in Essex, now the largest Masonic Province since the division of Kent. The nearest Masonic Home was Cornwallis Court in Bury St Edmunds and, although convenient for the north of Essex was not so for the remainder. Initially two potential localities were identified: one at Shoeburyness and the other, a period property, near Braintree in the village of Stisted. The latter, now known as Prince Edward Duke of Kent Court, is surrounded by Braintree Golf Club, giving scenic panoramic views of the countryside. The house, constructed in 1823 of gault bricks bonded in the Flemish manner, and its grounds had been requisitioned by the Army during the Second World War, but it was converted to a hospital in 1942,

ABOVE **Lord Harris Court, Sindlesham.** *Royal Masonic Benevolent Institute*

housing patients from the bombed out Boreham Hall Hospital near Chelmsford. When hostilities ended, the building was converted to house the frail and elderly until it finally closed in 1992. The County Council sold the buildings to the RMBI in 1995, and two years later the RMBI's architect John Ismay planned the restoration of the building to its original state. The Home opened in 1998 and houses 43 residents. The stable block has since been converted for dementia care.

Since the birth of the RMBI it has always had its friends and supporters. Dr Crucefix created the organisation with his friends who met in the evenings at Radley's Hotel in Blackfriars to plan the fund-raising events that would eventually lead to the Home at Croydon, and these fund-raising events have continued virtually unbroken in one way or another to the present day. Although arguably now in a different format, the ultimate aim is still to contribute funds to support the RMBI Homes and their residents. For many years the Provinces have held Festivals in support of the four central Masonic charities. Members of the Province are

LEFT **Lord Harris.** *Royal Masonic Benevolent Institute*

ABOVE **Prince Albert Edward Court, Porthcawl, South Wales.** *Royal Masonic Benevolent Institute*

encouraged to support the appeal and the amount raised is usually celebrated by a Festival dinner when the final figure is formally announced. The RMBI works closely with that Province, advising on how the appeal should be run and providing literature and promotional material. However, the RMBI does not interfere — it is the Province's Festival, and it will be their 'Party' at the end.

The RMBI now provides a comprehensive range of services to meet the needs of an ever-increasing number of elderly Freemasons. There are now some 1,100 residents within the Homes and over 3,000 living in the community who receive some form of assistance.

When the first Home in Croydon opened in 1851, patronages could be purchased that permitted voting rights. The 32 men and women living in the Home at Croydon were the focus, or more precisely the conscience, of the Craft, and no action was deemed too small to entertain them. They were if anything pampered, and as most came from the Home Counties they were often resented by members from more distant Provinces. Victorian and Edwardian Freemasons were proud of their generosity, and ever present at these functions were the two great RMBI dynasties — the Farnfields in the early days, and the Terrys from the 1870s until the late 20th century. These two families in their day

rarely if ever missed an event.

The Lodge of Tranquillity is an excellent example of the continual support given by individual Lodges. They began attending the Christmas celebrations at Croydon in 1896, when members would act as Stewards whilst the Playgoers Lodge would entertain the residents. The very first entertainment had the cinematography pioneer Birt Acres showing an early film of the Royal Family taken at Marlborough House. Today the members assemble at Victoria Station to travel to Hove, and the Master usually brings a cake for the oldest resident. In 2008, the members entertained 21 residents to lunch at the Brighton Masonic Centre.

However, the role of individual Lodges, although still relevant and welcomed, has now largely been superseded by the formation of Associations of Friends. In January 1972, the Masonic Press described the role of an Association of Friends as providing assistance to the Matron and additional companionship and comforts to the residents. These Associations of Friends started within months of each Home opening and have been very effective ever since. They convert a Home from a place for the elderly to pass their final years into a family home were living can be fun. The Matron at one of these Homes once stated that one of biggest problems she experienced was how to keep the residents occupied. The Associations of Friends stepped in and now provide films, plays, concerts and a range of games from Bridge to Bingo.

These Associations have been best described as follows:

In all RMBI Homes, a volunteer group of local Freemasons exist, called the Association of Friends. Each Association of Friends group has been established with the purpose of working with RMBI Homes to complement the service to residents. The groups are also a great opportunity for local Freemasons and their dependants to practically support the work of the charity.

The Association of Friends are independently registered charities and work to the following objectives:

Fund-raising and Events

A number of events and activities are organised each year to help raise funds for the benefit of residents in the Home. Working very closely with the Home Manager, members of the Association of Friends identify areas where practical assistance for the benefit of residents is required, purchasing items over and above that provided by the RMBI. For example, in all of our Homes, the Association of Friends have raised significant funds to provide minibuses and adapted cars for residents' use.

In addition, social events and entertainment for residents are organised and members actively volunteer within the Home.

Befriending Residents

Members of the Association of Friends play a pivotal role in befriending residents who have minimal or no contact with relatives. Their genuine acts of friendship provide comfort and reassurance to many.

Furthermore, the Association of Friends work closely with Lodges and other Masonic organisations to encourage their members and wives to also support their work. They also assist residents wishing to attend Masonic meetings.

Whilst the Homes are still there for those needing them most, as the charity has done since its foundation, they are now available to a wider range of Freemasons and their dependants who are prepared to contribute either totally or in part towards their accommodation. Some 60% of residents are self-funding, whilst 40% require some form of charitable support. Most Associations of Friends have two major fund-raising events — one at Christmas and the other during the summer — and these are invariably supported by their Province and raise substantial funds for their Homes. For

BELOW **Prince Albert Edward Court, Porthcawl, South Wales.** *Royal Masonic Benevolent Institute*

ABOVE **Prince Albert Edward Court, Porthcawl, South Wales.** *Royal Masonic Benevolent Institute*

example, the Earl of Cadogan's wife opened the first Spring Fair at Prince George Duke of Kent Court in June 1971, and it was a beautiful day when James A. Terry welcomed her. Some 6,000 programmes had previously been sold and 2,550 visitors turned up on the day. The Matron showed Lady Cadogan around the Home and gardens and they visited the innumerable stalls in the grounds. Miss Carrick and Miss Sedgeley, the newly appointed Matrons of Connaught Court and Devonshire Court, came to witness how it was done. The highlight of the day was a display of dance and movement presented by the Women's League of Health, and the event raised a total of £1,600.

On the fourth anniversary of the opening of Connaught Court in York the residents attended a sherry party hosted by their Association of Friends, and in the autumn of 1975 the Friends arranged a trip around the Yorkshire Dales. That year the Christmas celebrations at Devonshire Court began with a carol concert, and two days later the residents attended a musical extravaganza at a church in Melton Mowbray. As Christmas Day approached, the Friends held a wine party whilst listening to the Great Glen Hand Bell Ringers accompanied by a piano accordionist. On Christmas Day the Mayor attended a sherry party at the Home, and on the day prior to New Year's Eve the residents were entertained by an exhibition of dancing presented by the Marjorie Wise School of Dance. The ingenuity these Associations show in entertaining and assisting the residents never ceases to amaze. In Albert Edward Prince of Wales Court, Porthcawl, they are entertained by male voice choirs, whilst at Shannon Court a drum corps concert is held given by army cadets.

There are many residential, nursing and dementia units throughout the country, some of which are excellent whilst others may fall well below the standard required. However, the RMBI's Homes are distinct from the commercial sector by their Associations of Friends, who may often turn up just to have a cup of tea with an elderly resident on a Saturday afternoon. It is they who take the elderly Freemason to his Lodge and accompany a resident to hospital. There are many who work and do good deeds for the RMBI, from the President and the trustees to the Home Managers and their teams, but it is the Association of Friends from each Home that are the icing on the RMBI's cake.

In September 1968, David Alun Lloyd resurrected a 100-year-old fund known as the Good Neighbour Fund, originally raised from Lodge donations and contents of charity boxes. There were sufficient funds to pay for holidays at Eastbourne, Llandudno and Westcliffe-on-Sea, and these holidays have continued to the present day with little change, although the range of resorts has now increased to four with the addition of Bournemouth. These holidays are held for the benefit of RMBI annuitants or people receiving financial

ABOVE **Province of Dorset's Festival for the RMBI 1967.** *Royal Masonic Benevolent Institute*

LEFT **Lord Cadogan laying the Foundation Stone at Cadogan Court.** *Royal Masonic Benevolent Institute*

BELOW LEFT **Cadogan Court, Exeter.** *Royal Masonic Benevolent Institute*

assistance, e.g. Masonic Relief Fund, and are funded by the Friends of the RMBI, the Good Neighbour Lodge and various other Masonic charities around the country. Some holidaymakers are beneficiaries of their own Province, but all are selected by the Care Advice Teams.

Local Freemasons are key to the success; they arrange trips to various country houses, the theatre, points of Masonic interest and other entertainments over a two-week period. The highlight is a farewell gala dinner attended by the PGM or his deputy as well as a member of the Board of Trustees. A winter holiday to Malta helps those annuitants who may have respiratory-related illness or symptoms affected by the British weather, and is usually sponsored by Provinces.

The Friends of the RMBI was formed some years ago specifically to raise money towards the Good Neighbour Fund; this is primarily used to fund holidays for recipients of relief grants. They have now raised well over £500,000.

ABOVE **Cadogan Court, Exeter.** *Royal Masonic Benevolent Institute*

RIGHT **Noel Grout, former Chief Executive of RMBI.** *Noel Grout*

BELOW RIGHT **The Hon Edward Latham Baillieu at Queen Elizabeth Court.** *Royal Masonic Benevolent Institute*

Their first venture, in 1974, was to hold a large Grand Charity Ball at the Connaught Rooms under the patronage of Lord Mais, the then Lord Mayor of London. The entertainment was provided by Victor Silvester Junior and his Orchestra along with Roy Castle. This ball raised £2,500, which was duly presented to the Secretary of the RMBI. A roll of honour is collated and published each year of those members and friends who have contributed towards the fund.

On 10th February 1971, the Good Neighbour Lodge, formed from the many supporters of the RMBI, was consecrated in the Province of West Kent. The Lodge has at least two of its meetings away from Kent, usually in one of the Homes. They also contribute to the annuitants' holidays and other RMBI projects.

Over the last few years the charity has recognised that the demand for residential care is declining as funding from the state decreases; the population is also living longer and the demand for dementia care is becoming a national crisis. There is little understanding of the condition and often sufferers are just left or treated with a soporific drug. The RMBI has recognised that although the disease is incurable, the application of sympathetic and structured care can be beneficial and has since initiated a policy of training all its staff in dementia care. The various Friends and members of Associations of Friends have contributed towards projects such as dementia cafés and sensory and safe gardens. They are now, and have always been, an integral part of the work of the RMBI.

ABOVE **Queen Elizabeth Court, Llandudno.** *Royal Masonic Benevolent Institute*

LEFT **Queen Elizabeth Court, Llandudno.** *Royal Masonic Benevolent Institute*

BELOW **Noel Grout, Miss Carrick, the Matron, and the Duke of Kent at the opening of Zetland Court.** *Royal Masonic Benevolent Institute*

ABOVE **Zetland Court, Bournemouth.** *Royal Masonic Benevolent Institute*

LEFT **Zetland Court, Bournemouth.** *Royal Masonic Benevolent Institute*

BELOW LEFT **HRH the Duke of Kent opening Zetland Court.** *Royal Masonic Benevolent Institute*

LEFT **Cornwallis Court.** *Royal Masonic Benevolent Institute*

BELOW LEFT **Cornwallis Court.** *Royal Masonic Benevolent Institute*

BOTTOM LEFT **Ecclesholme, Manchester.** *Royal Masonic Benevolent Institute*

BOTTOM RIGHT **Ecclesholme, Manchester.** *Royal Masonic Benevolent Institute*

ABOVE **The Tithebarn, Great Crosby.** *Royal Masonic Benevolent Institute*

RIGHT **The Tithebarn, Great Crosby.** *Royal Masonic Benevolent Institute*

BELOW **Barford Court, Hove.** *Royal Masonic Benevolent Institute*

ABOVE **Barford Court, Hove.** *Royal Masonic Benevolent Institute*

LEFT **Jane Reynolds, CEO, and Lord Shannon at Shannon Court.** *Royal Masonic Benevolent Institute*

BELOW **Shannon Court, Hindhead.** *Royal Masonic Benevolent Institute*

LEFT **Shannon Court, Hindhead.** *Royal Masonic Benevolent Institute*

BELOW LEFT **Prince Michael of Kent and H. C. Cottrell, President of the RMBI.** *Royal Masonic Benevolent Institute*

BELOW **Official Opening of Prince Michael of Kent Court, Watford.** *Royal Masonic Benevolent Institute*

LEFT **Prince Michael of Kent Court, Watford.** *Royal Masonic Benevolent Institute*

BELOW LEFT **Prince Michael of Kent Court, Watford.** *Royal Masonic Benevolent Institute*

BELOW LEFT **Prince Edward Duke of Kent Court, Stisted, Essex.** *Royal Masonic Benevolent Institute*

BELOW **Prince Edward Duke of Kent Court, Stisted, Essex.** *Royal Masonic Benevolent Institute*

CHAPTER 14

TOWARDS THE FUTURE

Norman Jacobs, a member of the General Purposes Committee, replaced H. C. Cottrell as President of the RMBI in February 1996. He was a solicitor, the senior partner of Slaughter & May, and had decided to retire on his 60th birthday. As a consequence he was asked by the then Home Secretary to chair the Football Licensing Authority and oversee the implementation of the recommendations of Lord Justice Taylor after the Hillsborough disaster. He was also a Steward on the Boxing Board of Control as well as the Chairman of the International Bar Association's Committee on Sports Law.

For many years there had been attempts to restructure and reform the range of committees within the RMBI; each seemed effective for a few years and then almost inevitably became cumbersome and difficult to work. Bro B. O'Meara announced in 1997 the recommendations of the charity's Constitution Working Party, which took the following form:

Grand Patron
Her Majesty the Queen

Grand President
HRH the Duke of Kent (ex-officio)

Governors
MW Pro Grand Master (ex-officio)
RW Deputy Grand Master (ex-officio)
Plus four other Governors to be appointed and selected by trustees

Trustees
One President appointed by MW Grand Master
Five Nominees chosen by trustees but ratified by MW Grand Master
Six Appointees (including Chief Executive, RMBI) appointed by trustees

Representative Forum

A final Board of Directors consisting of the 12 trustees was presented to the Committee of Management at the 1998 AGM.

Jane Reynolds and John Moore, the Chairman of the Board of Trustees, now reported that the RMBI was in the process of purchasing a property in Doncaster, specifically for assisting young people with severe learning difficulties. This would be a new venture for the RMBI, as up until now it had never worked within the community. It was felt that the property, known as Harry Priestley House, would be best run by a separate company, Masonic Care Ltd, which had its own Board of Directors. Initially funds were provided by the Province of Yorkshire (West Riding) and the Grand Charity, and RW Bro Derek Buswell, Provincial Grand Master for Leicestershire and Rutland, was appointed as its first Chairman.

Scarborough Court, now 30 years old, was beginning to show its age and there were concerns over its future. It was thought a more profitable site could be found either in Durham or Newcastle, but Durham was not considered appropriate and it was not realistic to update the current Home. What was required was a building that could accommodate individuals with mental frailty. This debate eventually became contentious, and, in the New Year, Kevin Harris, the Home Director for the Eastern Division, summarised the situation, stating that realistically there were but three options:

1. To refurbish the current structure.

2. To relocate the Home to another area.

3. To close the Home and relocate the residents in other nearby accommodation.

None of these suggestions were cost-effective and Kevin Harris stressed that currently the Home was not competitive with others in the vicinity, adding that the principle of relocating to a nearby site would be fundamentally wrong. In his opinion, the Home had been built in the wrong place and matters would only get worse, resulting in the only sensible option — to close the Home. However, it was clear that no matter how financially attractive this was, it would not be acceptable and would be opposed by the neighbouring Provinces.

About this time two influential people joined the Finance and General Purposes Committee; both would have a profound effect on the charity and Freemasonry. The first was Russell J. Race, from the Province of East Kent. He had been educated at Sir Joseph Williamson's Mathematical School in Rochester before obtaining a degree in economics at the University of Liverpool. Having been a corporate director at the stockbroking firm of Hoare Govett, he was therefore considered an ideal member of the RMBI's Investment Sub-Committee. Russell Race would eventually be appointed Deputy Provincial Grand Master of East Kent before being whisked off to London to become its first Deputy Metropolitan Grand Master and later the Metropolitan Grand Master. He remained a trustee of the RMBI until 2008. The other was Christopher J. Caine, who joined the Committee in September 1998, a businessman with an excellent understanding and knowledge of business law that made him the ideal person to introduce the various employment laws recently brought in by the government. He was soon appointed to the Salaries Sub-Committee and played an important role in merging the pay structures of the four Masonic charities before they eventually moved to Freemasons' Hall in 2008. He would become the Chairman of the Board of Trustees and the Deputy President, and in 2013 was elected a Grand Vice President of the charity. His commitment and energy during his time in office were exceptional.

Norman Jacobs retired and H. B. Smith was appointed President during November 1999. One of his first acts was to declare that the Finance and General Purposes Committee would, from then on, be known as the Board of Trustees in line with the newly recommended RMBI Constitution. The new Board of Trustees replaced disenfranchised earlier trustees, the Earl of Shannon, I. Mackenson-Sandbach, H. C. Cottrell and M. Jump and appointed them as Grand Vice Presidents. H. B. Smith suggested that, in recognition of their long service and support, H. C. Cottrell, R. J. Wade and P. Cornish should be nominated as Grand Vice Presidents of the RMBI. The new Board of Trustees would now meet four times a year, and a Supervisory Board, consisting of the President, the Chairman of the Board of Trustees and the Treasurer along with an elected trustee, would meet monthly with the CEO and his directors to concentrate on strategic and policy matters.

The problems at Scarborough Court were now coming to a head and a decision would inevitably have to be made on its future. Likewise Harewood Court was beginning to need considerable building attention and, with the cost now exceeded the value of the building, it seemed that the only viable option was to close it. Moreover, ever since the RMBI had taken over responsibility for the three Hannay Homes in Lancashire there had been financial problems. There were too many Homes in their vicinity and they were not cost-effective. The lack of demand for accommodation at Ecclesholme in particular now forced the RMBI to consider seriously deregistering the top floor and mothballing the rooms. It became obvious that at least one, possibly two, would have to be sold. Initially, the decision was to sell Ecclesholme and transfer the residents to Lytham St Annes, but this was later reversed, primarily because the catchment area within Manchester was greater than that of Fairlawn, and so the latter was closed. If The Tithebarn could be enlarged then perhaps Ecclesholme would become viable. Finally, the Chairman of the Board of Trustees, John Smith, expressed his sorrow that the pilot scheme at Harry Priestley House could not continue if it continued to make such losses. Amidst all these uncertainties the CEO, Jane Reynolds, decided to resign.

A new year brought a new CEO, when Peter Gray took up the post in his office on the first floor of the headquarters of the RMBI overlooking Freemasons' Hall. He faced a daunting situation — the potential closure of Harewood Court as well as at least one of the northern Homes. In addition, the future of Scarborough Court was in severe jeopardy, whilst the pilot scheme at Harry Priestley House was virtually on the rocks. The Homes that had been built predominantly to house fit, elderly Freemasons were now no longer appropriate for the more aged and infirm residents, thus the whole ethos of the RMBI would have to change.

The first good news came when Chris Caine, the Chairman of Masonic Care Ltd, together with Peter Gray, the co-opted Secretary, announced that Doncaster Borough Council had agreed to fund four residents in the 12-bed unit of Harry Priestley House and now, with an additional loan of £30,000 followed by a donation of £20,000 from the Province of Yorkshire, the Home was at last on a firm footing. Now there was a stable occupancy of 12 individuals, making Harry Priestley House a happy place.

Other good news soon came with permission to build a

LEFT **H. C. Cottrell, past President of the RMBI.** *Royal Masonic Benevolent Institute*

BELOW **Brian Smith, past President of the RMBI.** *Royal Masonic Benevolent Institute*

ABOVE **Chairman Christopher J. Caine presenting John Moore, past President of the RMBI, with a painting on his retirement.** *Royal Masonic Benevolent Institute*

12-bed extension unit for those with dementia at Shannon Court. It was hoped that soon every Home would be able to support dementia sufferers.

The continual deterioration of the fabric of the Homes, however, was an ongoing issue, and at Harewood Court it was hoped that a partnership with an independent company, the Retirement Lease Housing Association (RLHA), would eventually lead to them taking control of the building. In the meantime the residents were encouraged to form a residents' committee to speed up communications, thereby preventing confusion and misinformation. They were told that keeping the Home under the control of the RMBI was no longer an option, and it was emphasised that since its very conception, sheltered accommodation had never been the charity's core strategy. The cost of redeveloping Harewood Court had now reached the staggering sum of £7.5 million. However, the partnership did not last long — the RLHA and the RMBI soon went their separate ways. The RMBI continues to manage the Home, but the number of Freemasons housed there is diminishing.

Fairlawn at Lytham St Annes was eventually sold in 2001 and their Association of Friends began to wind up its affairs. Their funds were distributed between Ecclesholme, The Tithebarn, and the local Masonic Province. Fortunately most of the residents moved to neighbouring Masonic Homes, only two continuing to live at Fairlawn, funded by the RMBI, until the last one died in 2012.

Since the union, the Asylum for Worthy and Decayed Freemasons and the Royal Masonic Benevolent Institution for Annuitants had been administered by the RMBI, but from 1st April the Grand Charity took control of the annuitants' programme. This should not be considered as the break-up of the charity, however, as by that time the number of annuitants had shrunk from the many thousands in the 1930s to around 1,700. Traditionally each annuitant had received a Christmas present, and this continued under the management of the RMBI.

The main question over the next few years was the future of Scarborough Court. It was evident that a replacement was not going to be economical, yet local pressure insisted this was the only option. The Board therefore agreed to search for a nearby site where a more economical building could be constructed, and by July 2002 they had identified three potential sites. The most popular was in Chester-le-Street, and if not there then along the banks of the Tyne or in the market town of Hexham. But it soon became apparent that the only option acceptable to the local population was to rebuild in Cramlington. The Matron made it perfectly clear that neither she nor most of her staff would be prepared to move to a site beyond Cramlington, and this was also the verdict of most of the residents. The Board was split; most trustees were suspicious of a rebuild and one openly admitted that he would not support it. In 2007, Peter Gray gave a résumé of the debate since 2000 and a compromise was agreed on — to rebuild Scarborough Court a short distance from its current site. It was completed and officially opened in 2008 by HRH Princess Alexandra. Scarborough Court is a state-of-the-art Home, built using the latest environmentally friendly technologies, and provides high-quality and exceptional care.

In April 2004, Peter Gray announced that the charity had been offered accommodation, along with the other Masonic charities, in Freemasons' Hall and that he was in favour of accepting this offer, the current offices having become dated and cramped. The RMBI had owned the freehold since the early 1950s, and as a consequence it could either sell or let the current premises and benefit from the income. There was one problem — the occupancy of the ground floor and basement, which was leased by Toye, Kenning & Spencer, a clothing and jewellery manufacturer that specialised in Masonic regalia. The lease would eventually be purchased by the RMBI in 2015. In the meantime it was made clear by the rulers that the ultimate aim was to achieve full integration. This would need to be carried out in a professional and properly managed way and would inevitably take some time, progressing in stages, the first being a move to a common site.

In 2004, John Moore replaced Brian Smith, the Provincial Grand Master for Northamptonshire and Huntingdonshire, as the President of the RMBI, and Chris Caine became the Chairman of the Board of Trustees for the next four years. June 2006 saw major changes to the Board with the appointment of James Newman as Treasurer. A Yorkshire Mason who as a young Freemason had played an important role in the development of Connaught Court in York, he would hold this position for a number of years, eventually occupying the post of Chairman of the Board of Trustees. In 2013, he became its President.

In the early part of 2007, Peter Gray announced his retirement, which coincided with the retirement of John Moore. John Moore had been a supporter of the RMBI for

ABOVE **Brigadier William Shackell, former President of the RMBI.**
Royal Masonic Benevolent Institute

over 30 years, and at his retirement dinner Chris Caine presented him with a painting, *Sailing on the River Thurne* by David Eddington. He would be replaced as President by Brig Willie Shackell CBE, a retired Royal Engineer, who had for a number of years worked with SSAFA, the servicemen's charity. In May 2008, David Innes was appointed as Chief Executive. He had previously been employed to set up Canterbury Cathedral's £50 million global fund-raising appeal, helping to raise over £7.5 million in two years. Prior to that, he enjoyed 34 years in the Army as a military engineer and rose to the rank of Brigadier and the position of Engineer-in-Chief.

In recent years the charity has concentrated on redeveloping some of its elderly Homes and bringing many of them up to the standards required in the 21st century.

Indeed, new fire protection requirements meant that the Institution had to invest £6 million — a substantial sum but essential for the safety of the residents.

Now attention was given to updating James Terry Court and to developing its ability to house dementia sufferers. In July 2013, the Duke of Kent officially opened this state-of-the-art care home, which now exceeds all the latest government guidelines to ensure that residents and staff enjoy the highest level of comfort and safety. The refurbishment programme has equipped the Home with spacious en-suite bedrooms fitted with the latest mobility equipment and shower rooms. There are now new modern dining rooms, pamper rooms, roof-top gardens and terracing. This building makes the maximum use of space, with an excellent dementia wing with dedicated gardens.

The RMBI Homes had originally been designed for relatively fit individuals, and if any became too infirm they were often sent to a hospital or alternative institution in a better position to care for them. Many Homes were built with bowling greens and provided other activities specifically for the fit elderly person. Zetland Court had been built at the top

LEFT **Peter Gray, former CEO of RMBI.** *Royal Masonic Benevolent Institute*

BELOW **Harry Priestley House.** *Royal Masonic Benevolent Institute*

of a chine, a steep-sided valley cut through the cliffs by water, and residents had been encouraged to take advantage of this beautiful and shady setting to climb down to the beach. Now, with the average age of residents reaching 90 years, few are able or would even wish to attempt such a venture.

The population of the elderly in this country has rapidly increased and currently there are 10 million people over 65 years of age. Over the next 20 years this number is likely to double; three million of those are over 80 years of age, and this figure is likely to increase to eight million over the same timescale. A 20-year-old man now has a life expectancy of 84 years, whilst a male born today can expect to live to the age of 91. Likewise a woman born in the early 1980s can expect to live to 89, and a girl born now to live to 92. This has had, and will have, a substantial effect on pensions and a similar impact on the NHS. It is generally assumed that an elderly person is liable to seek admission into a care home as a consequence of a crisis. The Policy Studies Institute has quoted five main factors leading to such an event:

- Following a fall/fracture.
- Following an acute illness.
- A general deterioration in their health and their ability to look after themselves.
- As a result of increasing pressure on their carer.
- The effect of loneliness.

Entering a care home has certainly been made simpler over recent years, if the individual is financially independent. The difficulty arises if an elderly person cannot raise the full fees and other sources such as the local authority are called upon to make up the difference, with each body having its own rules relating to admission and financial support. In recent years restrictions in government funding have inevitably led to individuals having to remain in their own home, hopefully with the correct daily support, until time and circumstances make their admission into care an absolute necessity.

Prices will vary considerably, depending on the location and the facilities offered by the Home. In most cases the rate usually covers the basic needs such as care, meals and accommodation; other expenses, such as telephones and hairdressing, are additional. If an individual's assets and savings are less than £14,000 in England currently (£13,750 in Scotland and £22,500 in Wales), the local authority may pay for the residential and nursing care; otherwise individuals will have to find the full costs themselves.

There is, however, another factor that has slowly but surely increased as the population has grown older and that is

dementia, or senility as it was known in previous generations. The RMBI made the decision in 2007 that it would have to adapt in order to manage the situation. At that time 8% of its occupants were classified with the condition, but the demands were increasing. Nationally there are 800,000 people in the UK with a form of dementia, with 1 in 14 over 65 years of age. The prevalence of the condition is as follows:

- 40-64 years: 1 in 1,400;
- 65-69 years: 1 in 100;
- 70-79 years: 1 in 25;
- 80+ years: 1 in 6.

It is now estimated that one-third of individuals over 95 years of age suffer from dementia of one form or another, resulting in 60,000 deaths per annum. The cost to the country is in excess of £17 billion per annum, and this will inevitably increase.

The initial response of the RMBI was to increase the number of dementia beds it could safely administer. It was estimated at the time that the cost of caring for an individual in the final stages of the disease was about £100,000 and would be so expensive as to be prohibitive, but the appointment of Debra Keeling as Deputy Director of Care, who had had a great deal of experience with the various forms of dementia, changed this basic thinking. With the average age of the residents approaching 90 years of age, it was evident that many already had the condition, and the answer was to adapt the Homes so as to care for those with the early onset of the disease whilst attempting to delay progression to the more acute phase, at all times making their lives as full and enjoyable as possible. Since then the RMBI has endeavoured to reorganise the Homes not only to cater for the healthy resident but also to integrate those in the varying stages of dementia. The RMBI strategy plan for dementia, approved in 2009 as a five-year programme, is currently being rolled out in a phased approach to its 17 care homes throughout England and Wales.

There are many forms of dementia; some are treatable, whilst others are less responsive to therapeutic compounds. The four most common are:

- Alzheimer's;
- Vascular Dementia;
- Dementia with Lewy Bodies;
- Frontotemporal Dementia.

Dementia affects not only those with the condition but sadly

their families and those living and working with them. There is also a national ignorance about the causes and effects of the illness. Therefore, the first and immediate step to take was education, to understand the various forms of the disease, its treatment and the most effective way of caring for those affected. Education was not to be restricted to the staff but was also to be given to the relatives as well as the other residents living within the Home. The Grand Charity initially donated £60,000 to train the staff in three of the Homes, and since then it has been cascaded down to all. It is now included in the induction process of all new staff, and most senior managers are now encouraged to complete the diploma, a more comprehensive study in treatment and handling, run by Dementia Care Matters.

The disease is currently incurable and will inevitably progress. It is then that those suffering from it will need to live, for their own protection, in a secure and safe accommodation, so areas within the Homes will have to be redesigned for such purposes, which is ongoing and expensive. It is the intention that eventually all Homes will have a secure dementia unit. These will often have a sensory garden, usually with a creative circular path that will inevitably bring the individual back to where they have started, as well as water features and other designs that are pleasing to the eye and bring a feeling of contentment and peace. The garden, as with every part of the Home, is recognised as the personal home of each resident, but in the secure unit the physical presence of a front door is important

as part of the therapy. There is either clear evidence of a front door at the entrance to the unit or alternatively each bedroom will have its own front door. Placed by the side of door to their room is a memory box containing items that mean a lot and are recognisable to the individual. Its purpose is to stimulate the memory, and it often contains photographs of loved ones and artefacts that have played an important role in their lives.

In recent years the Homes have been introducing Sonas apc, a system pioneered by Sister Mary Threadgold, a speech and language therapist in Dublin. The word 'sonas' is Gaelic, meaning well-being, joy and contentment. Each session takes approximately 45 minutes and is designed to stimulate the five senses: touch, sight, smell, taste and hearing. The aim is threefold:

• To activate the potential for communication that has been retained by the older person with communication impairment.
• To encourage the creation of an environment that facilitates communication.
• To have activation of potential for communication recognised and accepted as an essential part of care planning for older people.

ABOVE AND THIS IMAGE **New Scarborough Court, Cramlington.**
Royal Masonic Benevolent Institute

This works, in an example of smell, by presenting an individual with a spice and asking what the aroma reminds them off. Depending on the spice they may say Christmas, remembering the spices put in a Christmas cake. Equally a particular song may stimulate a certain memory locked in the brain. It has been recognised that, after a number of sessions, individuals may respond in various ways such as clapping or humming.

In recent years there have been innumerable scandals relating to the care home industry. These include physical and verbal abuse, standards of care, welfare of vulnerable individuals, and many other acts of cruelty. The RMBI has always had a policy of no tolerance of this kind of behaviour. It provides only the very best for its residents, but in a society that requires proof of ability and compliance, it has always been necessary to conform to certain accreditation in order to demonstrate to the world that we practise what we preach. To this end, the charity has taken part in a range of quality control schemes, and recently a government-led national scheme has been introduced. The Care Quality Commission (CQC) inspects hospitals, care homes, people's own homes, dental and general practices against nationally defined standards. It currently inspects hospitals, care homes, domiciliary care services annually and dental practices biannually. The inspections occur without notice being given, so that assurance can be confirmed that the criteria are being met on a day-to-day basis.

These national care home standards have to demonstrate the following criteria:

- That care, treatment and support meet the residents' needs.
- That the Home is a safe environment.
- That the staff have the correct skills to carry out their job.
- That a system is in place that regularly demonstrates that all the above criteria are inspected to prove that they are properly carried out.

TOP **James Newman, President of the RMBI.** *Royal Masonic Benevolent Institute*

ABOVE LEFT **Refurbished James Terry Court.** *Royal Masonic Benevolent Institute*

LEFT **Roof Top Dementia Garden at James Terry Court.** *Royal Masonic Benevolent Institute*

Five questions need to be demonstrated by each Home to gain accreditation:

- Are they safe?
- Are they effective?
- Are they caring?
- Are they responsive?
- Are they well-led?

Satisfying these criteria requires a great deal of work. The very nature of the system is labour-intensive and therefore costly, but the end product should guarantee that the RMBI practises what it preaches. To alleviate the pressure on staff, the organisation is introducing various computerised programmes to assist the carers in carrying out their duties satisfactorily in an efficient, correct and provable manner.

Other computerised systems are being introduced across the services to decrease other labour-intensive duties that often fall on the Home Manager, such as clocking-in and timetabling staffing duties. The end product hopefully should make the organisation more efficient, effective and streamlined.

But what is the future of the organisation as a whole? The RMBI was the third of the Masonic charities. The first was the Royal Cumberland Freemasons' School for Female Objects, established in 1788 by the Chevalier Bartholomew Ruspini, and followed a few years later, in 1798, by a similar institution for boys. These initial two charities were eventually amalgamated into the Royal Masonic Trust for Girls and Boys. The third charity, as mentioned, was the RMBI, a fusion of the Asylum for Aged, Worthy and Decayed Freemasons and the Royal Masonic Benevolent Annuity Fund. Then came the Freemasons Grand Charity, which although it could trace its origin back two hundred years, was formed in 1980 as consequence of the Bagnall Report. Finally, there was the Masonic Samaritan Fund formed in 1990 to support Freemasons and their dependants with medical needs as a consequence of the closure of the Royal Masonic Hospital. These charities were,

for many years, independent in every way, barring their duties to the members of the United Grand Lodge of England. They had separate headquarters and each had its own President, Board of Trustees, Chief Executive and staff.

The four charities agreed to move into central accommodation within Freemasons' Hall in 2008. The rulers at the time made it clear that this was the start, and that further mergers would occur at some time in the future. A large area beneath the Grand Temple and the Sussex Corridor was made vacant and redesigned into four distinct glass units denominated by the four charities. They now all share a common entrance, staff room and other facilities, but more importantly work increasingly closely together.

In recent years further elements have been centralised, such as working conditions and payroll facilities, and Freemasonry Cares, a Craft-wide communication initiative, has been successfully launched.

In 2013, Brig Willie Shackell went to the Masonic Samaritan Fund to become its President, whilst the Chairman of the Board of the RMBI, James Newman, replaced him as President, leading the charity into the new and exciting areas that will inevitably confront it.

Over the many years that Freemasonry has existed it has had as its principal tenets brotherly love, relief, and truth. Provided it maintains these initial guiding lights, the objectives of the current charities, and the RMBI in particular, will continue in whatever form circumstances and time dictate.

RIGHT **Ruspinni presenting the children to the Prince of Wales..** *Royal Masonic Benevolent Institute*

INDEX

Tilley, Vesta 98
Time versus Life: An Enigma 25
Times, The 21, 72, 114
Tipper, Bro 89
Tithebarn, Great Crosby 129, 150, 151
Tobin, John 38
Tolpuddle Martyrs 31
Tombleson, Bro 69
Tooting Cemetery 45, 85
Tory Party 30, 64, 66, 69
Toye, Kenning & Spencer 152
Trinity College, Cambridge 53, 65, 95
Truman, J. O. 25
Truro 94
Tucker, William 72
Turner sisters 62
Turner, Miss 55, 59
Turner, Mr 62
Turton, A. E. 104
Turton, Bro 123
Tuscan Lodge 42
Tyedeman, Richard 129
Tyne, River 151

Union Workhouses 15, 33, 77, 96, 97
United Grand Lodge of England
  (UGLE) 29, 32, 34, 36, 39, 40,
  48, 49, 51, 52, 55, 56, 58, 59, 60,
  63, 65, 66, 68, 70, 72, 75, 79, 80,
  84, 86, 102, 113, 116, 118, 120,
  124, 132, 158
United Kingdom 154
United States of America 32, 69,
  102, 112
United Strength Lodge 90
Unity, Peace and Concord Lodge 20
Unlawful Societies Act, 1799 31
Upper North Gloucester St 25
Urban Lodge 90
Urban Workhouses 8

Vacant Chair, The 88
Van Rymsdyk, Jan 23
Vanity Fair 132
Vascular Dementia 154
Vassar-Smith, Richard 103
Versailles, Treaty of 103, 122
Victoria station 137

Victoria, Princess 81
Victoria, Queen 30, 62, 63, 81, 82,
  86, 89, 92
Vink, Charles 60
Voltigeur 75
Wade, Roland J. 135, 150
Wales 15, 154
Wales, Albert Edward, Prince of
  82, 85, 86, 87, 92
Walton, Bro 74
Wandsworth, London 102
War Loans 112
War Office 116
Ward, Constance Harriett 98
Warham Road, Croydon 130
Warwickshire 98
Washburn, Henry 88
Waterloo, Battle of 26, 65
Watford 135
Watkins, Bro 43
Wayte, Dorothy Margaret Anne 98
Wayte, J. A. 92, 98
Wayte, John Woollaton 98, 112
Wayte, Samuel Wilfred 98
*We'll Keep a Welcome in the
  Hillsides* 129
Webb, Bro 99
Wellington School, Somerset 102
Wellington, Duke of 30, 68
Wells, Miss 76
West India Arms Tavern, Blackwall 37
West Kent 82, 141
West Kent imperial Yeomanry 104
West Lancashire 129, 134
West Riding of Yorkshire 149
Westcliffe-on-Sea 139
Westminster and Keystone Lodge 82
Westminster Hall 98
Westminster School 66
Weybridge 104, 131
Weymouth 26
Whig Party 27, 30, 64, 70
Whit, Miss 63
White Horse of the Peppers, The 42
White, Joseph 42
White, William H. 34, 52, 58, 66
Whitehall 92
Whitmore, John 67, 68, 69, 70, 71,

72, 74
Wilkins, John 114, 120
Willett, William 122
William IV, King 26, 30, 39, 40
William Taylor 20
Williams, John 104
Williamson, Sir Hedworth 84
Wilson, Bro 70, 72
Wimborne, Lad 132
Winchester College 108
Windmill Hotel, Croydon 76
Windsor 30
Winpenny, Jonathan 134
Witham Lodge 65
Woburn Place, St Pancras 108
Women's League of Health 139
Wood, Benjamin 58
Wood, John 50, 51, 52, 53, 54, 56
Wood, Stacey 51
Wood, Thomas 42, 46, 52
Woollen, Matthew 114
Woollen, Thomas Henry 114
Workmen's Compensation Act, 1897
  96
Worshipful Company of Clockmakers
  16
Worshipful Company of Fruiterers
  122
Wren, Christopher 16
Wright, Gertrude Mabel 102
Wright, W. L. 66, 69, 70

Yarborough Lodge 92
Yarborough, Earl of 76
York, Duchess of 111
York, Duke of 110, 111, 112, 114
Yorkshire 150
Yorkshire Dales 139
Yorkshire Hussars Yeomanry 108
Ypres 99

Zetland Court 132, 153
Zetland, Countess Sophia Jane 84
Zetland, Marquess of 121